KNOWING
OTHERWISE

Alexis Shotwell

KNOWING
OTHERWISE

RACE, GENDER, AND IMPLICIT UNDERSTANDING

The Pennsylvania State University Press
University Park, Pennsylvania

Library of Congress Cataloging-in-Publication Data

Shotwell, Alexis, 1974–
Knowing otherwise : race, gender, and implicit understanding / Alexis Shotwell.
p. cm.
Summary: "Draws on philosophers, political theorists, activists, and poets to explain
how unspoken and unspeakable knowledge is important to racial and gender formation;
offers a usable conception of implicit understanding"—Provided by publishers.
Includes bibliographical references (p. 157) and index.
ISBN 978-0-271-03763-9 (cloth : alk. paper)
ISBN 978-0-271-03764-6 (pbk. : alk. paper)
1. Blacks—Racial identity.
2. Gender identity.
I. Title.

E185.86.S586 2011
305.896—dc22
2010025710

CONTENTS

ACKNOWLEDGMENTS

It is difficult to put into words the web of connections that has sustained this book over the years. My first and deepest thanks go to the teachers and mentors who helped this work grow: Sue Campbell, James Clifford, Lorraine Code, Angela Davis, Barbara Epstein, Donna Haraway, and David Hoy. They are extraordinary scholars, unparalleled interlocutors, and exemplars of principled, warmhearted, cheerful living. I anticipate spending much of my life attempting to follow their examples, and I am honored to have had the chance to work with them.

Intellectual community is a blessing I have experienced in abundance. Thank you to the participants in conferences at University of Wisconsin–La Crosse, Harvard University, Purdue University, Amsterdam School of Cultural Analysis, City College of the City University of New York, UC Davis, UCLA, University of Dayton, Simon Fraser University, and colloquia organized by the Society for Women in Philosophy, Pacific Division, Dalhousie University, the Canadian Society for Women in Philosophy, the Association for Feminist Ethics and Social Theory, and the Society for Existential and Phenomenological Theory and Culture. Thank you also to the University of California, Santa Cruz's Friday Forum. I have been fortunate to find supportive colleagues at Laurentian University in the Philosophy and English Departments, and I thank them as well. My undergraduate and graduate students at Laurentian have provoked me to think through these issues anew almost weekly.

The staff and readers for Penn State Press renewed my faith in academic publishing. Thank you to Sandy Thatcher for editorial guidance, Kathryn Yahner for meticulous support, and the anonymous readers who gave detailed and productive feedback on the book. Shannon Sullivan identified herself as one of these readers, and I am pleased to be able to thank her directly for past and future critical readings. Nicholas Taylor's lucid and careful suggestions for sharpening the text were a gift. I am grateful also to Laurie Prendergast for preparing the index.

My work has benefited from conversation, political work, and play with more people than I can name. Thanks to Pasi Ahonen, Aren Aizura, Max Bell Alper, Patrick Barnholden, Clare Bayard, Kim Bird, Bekki Bolthouse, Regan Brashear, Jessica Breheny, Marta Brunner, Sean Burns, Shana Calixte, Chris Crass, Lucas Crawford, Lisa Guenther, Mrinalini Greedharry, Kelly Fitzmaurice, Ami Harbin, Adam Hefty, Cressida Heyes, Rahula Janowski, Jennifer Johnson, Gary Kinsman, Joseph Lapp, Alice MacLachlan, Jim Maughn, Peter Murray, Scott Neigh, Michelle O'Brien, Justin Paulson, Pamela Perry, Chanda Prescod-Weinstein, Maia Ramnath, Michael Rasalan, Trevor Sangrey, Kim Tallbear, Kalindi Vora, Ryan Wadsworth, Marla Zubel, everyone in the Student-Worker Coalition for Justice, the Graduate Student Solidarity Network, Free Radio Santa Cruz, Sudbury Against War and Occupation, the transsomapolitics formation, and the Long Road collective. Scout Calvert, Ada Jaarsma, Nora Madden, James Rowe, and Rebecca Schein are shining friends and comrades. I also thank the Shotwells—Hudson, Janet, Vivien, and Gordon—for a constant stream of love, e-mail, and goodness. Above all, thanks to Chris Dixon for dauntless and unflinching conversation, meticulous reading, and all forms of sustenance.

Earlier formulations of parts of this book appeared in *Race and the Foundations of Knowledge,* edited by Joseph Young and Jana Evans Braziel, published by the University of Illinois Press (2006); *The Shock of the Other: Situating Alterities,* edited by Silke Horstkotte and Esther Peeren, published by Rodopi (2007); *Upping the Anti: A Journal of Theory and Practice* 6 (October 2008); and *Agency and Embodiment,* edited by Sue Campbell, Susan Sherwin, and Letitia Meynell, published by Penn State Press (2009).

PROLOGUE

Even though humans are more committed to language than other animals, we use more than words in every aspect of engagement with our lives. We are intricately and intimately connected with others and with the world, and most of these connections happen alongside, beneath, and in other spheres than the words we say and the propositions we formulate. We know how to say some things, and how to make claims and test them. This sort of knowledge—propositional knowledge—has been often understood as the only form of knowledge worth thinking about. We also know otherwise—we understand things that cannot be or are not spoken, and we may suspect that this form of understanding is important. In this book, I attend to this second form of knowing, which I call "implicit understanding." I argue that various forms of knowing otherwise than propositionally are vital to current possibilities for flourishing, expressing dignity, and acting.

I have two main aims: first to delineate the differences and the connections among four sorts of implicit understanding, and second to show how they are crucial to personal and political transformation. Indeed, it is often at points of transition that the work of implicit understanding is most palpable—when people shift their gender enactment, when they take up new political orientations, when they aim to create new social relations. Consider Dorothy Allison's narrative of feminist transformation: "When feminism exploded in my life, it gave me a vision of the world totally different from everything I had ever assumed or hoped" (1994, 167). Here, feminism offered a vision of the world that was new in two ways: it shifted an already present framework of presuppositions and provided different possibilities for future hope. Accounts of political transformation often highlight the new information and understanding involved in an individual's change. As Allison's narrative suggests, they can also create a changed context for one's assumptions and hopes. When this happens, political transformation takes root in something deeper than what one can say, offering new expressive possibilities. Such possibilities speak to the implicitly political frameworks of understanding.

It is important to think about this form of understanding. Every story I know about queerness and coming out, about gender and transitioning, about coming to political consciousness of racial formation and one's own place in it, of struggle for economic justice, of coming to crip pride, unfolds a complex web of understanding. In that web, conceptual knowledge changes—the information one has and one's ability to speak about it shifts, and people learn facts and figures they didn't know. But that changed propositional knowledge is thoroughly enmeshed with other forms of understanding—feeling, somatic experience, skills and competencies, presuppositions and common sense. Thinking about the always socially situated work of striving to create the conditions for complex flourishing requires a thick understanding of these aspects of our experience.

As I will show, there is wider range of such thinking than one might expect. This is true even within the discipline of philosophy, often seen (with reason) as most unfriendly to pushing the boundaries of propositionality and rationality narrowly construed. I am uneasily situated in relation to this discipline, sutured to philosophical topics and approaches by my interest in epistemology and political theory. I believe that it is possible to put people concerned about social justice in conversation with philosophers for the mutual aid of all concerned. This work is directed toward thinkers who are interested in knowledge—mostly philosophers—and also toward people looking to change the world—mostly social justice activists—(not mutually exclusive categories) because I believe that we need to consider implicit understanding far more deeply and synthetically from both directions.

SOME PRELIMINARY DEFINITIONS

"Propositionality" here names claim-making activity; to put something propositionally is to put it in a linguistically intelligible form that could be evaluated as true or false. "Implicit understanding" names our background, taken-for-granted understanding of being in the world: The implicit is what provides the conditions for things to make sense to us. The implicit provides the framework through which it is possible to form propositions and also to evaluate them as true or false, and is thus instrumentally important. Implicit understanding is also non-instrumentally important. It not only helps provide the conditions for propositional work, it also occupies its own epistemic and political terrain, and in itself is vital to flourishing. That is, living well involves substantial implicit content, perhaps unspeakable but central to the felt experience of manifesting dignity, joy, and contingent freedoms. While there is reason to consider implicit understanding a form of knowledge, it may not be verifiable in the same way as propositional knowledge. In what follows I will for the most part use "implicit understanding" as an umbrella term, though at various points I will also use "knowledge" out of respect for specific texts' use of the term. As I explain below, my primary analytic attempts to avoid a split between what we can and cannot say in a coherent sentence. Rather, I begin from the stance that this split is inadequate to our epistemic and ethical experience of knowing. Implicit understanding is both epistemically and politically salient, and I inquire into this twined salience. Notice, then, that I am trying to shift the terms of a conversation about the difference between propositional and nonpropositional knowledge in order to understand the ways these categories are themselves inadequate. Rather, I believe that they at least interpenetrate and may be co-constituted in ways that are most visible when we concern ourselves with the political.

I distinguish among four different sorts of implicit understanding: practical, skill-based knowledge; somatic or bodily knowing; potentially propositional but currently implicit knowledge; and affective or emotional understanding. In the chapters to follow I will situate each more thoroughly in relation to some key theorists; let the following stand as a gestural key to what I will discuss in more detail. Although I distinguish the differences among these four kinds of understanding, I don't think it is possible to think about them as though they were not intimately and necessarily connected.

First, skill-based "know-how," developed through practice. Skills, like being able to knit a sweater, or being able to swim, are "known" only insofar as one has the ability to exercise them. A person can tell me many things about how to swim, but I will not know how to do it unless I actually acquire the understanding of moving in particular ways in water. Losing the ability to swim means, over time, losing the knowledge of how to swim. Many examples of this sort of knowledge relate to things that you could say about them; knowing how to swim, or how to pound a nail effectively, for example, are skills that can be improved by someone who is good at them saying things to us about how to do them better ("Maybe if you turn your head less when you take a breath your stroke will be smoother" or "Hold the hammer farther back along the handle").

A second sort of implicit understanding, connected to the first, is knowledge people have at the intersection of their bodily and conceptual systems. What does it mean to feel good in one's body? To have a body image? To shake hands in a way that conveys friendliness, confidence, or aggression? This sort of somatic knowledge is bodily and social, and thus it is always political. Being gendered, for example, is intensely somatic while also complexly social and relational; feeling like a girl, a boy, or some genders we don't have words for involves our corporeal sensorium and also a social uptake of our bodily ways of being in the world. While it might be tempting to think of bodily knowledge as somehow pre-social, pure, or free from enculturation, it is more precise to see how our felt experience of embodiment constellates social worlds with material realities.

A third species of implicit knowing is knowledge that could be put into words but is not, now, in that form. Moreover, "now" is always shifting; what stands as implicit sometimes moves under the surface of propositional knowledge and can be brought into explicitness. There is always a great deal that could be said but is not—and perhaps has never been—put into words. Other propositions have become foundationally assumed to the extent that we rely on them without conceptual consideration. Potentially propositional knowledge stands as commonsense; it provides the foundation from which we reason, or is heuristically unspoken. In sometimes benign and sometimes troubling ways, this form of understanding goes without saying or is contingently unspeakable. When it carries political judgment, the difficulty attached to drawing potentially propositional, commonsense knowledge into conceptual thought may restrict people's perceptions and actions.

Finally, the category of affect and feeling can be understood as a kind of implicit understanding, not fully or generally propositional or considered a kind of knowledge. "Affect" is increasingly coming to name a previously under-theorized dimension of racial formation, queerness, gendered norms, and class delineations. I understand affect and its relations—emotions and sensibilities, among other labels—to name nonpropositional but energetic and moving feelings that texture and tone our experience. Sometimes these feelings have conventionally accessible labels like "happy" or "sad" and sometimes they are inchoate and slippery, suffusing or torquing our experience in ways that may be overwhelming and inexpressible.

Again, these four facets of implicit understanding are always experienced in co-constituting relation with one another. We will not have affect without bodily being, both social and skillful, and feeling may point to or be the nascent form of something that could be put into words—and the same can be said for any configuration of implicit understanding in which we prioritize one of these four. Still, it is important to delineate the differences among these in order to understand more completely ways of knowing too often rendered useless, irrelevant, or beneath reason. Even theorists who attend to one or the other of these other forms of knowledge collapse many forms of implicit understanding into the sort they examine. Doing this preserves a binary relationship between propositional knowledge (knowledge proper, we might say) and everything else—which is then rendered extra-epistemic.

Consider a relatively simple, concrete example: an out-of-true bike wheel, so warped that it hinders bicycle riding—the rim runs against the brake pad, and therefore the bike can't move. What are the epistemic issues involved in fixing this wheel? In what way, if any, is this wheel political? Skilled knowledge is clearly present here. Knowing how to true a bike wheel is a learned capacity. The mechanics who taught me how to do this, along with the books I've read about building wheels and truing warped wheels, all explained in words and propositions aspects of the process, and their words shaped my practices. Actually working on wheels and learning how to apply those words opened a different sort of knowing relation with wheels. At a certain (not very high) level of skill, truing bike wheels is a skill that is rendered in words only imperfectly and approximately. The proof of having the knowledge is exercising it and creating a successfully trued wheel, perhaps reliably and repeatedly. Socially situated embodiment is also complexly involved. I was raised as a girl and live as a woman in a social world that does not habituate girls and women to handle tools and know our own strength in their use. This aspect of gendering was obvious to me when I worked as a volunteer mechanic teaching people how to fix their own bikes in a bike tool co-op. I noticed that being able to teach a skill (like truing a wheel) to women in particular depended on creating new bodily ways of being, which involved pushing back on a weight of history that assumed that girl children and women adults didn't need to use wrenches. I am generalizing, of course; not all girls and women are raised to be incompetent with tools—people like me, the eldest child of a maker and fixer sort of father, may be given more room to shape our bodies and identities around these competencies. Having an orientation toward the world such that the skills of truing a wheel come reasonably easily depends greatly on the social world in which one dwells, creating habits and tendencies that intersect with skills and know-how.

Aspects of this political-epistemic situation could be put into words. Teaching someone how to true a wheel involves evoking both the know-how and the socially situated bodily knowledge involved in the work—one might give some directions that help develop the skill ("You can think of this spoke like a screw, see? It tightens when you turn it in this direction") or the habitus ("Yeah, sometimes it's hard to feel confident about how far to turn the spoke wrench. You can just fiddle with it"). There are other sorts of commonsense understanding involved, too—assumptions about whether it's worth fixing a broken wheel, about what sort of people are able to learn how to do this work, about whether it's demeaning to get one's hands dirty in working. There are also various implicit contents to the material situation of the bike's wheel. In the shop where I volunteered, there were two main groups of people who came in to use the free services and cheap tool time: bike hipsters with a do-it-yourself aesthetic, often committed to bicycling with an equal mix of style and environmentalism; and noncitizens, barred from getting driver's licenses and therefore dependant on bike transport to get around. These groups shared economic reasons for fixing their own bikes, perhaps along with other sorts of joys in biking and fixing bikes. Thinking about what was going without saying in that space reveals an array of potentially propositional knowledge, some of it quite salient to the fact of the out-of-true wheel. But almost all that understanding goes without saying in ways that could be brought into propositional consciousness. Much what is unspoken or unspeakable is also political, such as the differences between undocumented and documented people and their reasons for riding bikes. Finally, there is affective content to the broken wheel and its fixing. It is frustrating to not be able to ride one's bike, and it's hard to learn how to true a wheel. It is satisfying and empowering to be able to do this sort of work, and it's a joy to be able to ride again. So: frustration, irritation, confusion, competence, confidence, happiness, joy—and more. In this situation, not much of the affective content is clearly tied to propositional knowledge (as it might be in a statement like "something felt fishy," where "feeling fishy" signals a way of knowing). Still, the feeling involved is important to the possibilities for truing the wheel or interacting with it in other ways.

To move from reasonably simple objects of knowledge to something more involved, like discovering feminism, underlines the salience of implicit understanding in all its complexity. One way to think about political transformation is epistemological; we gain access to new knowledge about things, new standards for justification, or different practices of knowing.

Of all the things feminist theory has given philosophy, feminist epistemology is one of the most significant. Interventions in traditional epistemology have come from feminist scientists and feminist philosophers of science who argue that the production of knowledge is intimately tied to the position of knowers within social and political networks. They examine the production of knowledge as a situated and invested category in scientific practice and society more generally.[1] Feminist epistemologists offer compelling arguments against any conception of an isolated knower whose knowledge is fungible, discrete, and infallible. Rather, they give an account of a situated knower whose standpoint is achieved, whose knowledge is connected to a network of social relations, and whose very being is co-constituted with others.[2] The quality of knowledge changes with the position of the knower, and there are some things knowable only from particular knowledge positions.[3] There turn out to be many "ingredients" in knowledge, a great number of which are explicitly disallowed by more traditional or conventional theories of knowledge.

Among the ingredients implied but under-theorized even in feminist epistemology is the category of implicit understanding I have been exploring: the unspoken and unspeakable frameworks of our propositional, claim-making activity. Our epistemic resources are thus impoverished, particularly if we are looking for epistemic accounts that can help address the relationship between knowledge and political change. I propose that the implicit is a crucial yet under-interrogated element in knowledge. We do not have an adequate epistemology without an account of how the implicit is at play in the construction and verification of knowledge. The epistemic salience of implicit understanding becomes particularly clear, as I will show, when we examine racial and gender formation with an eye toward the epistemic work involved in stabilizing them as political categories.

For something to be unspoken, perhaps unspeakable, is for it to be inaccessible in a significant way—and not only to conventional Western philosophy. Often pride of place is given to knowledge we can evaluate as true or false and that we can put in the form of a proposition. This is the case even when intuitions and "gut feelings" are seen as important to our decisions and actions. It matters, for example, whether racism—and race itself—as an

---

1. See Code 1987, 1991, 2006; Haraway 1991, 1997; Harding and Hintikka 1983; Harding 1986, 1991; Hartsock 1998; Keller 1983.
2. See Hartsock 1998; Hill Collins 1991; Babbitt 1996; Antony and Witt 2001.
3. See Harding 1991; Smith 1987, 1990.

ideological construction is significantly unspoken and unspeakable. I will argue that racialization, racism, and racial formation involve significant implicit understandings; the nonpropositional is important to forming the background of "race." Similarly, the norms through which gender is formed and enforced can be seen as implicit in several of the modes I laid out above. Implicit understanding helps produce our experience of knowing as a coherent one. It might play an especially crucial role when our understandings are challenged, when they shift or change. While it is clearly important to social justice work to change laws, how people speak, and what gets said, such transformations rely on implicit frameworks of understanding and may also create new constellations of tacit knowing.

I situate the concept of "the implicit" within a polythetic field of overlapping terms, uses, and meanings. The theoretical field of "implicit understanding" is not unmarked terrain or new territory. Rather, this is an already multiply mapped topography. In more and less explicit ways, thinking about the implicit is woven through thinking about almost anything. Where the implicit appears explicitly, it tends to be thoroughly enmeshed in the specific context of its production. The various "maps" of the field, then, are drawn with varied materials, interpreted by diverse legends, and read by focusing on differently salient aspects of the landscape. The area treated by one outline might exceed the area of another in some ways but fall short of its mapping in others. To think about several such mappings together is to construct a palimpsest by addition—layering many images of a potential field on top of one another such that some lines are reinforced across iterations, others shifted and blurred by near matches, and others marked off by singularity. Like any map, these are made for a purpose.

In the palimpsest I create, the implicit may be visible primarily at sites of a certain rupture in habitual activity, or points of breakdown in our conception of our selves. When our own self-conception reveals itself as contradictory or—as in some moments of strong emotion or unpremeditated reaction—as simply unexpected, there is the possibility of "seeing" our implicit understanding. Likewise, the experience of one person's network of understanding catching on another person's could produce a revealing disjuncture. And this disjuncture could be the product of, and productive of, joy as much as discomfort. Take another bicycle example, this one from Terri Elliott's essay "Making Strange What Had Appeared Familiar." Elliott imagines that she has inherited a one-speed Schwinn with a bent rim, low air in its tires, and a too-high seat. In her words: "But it's my first bike. I balance precariously, I struggle up hills, I think to myself, 'So this is biking, huh? Maybe roller-skating will be more fun.' Then a friend of the family visits with a beautiful new ten-speed that's just my size. She lets me try it, and I'm amazed at how fast I can go—so effortlessly" (1994, 431). In this example, Elliott's original bicycle provides a framework for understanding what it is to ride a bike, and the friend's bike shifts that understanding through offering the opportunity for a different practice. Dorothy Allison's account of discovering feminism indicates that the "explosion" of feminism offers a more complex account of this kind of political transformation. Feminism—figured as an explicit knowledge, a set of practices, transformed social relations, and more—enabled her to move from a web of implicit understanding that systematically derogated the possibilities for a positive lesbian identity, to a worldview that gave her material and psychological resources for flourishing within that identity.

My stakes here are personal, philosophical and political, including a wish to begin to address my own role in inequitable distributions of resources, attention, and possibility. The trajectory that brings me to this reading of implicit knowledge begins with my experience as an undergraduate philosophy major and the frameworks of apprehension active in that discipline. It was assumed that we were all working and thinking in terms of at least potentially clear truths. Within reason, philosophy students are expected to encounter texts on an equal footing, able to obtain a measure of objectivity. Perhaps because of this assumption, I could see some places where those suppositions broke down—particularly around the anomalies of a deeply gendered gender-neutrality.

My experiences of conceptual breakdowns were in many ways perfectly generic: noticing professors who regularly called on men in a philosophy classroom by name but who routinely failed to call on women, got our names wrong, or expressed gratified surprise when one of us would provide a competent response to a question. My own feminist transformation was not a product simply of the conceptual content of an introductory feminist theory course. It was also a result of the experience of finding myself in the contradictory identity terrain inhabited by an undergraduate woman in a philosophy department. Because I took delight in studying philosophy, I had a particular stubbornness about staying in the discipline; the pleasure involved in the work gave me a kind of entitlement to the field. That entitlement was the condition for being indignant about the sexism endemic to philosophy as a discipline. But other sites of my experience did not provoke such indignation. There are levels of implicitness, some moving into explicit consciousness, some becoming a background, and others occluded. For example, it was very easy for me to be white in my undergraduate philosophy department.

The fact that my gender was noticeable to me yet my whiteness remained unnoticeable indicates the manifestation of a network of implicit understanding, expressed along interwoven and twisting axes of race and gender. My class position, as someone able and expected to go to university, functioned as a root condition of possibility, the hinges on which axes of race and gender turned. Given that condition of possibility, my enjoyment in studying philosophy and my resistance to the constraints of being a woman undergraduate in a philosophy department together highlighted something about the place of gender in philosophy. That is, gender is assumed to be out of place, or inappropriately placed, when it appears in the philosophical framework. Since "woman" is the primary gender formation marked as gendered, to be a woman doing philosophy is to illuminate implicit understandings about gender. Similarly, race and ethnicity are often supposed to be nonphilosophical categories in ways that naturalize whiteness. The smooth functioning of whiteness and class privilege in my own experience indicates one function of implicit understanding: to facilitate the assumption of sometimes harmful norms in ways that perpetuate them. If classist, racist, and sexist practices implicitly define a field, being comfortable in that field involves deploying and benefiting from those practices. The implicit is significant even—perhaps especially—when it remains implicit.

The intersection of inarticulate frameworks of understanding with systems of power, then, is sometimes visible in the exercise of dominative privilege. While implicit understanding always moves in relation to power, thinking about the implicit as it manifests in "unconscious" prejudice, for example, highlights the relevance of having an account of the inarticulate for doing anti-oppression work. Theorists of race and ethnicity have used the notion of a "racial common sense" to get at the idea that there are substantial inarticulate, and possibly inarticulable, elements of racial formation. Understanding common sense as an implicit ground of self-formation provides resources for more adequate theorizing of this realm, and also a potential approach for shifting implicit understanding and introducing new ways of being. Therefore, implicit understanding can create the conditions for political transformation, but it can also block such transformation.

I am thinking, for example, of a guest lecture I gave to a class on white-ness (the fourth chapter of this book came out of this lecture). I talked about negative affect and whiteness, outlining why many antiracist activists argue that white guilt is an ineffective yet frequently invoked root for action. Mid-way through, I paused to invite questions, and a student in the back of the class put up her hand and said, "You mean, kind of like this class." Taken aback, I asked her to elaborate. She did, saying several things that connected with what I'd been arguing, and giving what seemed to be an accurate ac-count of some of what had happened in the classroom space. She offered a coherent account of the challenges she had encountered when talking about race and whiteness during that term. Along with this conceptual account, several forms of implicit understanding came into focus. The student was, it seemed, rendering some of what for her had remained temporarily unspoken in the classroom, and she was talking with emotion about her feeling. There was an affective dimension for the rest of us, as well: I experienced panic, worry about whether the professor in whose class I was lecturing was feeling attacked, relief that a student was unpacking some of the subtext implied in talking about white guilt, fear that I would botch my response, and more. Though I cannot be sure, it seemed to me that others in the room were ex-periencing an affective shock—everyone suddenly seemed more awake and focused. The host professor later confided that she felt a lot of fear at this moment, based on past interactions with the students in the class.

These feelings don't in themselves constitute understanding. Seen in the context of a matrix of implicit understanding shot through with propo-sitional knowledge, though, we can see how affect might be important to the epistemic situation. If the purpose of that class was, as it was titled, "Theo-rizing Whiteness," it matters if having a feeling, like guilt about whiteness, attaches to panic about discussing the topic evoking that feeling. Depending on one's political perspective, these feelings, including the ways they might show up through embodied understanding and including the previously un-speakable knowledge they might disclose, can enable or block the process of coming to conceptual understanding.

The student, then, was drawing attention to some affective and presup-positional aspects of the learning situation, and in a significant way intensi-fying and manifesting some of the implicit understanding I was gesturing toward in my discussion. At the same time, there were other things that re-mained implicit in her question in troubling ways, contributing to the stabi-lization of harmful classification. For example, though the class composition seemed to be unusually diverse by race and ethnicity, her question posited a white subject experiencing white guilt. This is an example of implicit understanding's regressive political and personal significance. Discursive situations that carry political content are always freighted with an affective, embodied, and unspoken charge. And implicit understandings of race and ethnicity, of disability, of class, of fatness, or of gender variance, for example, often work against transformations of those categories. The assumptions my questioner made, the class's affective shock, my response, and a complex network of other features of that experience, could work toward some kind of antiracist transformation. More often, though, I think such experiences evoke a kind of frozen response that short-circuits this kind of political change.

So, in this example, if talking about whiteness brings up panic in white people, who then shy away from talking about race, there is an immediate way that exploring or changing racialized propositional knowledge might be impossible. In particular, people who benefit from or are not targeted by racial inequity are usually not open to hearing and understanding information about the injustices that accompany racial formation. More important, though, is the epistemically salient weight of nonpropositional content attached to whiteness. Consider the difference between reading a quantitative study depicting statistics about white people feeling aversive toward people of color and encountering this feeling in person; consider the difference between hearing someone talk about the fear and shame that might be brought up for white people in talking about whiteness and feeling that fear and shame oneself. Studying theory or supposedly empirical results of studies will only indirectly point toward or approximate the web of understanding abstracted in such scholarship.[4] As I will argue in more detail below, feelings, implicit prejudices, and bodily responses constitute a significant part of racial formation itself. Insofar as political transformation of racialization is desired, these implicit dimensions are important.

This book is a product of feminist philosophy. It can be understood as an attempt to read key sites of racial and gender formation through a feminist lens and using the resources of feminist philosophy. Gender is salient throughout as I attempt to engage and resist what Tina Chanter has identified as a theoretical impasse, in which feminist theory permits race, class, and gender only

---

4. My colleague Pamela Perry and I wrote a paper examining how sociologists interested in whiteness deploy various categories of knowledge along these lines. See Perry and Shotwell 2009.

to "play second fiddle to gender, which will continue to operate as if it were neutral with regard to these secondary, derivative, differences while it in fact retains the middle-class privilege of white heteronormativity." At the same time, as Chanter argues, this problem is replicated in race theory, which at times "has allowed the concept of race to remain at the center of its analyses. Feminist theory thereby continues to marginalize the experience of its racialized others, just as race theory continues to marginalize its gendered others." Further, as Chanter puts it: "In efforts to take seriously the fact that gender has relied upon an inarticulate, indeterminate notion of race, or race has a repressed gendered history, theorists have rendered determinate those racialized or gendered histories that have been left indeterminate. . . . Yet corrective analyses systematically encounter the problem of reinventing new forms of marginalization in the very attempt to redress hegemonic relations" (2006, 87–88). I have, no doubt, fallen prey to these and other pitfalls in my attempt to render legible the concept of politically salient implicit understanding, using methodologies and examples from critical race and gender studies. By attending to precisely the inarticulate and indeterminate aspects of political epistemologies, however, I believe it is possible to work against the center-margin logic that Chanter critiques.

I argue that the implicit is central to the project of creating political consciousness in a transformative mode. Without being able to think and talk, to feel and move through various forms of implicit understanding, we are not able to work explicitly with and on our implicit, affective, tacit, and embodied experience of the world. If such work is central to the political transformations individuals experience, it is equally central to broader political change. In part 1, I attempt to create a useful map, in the form of a palimpsest, of some theories of implicit knowledge. In chapter 1, I offer some theoretical resources for thinking about implicit understanding through a fuller account of philosophers who have given various account of such knowing. In chapter 2, I draw on that palimpsest to think about racialization and commonsense gender formation, working through Wahneema Lubiano's and Antonio Gramsci's writing on common sense. I argue that racial and gender formations are to a significant degree inarticulate and potentially inarticulable, and thus that we need an account of the inarticulate to address these categories. I use the map of the first chapter as a resource, altering and redrawing it in relation to the terrain I encounter in thinking about "race" and "gender." In chapter 3, I examine the socially mediated conditions for transformative understanding, re-situating Bourdieu's notion of socially mediated embodiment in a philosophical history of aesthetics and politics—a history that stretches from eighteenth-century theories of art to current theories of protest and social change.

The second part of this book grounds and extends the philosophical method of part 1 to explore why implicit understanding matters. The accounts I draw on in part 2 act as correctives, affirmations, and supplements to the concerns and methods presented by the more traditional philosophers discussed in part 1. In chapter 4, I weave together themes from chapters 2 and 3 (on racialized common sense and on socially situated embodied experience) to consider feeling bad about whiteness. I argue that while antiracist activists and theorists often critique the utility of white guilt, there is good reason to talk about the affect of shame as a politically viable route to antiracist transformation. In chapter 5, I expand my discussion to look at solidarity as a complex individual and collective stance and action. I am specifically interested in the solidarity white people might be able to extend to racialized "others." In chapter 6, I extend my inquiry into normalized common sense and embodied sociality. I consider theorists writing on transsexual and transgender theories of embodied understanding, and argue for a kind of socially situated knowledge practice.

The task of the second half of the book, then, is to look for sites where implicit understanding's effects and calls are particularly visible, starting from them in order to talk about the political and epistemic salience of implicit understanding. Chapter 4, on shaming, is interested in how affect might offer a politically transformative experience of implicit understanding. Chapter 5, on solidarity, is an example of how potentially propositional understanding can block one's political aspirations, and how a non-reductive affective stance can deploy what Gadamer thinks of as an openness to the space of a question—in this case, a deep ethical relationship with difference. And the final chapter engages how transformations of our embodied knowledge have to do with our political and social world, and how such transformation motivates political change. That is, while part 2 moves topically from issues in race and ethnicity to issues in transgender liberation, it is also topically focused on three of the four areas of implicit understanding I have just laid out; chapters in that section can be read either under the rubric of a race/gender analysis or as a typology and grounded explication of several sorts of interlinked implicit knowing.

Most books are in some way still images of moving objects, and this is particularly the case for intellectual areas in formation. Given more time, I would engage here with the developing fields that speak to affective and somatic cognition (Protevi 2009; Gallagher 2005; Noë 2009), the uses of pragmatism (Sullivan 2001), and the significance of Maurice Merleau-Ponty's work on phenomenology and embodiment (Merleau-Ponty 1962; Weiss 1999). I believe there will be much more work on implicit understanding, and hope here to offer some contributions to currently under-theorized areas of that work. *Knowing Otherwise* dwells at the intersection of several areas of interest, presenting multiple points of attachment and grappling with the frictions that follow from disciplinary crossing. It is written for people who are interested in thinking about race and racism, who find themselves infatuated with unlikely philosophers, who suspect that attending to nonpropositional ways of understanding might help us know the world differently, who want to understand the sensuous import of how race and gender are braided together. As such, I hope the book will spark questions, perhaps more than it resolves, and open space for working with our political and philosophical presuppositions.

PART ONE

MAPPING IMPLICIT UNDERSTANDING

ONE

THEORIES OF IMPLICIT UNDERSTANDING

In the Anglo-American analytic philosophical tradition, there is relatively little attention paid to the fourfold category I am calling implicit understanding. Even so, there has been some significant work both squarely within and alongside this style of philosophy. In this chapter I aim to show how a range of theorists have articulated aspects of implicit understanding. Despite the often narrowly focused views of theorists who have discussed implicit understanding, I argue that we ought to see these forms of understanding as complexly related and interdependent. Simultaneously, it is important to clearly distinguish and delineate among different ways of knowing. Theorists who call on a conception of something like implicit understanding too often gesture toward a woolly and imprecise grouping of various sorts of knowledge in unnecessarily sloppy ways. Following the taxonomy suggested in the prologue, I will briefly discuss the work of exemplary theorists of implicit understanding as they speak to nonpropositional or skill-based knowledge, socially situated embodied knowledge or habitus, potentially propositional knowledge, and affect. Throughout I argue for an integrated account of how these forms of understanding are interrelated and co-constituted.

Much epistemological study has been devoted to propositional knowledge and to questions around knowing—what is an adequate analysis of belief, certainty, justification, grounds for knowledge claims, or truth. The knowledge discussed in many beginning philosophy texts centers around the classic proposition "S knows that p." "Knowledge" is often understood to name a subject's (S's) true and justified belief that something (p) is the case. Thus "S knows that p" if and only if S is justified in her belief that p, and p is true (perhaps with appropriate responses to Gettier problems). For example, Robert Audi frames the notion of knowledge in this way: "It looks as if we have a very substantive threefold necessary condition for (propositional) knowledge. Specifically, it seems that knowledge is at least justified true belief: that one knows something only if one believes it, it is true, and one's belief of it is justified" (1998, 215). Though widely contested even in conventional epistemology, this claim has appeal. It is somewhat testable, intuitively plausible, and offers the possibility of verifiable knowledge. But defining knowledge as "true and justified belief" (with appropriate caveats) does not take into account the importance of an implicit framework of practices, understandings, and situated knowledges to propositional knowledge. Most of this framework is not an explicit part of "true and justified belief"; rather, it is implicit in the judgment of truth and justifiability and enables the exercise of that judgment. What matrices of understanding might position what is known? *P* exists only in relation to a framework of assumptions, practices, presuppositions, suppressed propositions, emotions, and more. This framework conditions the possibility of knowledge, and accordingly of purposive action and political change. It is particularly salient to understanding the norms governing gendered, racialized political formation.

When I've discussed this book with conventional philosophical audiences, by far the most common comment at this stage of the conversation is, "You mean, like John Searle's conception of the Background?" For readers familiar with this literature as well as for those who have never heard of Searle, this question is a good chance to address the problem of failing to recognize important aspects of implicit understanding, and also the problem of how to carefully delineate a precise conception of this sort of understanding. Searle defines the Background as "the set of nonintentional or preintentional capacities that enable intentional action" (1998, 129). He is interested in how truth conditions for sentences (for example) require a "Background of capacities, dispositions, know-how, etc., which are not themselves part of the semantic content of the sentence" (130). Further, he extends this account to argue for the necessity of the Background to other sorts of intentional states. I agree with Searle in his general sketch of the import and function of what he calls the Background. I am, however, shocked at how very general and gestural his account in fact is[1]—he does very little to explicate what exactly the Background is, though he offers a (nonexclusive) list of seven ways it manifests.

---

1. It is striking to reflect on the broad-strokes treatment by which Searle intends to situate his conception in the history of philosophy: "My discussion of the Background is related to other discussions in contemporary philosophy. I think that much of Wittgenstein's later work is about what I call the Background. And if I understand him correctly, Pierre Bourdieu's work on the 'habitus' is about the same sort of phenomena that I call the Background. In the history of philosophy, I believe Hume was the first philosopher to recognize the centrality of the Background in explaining human cognition, and Nietzsche was the philosopher most impressed by its radical contingency" (132).

It troubles me that his conception so often fills in for more substantive talk about this very rich, nuanced, and vital aspect of our epistemological experience. So one of my central motivations here is to lay out some of the precision we might access in conceptualizing implicit understanding, without mashing all different forms of it together.

My other central motivation is to offer some thicker resources for an account of political transformation that relies on forms of implicit understanding. My starting point here is Susan Babbitt's generative work on dreaming "impossible dreams" and doing political work to go along with them. Indeed, Babbitt is my starting point for this project altogether; I read her book *Impossible Dreams* and wanted to contribute a more fine-grained epistemic story to flesh out some of her work. I follow her in seeing liberal individualism as an inadequate resource for political decision making and transformation. I'll begin with Babbitt's account in order to show why it is important to have an epistemological story that includes implicit understanding from the point of view of social and political philosophy.

One of Babbitt's central questions is: What kinds of implicit content might be necessary in order for people to undergo radical shifts in conception and action? Making claims about political, social, and personal transformations, as many theorists do, involves the danger of making claims about others' perceptions of their lives—both epistemically and politically. That is, political theorists often attempt to give an account of not only how other people live, but how they should live, and what they should dream of. Theorists have attempted to work with this danger in a number of ways. Liberalism is a particularly influential account of how to work with the tension of acknowledging individual agency while also making judgments on others' decisions. Babbitt's articulation of personal transformation contests the liberal account of interests. She is interested in how people imagine or dream of worlds that do not yet exist—how we dream what she calls "impossible dreams." She argues that in many cases personal transformation is a significant contributing factor to one's ability to determine one's objective interests, and that nonpropositional knowledge, as she calls it, is crucial to such transformations.

Contrast this notion with a Rawlsian liberal view of rational decision making. The liberal view of better and worse states of being rests on the premise that there is a strong connection between rational decision making and the determination of objective interests. This approach can be seen in John Rawls's work *A Theory of Justice*. On Babbitt's reading, Rawls's argument takes it that a person's rational choice is what she would choose to do under a number of conditions. In order to make a rational choice, in Rawls's sense, that person must first have the ability to think rationally, to reason. Second, she must possess comprehensive information about the choice she is making. Third, she must have the ability to "vividly imagine the consequences of her actions" (Babbitt 1996, 40). These three conditions are sufficient, on the liberal view, to make a rational choice about one's best interests. Two aspects of this view are important to Babbitt's account of rational deliberation, which amount to two unstated premises about the person making a decision. First, the complete information required for rational choice is taken to be propositional information—the sort of knowledge one could easily convey in speech and assess through reason. Second, the liberal view as expressed by Rawls takes it that the self a decision maker projects into the future is a self unchanged from the present. In other words, the self she vividly imagines as she makes a rational choice is fundamentally the same self as the one deliberating.

Babbitt argues that these premises exclude "complete access to a different kind of knowledge—knowledge people possess in the form of intuitions, attitudes, ways of behaving, orientation, and so on" (50). She thus sees nonpropositional knowledge to be an important kind of knowledge, and argues that it is the source of transformation experiences. As I note above, Babbitt understands certain sorts of transformation experiences to be key to the work of flourishing. She argues that changes in one's nonpropositional understanding are crucial to developing the ability to think and act outside of oppressive or inadequate norms. Babbitt uses the term "nonpropositional understanding" interchangeably with "implicit understanding" and "nonpropositional knowledge." She includes in this category intuitions, beliefs, ways of behaving, orientation, and feelings. Babbitt thinks that this sort of knowledge is important, in part, because it gives people the resources to understand ideological oppression to which they may be subjected. Because such an understanding can amount to a change in people's interpretive position, it is doubly inadmissible as a candidate for the liberal view's use of knowledge. I agree with Babbitt's account of the centrality of implicit understanding to political transformation on personal and political levels. But as with Searle, though to a far lesser extent, I find that her conception of implicit understanding is insufficiently worked through, attending as it does primarily to the effects and uses of this sort of knowing and only in passing delineating the differences among intuitions, beliefs, ways of behaving, feelings, and so on.

In the remainder of this chapter, then, I flesh out models of implicit understanding. I begin with an account of ontologically nonpropositional understanding, focusing particularly on Hubert Dreyfus and Michael Polanyi, then move on to a discussion of socially situated embodiment and the notion of the habitus. I next consider potentially propositional knowledge currently unspoken, with a discussion of Hans-Georg Gadamer. Finally, I discuss models of affective or emotional understanding, looking in particular at the conditions for expression of feeling as laid out by Sue Campbell and, differently, Deborah Gould. To conclude the chapter, I turn to Audre Lorde's compelling synthetic view of how these forms of understanding interpenetrate and co-constitute one another.

SKILLS/KNOW-HOW/ONTOLOGICAL NONPROPOSITIONALITY AS A BASE FOR PROPOSITIONAL KNOWLEDGE

Hubert Dreyfus articulates a kind of nonpropositional understanding, discussing it primarily in terms of skills, which he sees as manifestations of practical understanding. For Dreyfus, the background is not representative; it is a "non-cognitive precondition of all understanding" (1985, 233). "Non-cognitive" here seems to name a necessarily presupposed, unspeakable understanding. Dreyfus unpacks the concept in reference to Heidegger's articulation of the fore-understanding, looking at three ways that explicit understanding relies on or involves pre-understanding: *vorhabe,* or fore-having—the totality of what has already been understood or practiced; *vorsicht,* or fore-sight—the approach or way of interpreting what has been understood in the *vorhabe;* and *vorgriff,* or fore-conception—the conceptual frame through which the interpretation is evaluated. Dreyfus's intervention takes place in dialogue with Hans-Georg Gadamer's understanding of prejudices, discussed below. Dreyfus argues that Gadamer's account fails to incorporate nonpropositional dispositions into the terrain of prejudices, thus eliding an important aspect of our capacity to understand the world.

A salient feature of practical understanding is that it takes place against a background of culturally shared practices. Dreyfus writes: "Although practical understanding—everyday coping with things and people—involves explicit beliefs and hypotheses, these can only be meaningful in specific contexts and against a background of shared practices . . . we acquire these social background practices by being brought up in them, not by forming beliefs and learning rules" (231). The background, for Dreyfus, is made up of practices—habits and customs—"embodied in the sort of subtle skills which we exhibit in our everyday interaction with things and people" (232). Such skills are not beliefs, implicit or explicit, and to treat them as though they were would involve a basic distortion; although it is possible to translate some of what makes up a particular skill into propositions, this kind of translation is thoroughly inadequate to capture the mastery of a skill in propositions. The hermeneutic circle takes place "not only on the background of explicit or implicit assumptions but also on a background of practices (the *Vorhabe*) which need not—and indeed cannot—be included as specific presuppositions of the theory, yet already define what could count as confirmation" (234). Dreyfus is presenting here a background constituted of three main components: explicit assumptions, implicit assumptions, and practices, skills, or nonpropositionalizable epistemic "contents," which are neither beliefs nor assumptions. But Dreyfus is somewhat ambiguous on this point. He lays out a picture of the background that includes various sorts of assumptions, but he is also committed to the notion that the background has constitutive, practice-based aspects, free from beliefs and assumptions (perhaps the "propositional" components of the background). He argues: "All our knowledge, even our attempt to know the background, is always already shaped by what might be called our implicit ontology, an 'ontology' which is in our practices as ways of behaving towards things and people, not in our minds as background assumptions which we happen to be taking for granted" (234).

While Dreyfus may not be justified in thinking that prejudices are solely practical understanding, his discussion of the skills and practices highlights an important aspect of the implicit. His work is significant for this delineation of this "implicit ontology" expressed though our practices—an ontology that is not just contingently taken for granted but rather foundationally nonpropositionalizable. For Dreyfus, implicit ontologies are necessary for conventional epistemic work to proceed; we cannot have a structure of knowledge that presumes everything epistemic is potentially propositional. Rather, at some point there must be a ground that propositional knowledge rests on.

Michael Polanyi's discussion of tacit knowledge situates itself similarly as a discussion of practical knowledge—what I have been expressing in terms of ontologically nonpropositional epistemic content to our experience. One of Polanyi's central claims is "that *we can know more than we can tell*" (1967, 4). His articulation of tacit knowledge is also an articulation of the interested role of the knower; Polanyi is committed to the understanding that all knowledge is knowledge held by a subject who cares about what she knows. Understanding (knowledgeable understanding, in any case) might here have the sense of both comprehension and sympathy. In Polanyi's words, "Into every act of knowing there enters a tacit and passionate contribution of the person knowing what is being known, and that this coefficient is no mere imperfection, but a necessary component of all knowledge" (1962, 312). The tacit, for Polanyi, inculcates the personal into knowledge; someone is always involved in knowing. In this regard, Polanyi is also interested in the emotional and passionate aspects of our knowing.

While Polanyi considers skills to be paradigmatically tacit—in somewhat similar ways to Dreyfus—he argues more strongly for the notion that there is always a tacit framework to explicit knowledge, and that it is thus a mistake to limit our conception of epistemology to the articulate. He writes: "While tacit knowledge can be possessed by itself, explicit knowledge must rely on being tacitly understood and applied. Hence all knowledge is either tacit or rooted in tacit knowledge. A wholly explicit knowledge is unthinkable" (1969, 144). Thus Polanyi's theory of meaning argues that the inarticulate is the foundation of explicit meaning; the explicit is meaningful only in the context of, and because of, a matrix of unspoken knowledge. For him, this inarticulate coefficient of knowing is not only contingently inarticulate—it is necessarily unspeakable.

Polanyi is most convincing in his description of the significance of the (nonmystical) ineffable in his thinking on various sorts of expert knowledge. Drawing on examples of scientists, medical doctors, and skilled workers, Polanyi argues that although such knowers

> can indicate their clues and formulate with maxims, they know many more things than they can tell, knowing them only in practice, as instrumental particulars, and not explicitly, as objects. The knowledge of such particulars is therefore ineffable, and the pondering of such particulars is an ineffable process of thought. This applies equally to connoisseurship as the art of knowing and to skills as the art of doing, wherefore both can be taught only by aid of practical example and never solely by precept. (1969, 88)

Skills, like swimming, bicycling, or playing the piano, are always integrated and made subsidiary in knowledgeable practice; they can be improved by formulating precepts and maxims but will always need something more than words can say.

Polanyi lays out his conception of tacit knowledge in relation to three interrelated continua: subsidiary and focal awareness; proximal and distal objects of attention; and a "from-to" attention. Tacit knowing occupies the subsidiary, proximal, and "from" end of these continua, and includes the skills associated with embodiment; explicit knowing has to do with the focal, distal, conceptual, and "to" terms in the equation. Subsidiary and focal awareness are together key to one's understanding of the relation of parts to a whole; Polanyi thinks that the particulars of a thing—something in the world, a thought, an intention—can be noticed either in their discrete traits or in terms of their relation to a "comprehensive entity." This aspect of his thinking on the subsidiary is very much indebted to his reading of Gestalt psychology, and the notion in that field that all understanding of parts takes place only in the context of an apprehension of the whole those parts constitute.

The subsidiary is tacit in that, through attending focally to something, we necessarily cause other things to stand in the background. We attend to something, and in so doing attend also from something. Polanyi writes, "Knowing is a process in two stages, the subsidiary and the focal, and these two can be defined only within the tacit act, which relies on the first for attending to the second" (1969, 179). Polanyi's examples of this process range from the exercise of physical skills to the exercise of conceptual attentions. In using a hammer to hit a nail properly, the impact of the hammer's handle against our hand may be less present to our attention than the impact of the hammer's head against the nail—for Polanyi, we've extended our attention through the hammer toward its goal, rendering focal the impact of hammer on nail and subsidiary the impact of the hammer on our hand. Similarly, in terms of conceptual attention, Polanyi argues, "we may say that a scientific discovery reduces our focal awareness of observations into a subsidiary awareness of them, by shifting our attention from them to their theoretical coherence" (1969, 140). The act of apprehending something focally effects a kind of integration of its terms—to have focal awareness of something is to understand it as a whole, and thus to understand it in terms of component, subsidiary parts. Knowing involves always a kind of orientation from a tacit matrix of proximal understanding to a distal object of attention. It is an act that creates a personally integrated subsidiary knowledge and a corollary distal pole—one that is distanced in the process of being attended to.

The relation of the proximal and subsidiary to the distal and focal is one of utility; as in using a tool for an end, that which we tacitly rely on functions as a tool for focal attention. And in using the tacit as a tool, we orient ourselves along the lines of what has become our subsidiary awareness: "*This reliance is a personal commitment which is involved in all acts of intelligence by which we integrate some things subsidiarily to the centre of our focal attention.* Every act of personal assimilation by which we make a thing form an extension of ourselves through our subsidiary awareness of it, is a commitment of ourselves; a manner of disposing ourselves" (1962, 61). In this sense, again, knowledge is personal knowledge. But Polanyi argues that it is not subjective. Rather, a necessary and ubiquitous feature of knowing is the presence of a knower, and that knower commits herself to a stance in the act of knowing.

As I've mentioned, however, we need a more expansive understanding of the implicit—one not restricted to the potentially propositional, but rather one that accounts for the subjective experience and effect of practices, habits, and skills. Richard Shusterman's formulation of somaesthetics speaks to aspects of this form of implicit understanding, and also bridges conceptions of socially situated embodiment. Drawing on a range of philosophers in the continental and pragmatic philosophical traditions, Shusterman explores three branches of somaesthetics: "the analytic study of the body's role in perception, experience, and action and thus in our mental, moral, and social life; the pragmatic study of methodologies to improve our body-mind functioning and thus expand our capacities of self-fashioning; and the practical branch that investigates such pragmatic methods by testing them on our own flesh in concrete experience and practice" (2008, 139).

Surveying the contributions to philosophies of embodiment made by Foucault, Wittgenstein, Beauvoir, James, and Dewey, Shusterman makes a compelling argument for the importance of seeing the body as both foundationally nonpropositional and as a rich site for intentional and mindful self-cultivation. His work is particularly fruitful in its insistence that bodily habits can be attended to and transformed: "Somatic feelings can be transformed through training because they are already the product of training" (130). This insight is significant in part because it helps Shusterman make the case that while the somatic contents of our experience may be foundationally unspeakable, they can be brought into conscious attention and worked with.[2] In this

---

2. It is interesting to note the ways that Shusterman's own implicit prejudices inflect his very insightful account of bodily practices. For example, when he turns toward thinking about how

sense, "implicit" understanding is a misnomer: all four forms of knowing I discuss can be quite definitely explicit, present, suffusing, and so on—and to varying degrees, all of them can likewise be worked with, though not primarily through propositional consideration and logical analysis.

SOCIALLY SITUATED EMBODIMENT/HABITUS

Pierre Bourdieu's discussion of the habitus as a matrix of implicitly carried and transmitted understandings articulates a link between embodied under-standing and the creation of certain common senses. Where Shusterman fo-cuses on the formation and transformation of bodily dispositions, Bourdieu looks to the social effects of somaesthetic practices. He defines the habitus as "systems of durable, transposable dispositions, structured structures pre-disposed to function as structuring structures" (1990b, 53). The habitus per-sists over time, and can be deployed outside the context of its production. A habitus integrates "past experiences, [and] functions at every moment as a matrix of perceptions, appreciations, and actions" (Bourdieu 1977, 83). The term "habitus" names a tendency, too, to perpetuate the mode of attention and interaction it manifests—the matrix of perceptions, assumptions, and so on that function as structures are structuring in a normative sense. The habitus projects a future in the present, and through that reading helps to bring that future into existence (Bourdieu 1990b, 64).

The body is a significant locus of this sort of perpetuation of the habi-tus for Bourdieu. It displays and reproduces histories of its culture in the way we hold it, how we interact with objects in our everyday life, and how we interact with other people. Conceiving of the habitus as embodied accounts for how knowledge might be transmitted and understood without being conceptual—even potentially conceptual. Extending this idea, Bourdieu ar-gues that the habitus is also productive and expressive of the knowledge the body holds. On the first point, Bourdieu argues, "body hexis speaks directly

somaesthetic work might be politically salient, he characterizes queer desires as "deviant," arguing that somaesthetic reflection can "empower those homosexuals who are confused or troubled about having erotic desires and encounters that deviate from the heterosexual norm. By giving individuals greater clarity about their feelings, such mindful body consciousness can enable anyone with deviant desires to acknowledge, inhabit, and manage these feelings better (which need not mean to stifle them)" (131). At points like these, despite laudable political intentions, Shusterman's work has a dismaying tendency toward ableist, fat-phobic heterosexism that is neither necessary nor implied by his broader philosophi-cal project.

to the motor function, in the form of a pattern of postures that is both individual and systemic, being bound up with a whole system of objects, and charged with a host of special meanings and values" (1990b, 74). That is, the habitus works on the level of an underlying system of physicality, but a physicality thoroughly imbricated with the social practices and conceptions of that physicality. It is not that the concept "habitus" expresses a pre-social, natural, given, embodied state; rather, the habitus concretizes a social world.[3]

These manifestations encode also a variety of imperatives defining of the culture; they are almost moral values. In Bourdieu's words:

> One could endlessly enumerate the values given body, made body, by the hidden persuasion of an implicit pedagogy which can instill a whole cosmology, through injunctions as insignificant as "sit up straight" or "don't hold your knife in your left hand," and inscribe the most fundamental principles of the arbitrary content of a culture in seemingly innocuous details of bearing or physical and verbal manners, so putting them beyond the reach of consciousness and explicit statement. (1990b, 69)

The habitus, then, includes a component of "body hexis"—the implicitly inculcated and incorporated practical sense of what is acceptable and legible within one's culture and what is not. Within a particular culture, the principle expressed by "sit up straight"—or in the practice of sitting up straight—reveals a complex matrix of desired ends and undesired alternatives. And outside that particular culture, the same injunction will hold differently salient valences. In either case, the "seemingly innocuous details" end up implicitly bearing the weight of a whole cosmology, even if only in seed form.

A key aspect of Bourdieu's account of the habitus as embodied is the notion that it is transmitted implicitly through a pedagogy that encodes practices in the body, thus rendering the practices it teaches significantly inaccessible. The habitus allows for schemes "to pass directly from practice to practice without moving through discourse and consciousness" (Bourdieu 1990b, 74). It is itself inarticulate, though constantly expressive.

---

3. Judith Butler's discussion of the reproduction of binary categories of gender resonates with Bourdieu's account. Butler argues that Simone de Beauvoir's understanding of gender as a "historical situation" implies that the body "suffers a certain cultural construction, not only through conventions that sanction and proscribe how one acts one's body, the 'act' or performance that one's body is, but also in the tacit conventions that structure the way the body is culturally perceived" (1997, 407). The gendered manifestations of the habitus "happen" in the internal expression of the habitus *and* in the social perception of its expression.

The movement of culture into the body is effected in part through explicit means—outlining details of proper dining etiquette, for example—and in part through implicit means—through mimetically transmitted physical stances, for example. The habitus manifests implicit, culturally laden content in physical encoding.

These physical encodings have epistemic effect. The body does not simply carry cultural understandings and meanings—not in any way that those meanings could "wash off" at the end of the day. Rather, living a specific socially embodied habitus involves living and holding a specific past; it could be read as a kind of inescapable key to memory. And this characteristic is a result of the habitus forming one's identity in some significant way. The body absorbs an understanding of a culture and becomes that understanding. To be in one's body, then, performing enculturated acts, as we all always are, renders one subject to one's history. Bourdieu argues: "The body believes what it plays at: it weeps if it mimes grief. It does not represent what it performs, it does not memorize the past, it *enacts* the past, bringing it back to life. What is 'learned by the body' is not something that one has, like knowledge that can be brandished, but something that one is" (1990b, 73). The kind of knowledge expressed in the body's knowing is paradigmatically tacit—it is enmeshed and thoroughly incorporated cultural understanding. In some sense, to be a subject in culture rests on a constitutive relationship with one's bodily habitus.

Bourdieu writes that the "habitus—embodied history, internalized as second nature and so forgotten as history—is the active presence of the whole past of which it is the product" (1990b, 56). He suggests here the idea that the habitus includes not only a physical practical sense—what I read as a kind of skill-based, implicit understanding of oneself and one's place (multiply situated) in the world—but also some content of what may once have been explicit, expressible in words. To have forgotten something as history is in part to have forgotten it as propositional. And this process is a result of that history standing as "second nature"—as a subsidiary content to our focal interaction with the world.

To move in systems of forgotten histories—to possess a habitus—is to occupy what Bourdieu terms a "field": the objectified external history that corresponds to the incorporated history of the habitus. The field generates commonly held expectations and molds what counts as reasonable within it. It is the space through which habitus-bearing agents move. Bourdieu argues that the constitution of a field as common sense is a product of a kind of "objective consensus": "What is essential *goes without saying because it comes without saying*" (1977, 168). Applications of supposedly objective social norms, like laws, are bound to applications of principles that are unformulated and unquestionable.

Bourdieu articulates the specific relationship between field and habitus as the compliance with, and assent to, a system of presuppositions. He terms this "taking-for-granted" *doxa*.[4] Doxa—happening without conscious, articulate reflection (such that the "taking" is already a given)—gives rise to a deep misrecognition. Misrecognition is a kind of mystification necessary for the functioning of the field and for the production of social capital in the context of a field. It creates patterns of action systematically denying their own action—Bourdieu gives the example of an exchange of gifts, such that one is socially required to return a gift of equal or greater value for one received, but simultaneously to behave as though neither the reciprocation nor an assessment of its value were required. This sort of systematic, automatic, habitus-guided action produces a social world built on fabrication.

Bourdieu takes up the notion Marx and Engels elaborate in *The German Ideology* that "language is real, practical consciousness," arguing that "the boundary between the universe of (orthodox or heterodox) discourse and the universe of doxa, in the twofold sense of what goes without saying and what cannot be said for lack of an available discourse, represents the dividing-line between the most radical form of misrecognition and the awakening of political consciousness" (1977, 170). The formation of commonsense, self-perpetuating habitus in the form of doxa—that which goes without saying and therefore produces misrecognition—is thus unavailable for critical inquiry. The line between what goes without saying and what cannot be said demarcates also a line between commonsense subsidiary knowledge and an inarticulate knowledge that may be moving into explicitness. It remains unspoken because impossible within a field, but the fact of recognizing a lack in the field implies the possibility of its speaking. The possibility of awakening political consciousness, then, depends on the possibility of articulating new available discourses. I discuss the formation of common sense in more detail in chapter 2.

---

4. Doxa, for Bourdieu, is the species of "practical faith" tacitly required by any given field. It is "that undisputed, pre-reflexive, naïve, native compliance with the fundamental presuppositions of the field." In other words, "Doxa is the relationship of immediate adherence that is established in practice between a *habitus* and the field to which it is attuned, the pre-verbal taking-for-granted of the world that flows from practical sense" (1990b, 68).

POTENTIALLY PROPOSITIONAL KNOWLEDGE,
CURRENTLY NOT IN WORDS

While some forms of knowing—following Dreyfus and Polanyi—might be foundationally inarticulate in ways that do not necessarily imply social and political worlds, the habitus as Bourdieu describes it is inherently political. It carries content, a world in a gesture. There is this third form of currently unspoken knowledge: the potentially propositional but currently backgrounded content of our epistemic and political practices. Hans-Georg Gadamer thinks about this matrix of understanding as a network of presuppositions and prejudices underlying our hermeneutic capacities. I like his account particularly for its attention to the structuring effects of these prejudices and presuppositions.

Gadamer uses the term "prejudice" (or *Vorurteil*) to indicate something that operates unnoticed, something through which we hold ourselves open to understanding, and something that functions as a background condition for understanding. This variation in the use of the term indicates a certain flexibility in its definition, and also a breadth of application of the concept. In *Philosophical Hermeneutics*, Gadamer points to all three senses of the term: "The historicity of our existence entails that prejudices, in the literal sense of the word, constitute the initial directedness of our whole ability to experience. Prejudices are biases of our openness to the world. They are simply conditions whereby we experience something—whereby what we encounter says something to us" (1977, 9). I am thinking about prejudices as a kind of initial and continual positioning from which people interact with their world.[5]

A primary characteristic of a prejudice is that it often operates at a level we do not notice. It forms a substratum, a basis from which we move in understanding. Prejudices can be thoroughly unremarkable: "The fore-meanings that determine my own understanding can go entirely unnoticed" (Gadamer 1989, 268). They may be primarily based in unquestioned assumptions, and therefore it may require active work to bring a prejudice into view. In order to see a prejudice, it must cease to stand as a basic assumption. But prejudices are necessary to understanding—some of them must be called

---

5. I will follow Gadamer throughout this section in his usage of the word "we" as a general marker of beings that can understand things, that have presuppositions of this particular type, and that can shift their prejudices.

into question, but as they move into propositional, conceptual form, other aspects of their being recede into implicitness.

Gadamer further posits a necessary connection between language and understanding: "Not only is the special object of understanding, namely tradition, of a verbal nature; understanding itself has a fundamental connection with language" (1989, 396). Language is the medium for interpretation and understanding. The process of coming to understand a text or another person is a process of relationship through verbal interpretation: "There can be no speaking that does not bind the speaker and the person spoken to . . . this process is simply the concretion of the meaning itself" (397). Gadamer calls on the idea that language is deeply connected to our experience of the world; in fact, to the extent that the world is understandable, it exists linguistically. In his words:

> The world as world exists for man as for no other creature that is in the world. But this world is verbal in nature. . . . To have a world means to have an orientation (Verhalten) toward it. To have an orientation toward the world, however, means to keep oneself so free from what one encounters of the world that one can present it to oneself as it is. This capacity is at once to have a world and to have language. (443)

The hermeneutical capacity, then, is both to have a language, as the medium of understanding, and the attitude of the openness of a question—the stance from which one can question prejudices. But why is the second ingredient of this recipe important? For Gadamer, putting prejudices at risk is an essential activity in the process of coming to understanding. Without the process of questioning our prejudices, we are incapable of determining which are true and which false—a judgment that may come down to determining which prejudices are adequate to a text or a person, and which do not "work," in some sense.

In a 1957 essay, "What Is Truth?" Gadamer rejects on two grounds the idea that truth claims can be reduced to their propositional content. First, he argues that we understand a claim as true or false only in relation to a background, our prejudices and previous understandings. Second, truth claims are always, for Gadamer, positioned in a dialectic of question and answer. Gadamer is thinking of truth at least partially in terms of science, traditionally conceived. The truth of speech, on this view, is "determined by the adequation of the speech to the thing [die Sache], i.e., as adequation of the presentation through speech to the presented thing. From this stems the well-trusted definition of the truth from logic, as *adaequatio intellectus ad rem. . . .* In philosophy we call this propositional truth, keeping our eye on the fact that there are also other possibilities for the truth of speech" (1994, 36–37).

The other possibilities for the truth of speech are tied to non-objectifiable forms of communication through which interpretation and understanding happen; Gadamer says that we always "overstep" the logical form of the proposition in our communicative language. Language, he argues, is multi-vocal. It depends on a metaphorical ambiguity through which speakers are positioned. This positioning stands behind, or below, subsequent logical analyses: "And it is not such as the mere sum of propositions. For the propositions that intend to speak truth must satisfy conditions that are wholly other than those of logical analysis" (39). The problem, Gadamer argues, is that it is not enough to present "that which is present" in a proposition. This is because "the problem is precisely whether everything is so present that it can be presented in speech and whether presenting what can be presented does not block the recognition of what nevertheless is and is experienced" (39). That is, because there is a complex of prejudgments and positions surrounding our speech—because that is the condition for language—the pretense of rendering everything about an object in speech is simply pretense. Worse, the attempt to adequate speech to an object of understanding supposes that such full description is possible. The attempt itself forecloses an understanding of one's positioning, and thus openness to shifting one's prejudgments.

There are many things, Gadamer says, "that are true that we are not capable of recognizing because we are, without being cognizant of it, limited by prejudices" (40). So, the first objection to the notion that all truth, and all truth claims, can be contained in propositional form is that much of the determinates for truth lie outside of what can be said. This aspect of his account allows for the sort of fundamentally nonpropositionalizable content that other theorists argue characterizes the other three forms of implicit understanding I discuss here, though Gadamer does not spend much time on that which is not potentially expressible in language. Gadamer's second objection rests on the first: that every proposition presupposes more than it could say. He argues that propositions cannot be the limit of truth claims because propositions arise in response to a question; they refer outside of themselves. In his words: "Only those who comprehend these presuppositions can really judge the truth of a proposition. Now I maintain that the ultimate logical form of every proposition is the question. . . . There is no proposition that does not represent a type of answer. Therefore, there is no understanding of any proposition that does not take its exclusive criteria from the understanding of the question that it answers" (42).

The horizon of understanding for any proposition, and thus the criteria for evaluating its truth, rests on the origin story of a dialectic of question and answer. Gadamer argues that the truth of a proposition can only be determined in terms of its function as an address of a questioner, an I to a thou. It is at its base a relationship, of the sort that he posits as primary to language. Truth, in this account, must include the context of speech. It is a context that involves both the prejudgments and horizons of the speakers, the dialectic of question and answer, and, centrally, the acknowledgment of implicit content to epistemic judgments.

Gadamer's discussion of the movement of understanding as a movement of things into language, in combination with his understanding of what happens in foregrounding a prejudice, suggests that coming to better understanding is a process of prejudices coming into language. Indeed, Gadamer can be read to restrict prejudices to what is language-based and propositionally expressive.[6] Gadamer, in a passage that seems to support this view, writes:

> Thus the question that concerns us is the conceptual character of all understanding. . . . We have seen that conceptual interpretation is the realization of the hermeneutical experience itself. . . . The verbal formulation is so much part of the interpreter's mind that he never becomes aware of it as an object. . . . We must recognize that all understanding is interwoven with concepts and reject any theory that does not accept the intimate unity of word and subject matter. (1989, 403)

The interweaving of concepts and understanding implies that when a prejudice comes into language, in the move of understanding, it is coming into understanding because its nature is primarily propositional. That is, although it seems correct to read the nature of prejudices, in their pre-interrogated form, as implicit and therefore not propositional, it also seems to be a misreading to think of any prejudices as inherently nonpropositional, in the way that certain skills and practices might be. It seems that

---

6. Lawrence Kennedy Schmidt, in his book on prejudices in Gadamer's work, argues exactly this: *Vorurteil* is "essentially a concept or set of concepts" (2000, 159).

many of the sort of prejudgments Gadamer is interested in are prejudices that are always potentially expressible in language, even if they are never expressed.

Consider another approach to potentially propositional but presently unspoken epistemic content. Ludwig Wittgenstein's book *On Certainty* (1969) examines the grounding structures of propositional knowledge, and implies that those structures are currently implicit underpinnings. Further, Wittgenstein argues that the structuring of our propositions is the source of our certainty. I am primarily interested in what Wittgenstein calls "hinge propositions." On Wittgenstein's usage, hinge propositions are those which must stand fast for us in order for other propositions to make sense. They are "exempt from doubt, are as it were like hinges on which [doubts and questions] turn" (Wittgenstein § 341). They are assumed, constitute a stable background that we do not question, and make up a substratum of meaning. Hinge propositions provide the space in which testing of truth and falsity happens, and without which such interrogation could not arise (§ 83, 105, 205, 359, 410). It is important that hinge propositions be relatively fixed, for "we just can't investigate everything, and for that reason are forced to rest content with assumption. If I want the door to turn, the hinges must stay put" (§ 343). Wittgenstein elaborates:

> Much seems to be fixed, and it is removed from the traffic. It is so to speak shunted onto an unused siding.
> Now it gives our way of looking at things, our researches, their form. Perhaps it was once disputed. But perhaps, for unthinkable ages, it has belonged to the *scaffolding* of our thoughts. (Every human being has parents.) (§ 210–11)

Hinge propositions cease to stand fast, to be incontrovertible, at the point at which we can question them—the point at which we bring them back into play (§ 95–97). In Gadamer's terms, this is the point at which prejudices are put into play and rendered open to question. Hinge propositions are necessary to the epistemic system through which we are certain of things, and we make sense of any epistemic system in part through accepting certain hinge propositions. According to Wittgenstein:

> A totality of judgements is made plausible to us.
> When we first begin to *believe* anything, what we believe is not a single proposition, it is a whole system of propositions. (Light dawns gradually over the whole.)

It is not single axioms that strike me as so obvious, it is a system in which consequences and premises give one another mutual support. (§ 140–42)

The network of propositions is given to us not as discrete pieces of a
whole, but as a web containing those pieces. Wittgenstein thinks of hinge
propositions as those we cannot doubt, because to doubt them takes us out
of the bounds of the language game we are part of. Some of the examples
he gives are of the statement "I am certain that this is my hand," or "That
is a tree"—statements that may be acceptable in particular circumstances,
but generally are so assumed that it does not make sense to assert them. We
learn the language game through our experiences, which teach us what to
believe, what to rely on, and what is unquestionable. A system of beliefs is
learned experientially, as are hinge propositions. Wittgenstein says: "I do not
explicitly learn the propositions that stand fast for me. I can discover them
subsequently like the axis around which a body rotates. This axis is not fixed
in the sense that anything holds it fast, but the movement around it deter-
mines its immobility" (§ 152). If the movement around a hinge proposition
changes, that proposition can change as well. Both Gadamer's and Wittgenstein's naming of these potentially propositional but currently (contingently)
unspeakable forms of knowledge name something significant in epistemic
work. I turn now to a final form of implicit understanding, perhaps least
clearly legible as epistemically salient—the category of affect or emotion.

AFFECT/FEELING/EMOTION

In the other sections of this chapter, I have examined in some depth exem-
plar theorists I judge to have offered significant articulations of each facet of
implicit understanding. This is difficult for me to do regarding affective understanding, however, because the people who have shaped my understanding of feeling and emotion are so varied. Here, I tease apart two strands of
thinking on affect that I think help us understand its twined political and
epistemic importance, with the help of two thinkers who themselves con-
dense genealogies of thinking about feeling: Deborah Gould and Sue Campbell. Read together, these theorists offer resources from both queer theory's
affective turn and feminist philosophy of emotion.

Deborah Gould's recent book on American queer activism in response
to the HIV/AIDS epidemic forwards the argument that affect and political

feelings are a vital component of social movements. I discuss her work more in chapter 6, but here draw most specifically on her definitions of affect, emotion, and feeling. Gould argues that in the recent turn toward thinking about emotion, we can see emotion as "a crucial means by which human beings come to know and understand themselves and their contexts, their interests and commitments, their needs and their options in securing those needs" (2009, 17). Following the philosopher Brian Massumi, Gould defines "affect" as "nonconscious and unnamed, but nevertheless registered, experiences of bodily energy and intensity that arise in response to stimuli impinging on the body." Affect as Gould renders it is profoundly bodily—sensed and felt in the body but "inchoate and as yet inarticulable" (19–20). She, with Massumi (2002), understands affect as nonconscious, outside of ordinary awareness, and full of inarticulate potential.

Emotions, in contrast, name that part of affective experience that is stabilized and manifest through participation in a social world. Gould writes, "Where affect is unfixed, unstructured, noncoherent, and nonlinguistic, an emotion is one's personal expression of what one is feeling in a given moment, an expression that is structured by social convention, by culture" (20). One way to read this conception of the difference between affect and emotion is as a transition from implicit understanding to some level of explicitness. To illustrate Gould's sense of this transition, I quote her at some length:

> In this process of naming or approximately expressing what we are feeling, a transformation occurs, a reduction of an unstructured and unrepresentable affective state with all of its potential into an emotion or emotions whose qualities are conventionally known and fixed. Language and conventionalized bodily gestures thus in a sense "capture" affect, or attempt to. And that attempt gives specific form to an inchoate but pressing bodily sensation, shaping it, delimiting it, fixing it into the emotion or emotions that have been named or expressed. An emotion, in other words, brings a vague bodily intensity or sensation into the realm of cultural meanings and normativity, systems of signification that structure our very feelings. (21)

I appreciate the careful delineation Gould undertakes here, and I see her attention to these categories as more precise than many of the philosophers who have discussed feelings before her.

While I am compelled by this account—and will shortly add some philosophical resources to it from Sue Campbell's work—I also highlight

something of a false binary I believe Gould introduces through her differentiation of emotion from affect. The distinction seems to be between what is
inarticulable (affect) and what is articulated from that content (emotion)—
which would, of course, render the definition of affect inconsistent (as both
inarticulable and articulable). So, to back away slightly from the psychoanalytic and Deleuzian sources on which Gould draws, I see the difference between these formations tracing a line along a shifting boundary of what is
implicit and inchoate and what is explicit but still moving. In other words,
loosening the articulateness distinction between affect and emotion gives
us a more useable conception of these feelings—as paired concepts that together name something significant about what is felt but necessarily exceeds
the bounds of expression. The distinction Gould draws is useful, though, in
its articulation of a relevant difference between feelings that are more and
less socially stabilized. She calls "the entire phenomenon of affect and emotions, including those instances when the distinction is not of immediate
import," *feeling*, arguing that this noun calls up the sense of bodily experience and also the sense in which felt experience is in part a product of public
conventions of sensation (22).

Sue Campbell's conception of the relationship between feelings and expression is useful here for her germinal conception of the processes through
which affect is rendered expressible (or, contrariwise, made expressively impossible). Campbell offers a theory that accounts for how, in Gould's words,
systems of signification might structure our very feelings. Campbell begins
from the "conviction that there is more to the analysis of affect than can be
understood from an analysis of standard emotions" (1997, 5–6). That is, in
the relatively rare instances in which philosophers have theorized affect and
emotion, they have tended to focus on "big" or classic emotions—feelings
like sadness, vanity, love, or anger—and have ignored what Campbell calls
"free-style" or idiosyncratic feelings. Looking toward these more elusive and
local feelings, she articulates a powerful conception of the importance of
expressive resources for feeling. "To understand affect," she argues, "is centrally to understand both the activity of expression and the risks of expressive failure" (6). In ways particularly visible from the standpoint of heterodox
feelings, expressive possibilities and good-enough interpretive communities
shape the contours of the feeling itself. If our only expressive frameworks follow the lines of sight articulated through conventionalized feelings, Campbell argues that our felt life itself will be impoverished. Through expressive
acts, we stabilize and individuate affects and the objects of feelings—including currently heterodox or unknown feelings. Campbell thus proposes that

"we form our feelings through acts of expressing and, in doing so, attempt to make clear to others, or even just to ourselves, the personal significance of some occasion or set of occasions of our lives" (131). Interpretive work on the part of others who provide the context for this sort of expressive possibility is important, then, to the formation of feelings. Indeed, Campbell argues that feelings—both free-style and classic—are dependent "on publicly interpretable acts of expression" (181).

Campbell's account is important to the story I am trying to tell about implicit understanding in part for how it fleshes out Gould's description of the transition from affect to emotion. The expressive resources knowers might bring to bear on their affective experience matters to how and when we have emotions, and how those emotions get articulated politically. Feelings, then, surf the edge of a suffusive experience that is both personal and socially collaborative, both beyond the bounds of speech yet yoked to expressive possibilities. "Feeling," understood as a kind of implicit understanding, thus names in part how it matters for our intentions and attention to move in and out of experience, expression, and explicitness.

GIVING NAME TO THE NAMELESS: AUDRE LORDE'S SYNTHETIC ACCOUNT

To conclude this chapter, I turn toward Audre Lorde's synthetic account of the ways these forms of understanding, one that highlights the political stakes and implications of implicit understanding. "Poetry," Lorde argues, "is the way we help give name to the nameless so it can be thought" (1984, 37). Pierre Bourdieu quotes Jean-Paul Sartre: "Words wreak havoc when they find a name for what had up to then been lived namelessly" (Bourdieu 1977, 170). Richard Shusterman quotes T. S. Eliot, arguing that for him "the poet's role, by forging language, is to help us feel things that could not otherwise be felt, thus 'making possible a much greater range of emotion and perception for other men, because he gives them the speech in which more can be expressed'" (Shusterman 2008, 164). Read together, these claims articulate again the question of how something nameless, possibly heterodox, can be named—particularly if that naming might wreak havoc on a dominant articulation. These claims further substantiate Campbell's arguments for the importance of expression to the formation of feeling. With her conception of the erotic, Lorde offers a powerful understanding of how shifts in implicit knowledge might have to do with joy, and with a particular sort of embodiment. Through attending to her discussion of poetry and the erotic, it is possible to think about the implicit as a productive category—not simply a negation of propositionality. Further, Lorde shapes a holistic story of how the four forms of implicit understanding work together.

In common with each of the theorists I consider in this chapter, Lorde does not have the whole story on the implicit. Her consideration of it, however, provides this account with an indispensable mapping—one that lays out the terrain of the implicit as embodied, as underlying propositional knowledge, and as useful for liberatory change on the level of habitus. I give Lorde the last word here because her account of political change and personal involvement in that change offers an applied picture of the multifaceted epistemic-political matrix I think of as implicit understanding.

In her use of the terms "the erotic" and "poetry," Lorde effects a shift in meaning—she understands the erotic not as having to do simply with sex, or even sensuality, and she is not thinking of poetry (only) as spoken or written verse. Lorde defines "the erotic" as that which is "firmly rooted in the power of our unexpressed or unrecognized feeling" (1984, 53). It is that which provides a reference to joy and a reservoir of liberatory impulse. The first aspect of the erotic—as a kind of touchstone—works as a test and inspiration. This is the erotic as "an internal sense of satisfaction to which, once we have experienced it, we know we can aspire. For having experienced the fullness of this depth of feeling and recognizing its power, in honor and self-respect we can require no less of ourselves" (54). The erotic functions in this respect as a key to memory. The second aspect of the erotic, Lorde argues, is its capacity to offer "a well of replenishing and provocative force": through attending to the erotic, she writes of herself, "my work becomes a conscious decision—a longed-for bed which I enter gratefully and from which I rise up empowered" (55). This second aspect of the erotic addresses the use of working in conjunction with others, and of that relationship as a source for replenishing the erotic. The paradigm description of Lorde's erotic, then, has the dual sense of both underlining a "capacity for joy" and of providing resources to "pursue genuine change within our world" (57, 59). These are both affective feeling-scapes with political content. They are complexly embodied and social, and they offer paths toward multivalent transformation.

The erotic, then, constellates all four sorts of implicit understanding and shows how, although they may be discernible, they are interdependent. Lorde characterizes it as the "nurturer or nursemaid of all our deepest knowledge," arguing that "beyond the superficial, the considered phrase 'It feels right to me,' acknowledges the strength of the erotic into a true knowledge, for what that means is the first and most powerful guiding light toward any understanding. And understanding is a handmaiden which can only wait upon, or clarify, that knowledge deeply born" (56). Whether "dancing, building a bookcase, writing a poem, examining an idea" (57), the erotic names the aspect of experience against which we measure the livability of our lives and our capacities for flourishing. Underlying propositional knowledge, then, are bodily skills, habitus, feeling, and potentially propositional knowledge—each manifesting differently in the dance, the bookcase, the poem, the analytic work.

Lorde writes about poetry, in her particular sense, as a mode through which the potential inherent in the erotic can be realized. She argues that the interior framework of our perception of our lives is important to the lives we are able to lead. She discusses this notion using the concept of "poetry as illumination," which she defines as a space within which people are able to transform themselves and their world. In Lorde's words: "The quality of light by which we scrutinize our lives has direct bearing upon the product which we live, and upon the changes which we hope to bring about through those lives. It is within this light that we form those ideas by which we pursue our magic and make it realized" (36). In Lorde's sense, the quality of light by which we examine our lives is vital to our ability to imagine the change those lives can produce. If we see our lives in light that diminishes our selves, our desires, and our needs, we are less able to manifest those selves, desires, and needs. The concept of potentially propositional implicit understanding has a great deal in common with Lorde's notion of the quality of light within which we shape ourselves. The idea is that there is a backdrop, a space, that underlies and surrounds our expressive behavior and our perception. Poetry allows the expression of what Babbitt talks about as "the impossible dream"—that which we could not say, or necessarily think, before the poem. Lorde says this is "poetry as illumination, for it is through poetry that we give name to those ideas which are—until the poem—nameless and formless, about to be birthed, but already felt" (36). Poetry changes our presuppositions and background understanding—the light by which we perceive ourselves and our world—and both illuminates and forms that which was unseen. It expresses and creates an implicit understanding with liberatory potential, a seed of freedom.

Lorde sets poetry against a solely propositional knowledge. She calls for poetry—in her sense—as an agent for combining feeling and thinking.

Lorde thinks of this as a liberatory project, one that can refine and bring out the relationship between ideas and lived experience. Lorde argues that we "carry within ourselves the possibility for fusion of these approaches so necessary for survival, and we come closest to this combination in our poetry" (37). At the same time, Lorde thinks that the erotic, or the unspoken poetic, must be linked to more traditional ways of knowing. That linkage is the function of the poetic. Without it, we are unable to imagine futures that are different than our present. Because she sees great importance in the meaningful joining of propositional and nonpropositional knowing, Lorde claims that "poetry is not a luxury":

> It is a vital necessity of our existence. It forms the quality of the light within which we predicate our hopes and dreams toward survival and change, first made into language, then into idea, then into more tangible action. Poetry is the way we help give name to the nameless so it can be thought. The farthest horizons of our hopes and fears are cobbled by our poems, carved from the rock experiences of our daily lives. (37)

Poetry, in Lorde's sense, has some similarity with what Susan Babbitt calls "the impossible dream"—acting ahead of current reality in such a way that it changes that reality. It is sometimes necessary for a person to "choose what is not there to be chosen in a particular society at a time" (Babbitt 1996, 173). On Lorde's account, poetry is the mechanism by which people are able to imagine liberatory futures, able to choose what they can only imagine—or what they would have otherwise been unable to imagine.

Lorde articulates feelings and the exploration of feelings as a space within which audacious ideas can germinate and grow. They are necessary for change in part because they provide the proper environment, and in part because they are the source of changing what we attend to, what is salient for us. They make possible the conception of difficult-to-think propositional knowledge; through poetry, previously inaccessible ideas become accessible. In Lorde's words:

> Right now, I could name at least ten ideas I would have found intolerable or incomprehensible and frightening except as they came after dreams and poems. . . . We can train ourselves to respect our feelings and to transpose them into a language so they can be shared. And where that language does not yet exist, it is

our poetry which helps to fashion it. Poetry is not only dreams and vision; it is the skeleton architecture of our lives. It lays the foundations for a future of change, a bridge across our fears of what has never been before. (1984, 37–38)

Through poetry, what was unexpressed, and perhaps inexpressible, becomes communicable. It functions both as a descriptive tool and as a prescriptive one; poetry in Lorde's sense can both articulate what cannot be simply stated and create the conditions for that articulation. It is both the source and the nurturing force for liberatory transformation. Through these conceptions of the erotic and poetry, Lorde sets out a politically motivated picture of the relationships among our skills, habitus, currently unspoken knowledge, and affective understanding. As Gadamer and Polanyi argue, in some sense the politically motivated picture is the only one that matters: personal knowledge and the impassioned willingness to put our own prejudices into risky play are the only motivation for the kinds of mutual transformations among propositional and implicit understanding that Lorde imagines in her conception of the uses of poetry and the erotic. These sorts of transformations happen on the level of the habitus, and shift the core assumptions and deep beliefs that shape expressive and emotive possibilities for experience. Thus, in her account of political transformation, Lorde draws on each aspect of implicit understanding laid out above. I turn in the next two chapters to other synthetic accounts of how implicit understanding can be understood and mobilized in thinking about political change.

TWO

RACIALIZED COMMON SENSE

According to W. E. B. Du Bois, "The problem of the future world is the charting, by means of intelligent reason, of a path not simply through the resistances of physical force, but through the vaster and far more intricate jungle of ideas conditioned on unconscious and subconscious reflexes of living things; on blind unreason and often irresistible urges of sensitive matter; of which the concept of race is today one of the most unyielding and threatening" (1940, viii). Although Du Bois was writing in 1940, much of the intricate tangle of ideas around "race"—the problem of the color line—continues to bear the marks he describes. Race and ethnicity are ideas and realities that are often articulated in terms of their blind unreason, their conditioning by things unconscious and subconscious, their unyielding nature, and their threat. I am interested in beginning to chart one kind of path toward explaining why political categories like race and ethnicity might stand as "blind" and "irresistible"—as not subject to reason—but still commonsensical. Du Bois's work on this terrain has a contemporary resonance. Compare it, for example, to Mimi Nguyen's 2000 blog entry on talk shows and teaching about common sense: "Talk shows are notorious for ideologically asserting the authority of common sense, but when you look closer, what appears as 'common sense'—like, 'It's Adam and Eve, not Adam and Steve!'—is really deeply invested in racial and sexual hegemony." How, then, is commonsense racial formation imbricated with commonsense gender formation?

In this chapter, I argue that implicit, nonpropositional frameworks are a crucial aspect of gender and racial formation, and that we need an account of the implicit to address the maintenance and transmission of these norms. I explore how racial common sense is related to racialized and gendered "epistemologies of ignorance," gesturing toward how the two categories mutually constitute each other. Because I think the implicit plays a central role in maintaining "race" and "gender" as mutually constituting systems of domination, I find it necessary to address aspects of racial and gender formation that inhere in unspoken and contingently unspeakable understanding. In the United States, for example, the last fifteen years have seen a decided turn toward a rhetoric of "color blindness." As a stance toward race and racism, an aspiration toward color blindness brings together an uneasiness about race, a corollary attempt to erase its significance, and a liberal discourse of "freedom and equality for all." Such a rhetoric pushes key aspects of racialization into silence. As many theorists have discussed, the claim that not noticing race is an antiracist act undermines many explicitly antiracist projects; the gutting of affirmative action legislation is a product of such a process (see Bonilla-Silva 2003; Williams 1997).

I begin by examining the idea that understandings of "race" are significantly unarticulated—that they stand as commonsensical. My examination of this idea takes two tacks. First, I argue that theorists of race and ethnicity make use of the notion of common sense because they need a cluster of concepts that will express implicit aspects to racialization and gendering. Second, I argue that the category of "common sense" delineates implicit epistemic frameworks, which turn out also to be the grounds for ideology's connection to culture. I examine current feminist work on gender and epistemologies of ignorance, arguing that this scholarship parallels current critical race theories mobilizing the concept of common sense. In this chapter, I focus on tracking how key theorists discuss and deploy the concept of the commonsensical in their work; in the next chapter I gloss the origins of the notion itself in the history of philosophy of aesthetics. Throughout, my core contention is that in a range of ways theorists have shown the centrality of implicit understanding to political transformation of racialization on both individual and collective scales. In each case, it is useful to have a more closely parsed account of the various facets of understanding.

The theorists I draw on most centrally in delineating the concept of common sense are Wahneema Lubiano, for her incisive reading of cultural production, and the political philosopher Antonio Gramsci, for his nuanced account of the terrain of the commonsensical as a political formation. Lubiano offers a model of theorizing engaged in and arising out of struggle; her work on the movement of politics through culture presents the best sort of pessimism and optimism. Her theorization through taking films, newspaper articles, and songs as cultural artifacts of racist practice and anti-hegemonic resistance is particularly significant. Similarly, Gramsci exemplifies thinking deeply enmeshed in practice. I follow Stuart Hall in reading Gramsci both with an eye toward how he cannot be disentangled from his particular circumstance and with an understanding that this characteristic is central to Gramsci's promise. I value his account for its articulation of the commonsensical as a dense, contradictory, irreducible ground from which liberatory potential arises. Lubiano and Gramsci present compatible but different accounts of the role of ideology as productive of common sense; reading them together gives a nuanced picture of this production, and shows the extent to which common sense is the racialized ground on which culture promulgates ideology. Both lines of thought contest a liberal individualist account from the standpoint of more-and-less Marxian commitments—political and philosophical.

Many theorists of race and ethnicity working in the humanities have called on a conception of implicit understanding in their thinking about race and ethnicity. Shannon Sullivan's compelling reading together of psychoanalytic and pragmatist conceptions of habit and the unconscious makes the argument that "contemporary critical race theory cannot proceed effectively by assuming either that logical arguments against racism will convince racists to change their beliefs or that racism can be ended by conscious fiat" (2006, 22). Others working in critical race studies have made similar claims using the language of "common sense" to get at what I think are the political stakes of implicit understanding. Michael Omi and Howard Winant, for example, write that "race becomes 'common sense'—a way of comprehending, explaining, and acting in the world" (1994, 60). David Theo Goldberg explores how representations in racial discourse "draw their efficacy from traditions, conventions, institutions, and tacit modes of mutual comprehension" (1993, 46). Goldberg frames this underlying stratum as the preconceptual plane that underlies and shapes modernity's common sense (38, 43). Himani Bannerji relies on Gramsci's account to theorize the work of common sense in racialization. She argues that

> the history, ontology, and ongoing practice of an imperialist capitalist society appears to me to find its epistemology in the common sense of racism. Whereas clearly stated racism definitely exists, the problematic aspect for us is the common sense racism which holds the norms and forms thrown up by a few hundred years of pillage, extermination, slavery, colonization, and neo-colonization. It is in these diffused, normalized sets of assumptions, knowledge, and so-called cultural practices that we come across racism in its most powerful, because pervasive, form. (Bannerji 1995, 45)

These theorists are using the notion of common sense to get at what it is for racialization to be systematically woven through our social structure in such a way that everyone is subject to particular racial formations. This is in part a cultural process. How does a Gramscian understanding of common sense help someone in theorizing race and racism? It seems that Gramsci's notion of common sense (particularly as it relates to his articulation of ideological hegemony) is appealing in part because it gives a framework for thinking through how what is spoken hooks in to what is not expressed in words but is still known. It opens a way of thinking about how the unspeakable can be mobilized for political ends. Or, in other words, it might be that speaking of "common sense" is calling up, among other things, a way of thinking about how the implicit is involved in race and ethnicity. I am interested in the complex of unarticulated beliefs, feelings, habitus, inclinations, attitudes, emotions, first-pass responses, and so on, that underlie and shape racialized, gendered understanding.

This chapter addresses a number of interlinked questions: Is Gramsci's conception of common sense also a conception of implicit understanding? Why might it be important that there be some component of people's understanding that is not in words? How have some theorists of race and ethnicity taken up Gramsci's discussion? How might gendered common sense be understood as racialized, and how might racial common sense be understood as gendered? Beginning to answer these questions requires an attention to how both common sense and the implicit might figure in racial formation, gender formation, racism, misogyny, and heteronormativity. These questions concern also the connection between culture and ideology. The network of gender and racial formation involves significant taken-for-granted, often implicit, understandings. I will argue that such commonsense knowledges provide the connection through which culture and ideology affect one each other, exploring how cultural formations might change or affect racial formation on the level of everyday ideology.

GRAMSCI AND COMMON SENSE

I opened by suggesting that Gramsci takes common sense to inhere in everyday unconsidered conceptions—what I have been referring to as that which is taken for granted, understood, implicit, nonpropositional, and tacit in our ways of understanding the world. For Gramsci, the consciousness implicit in a person's activity—the person's common sense—is a significant part of ideology. Gramsci argues that "common sense is an ambiguous, contradictory, and multiform concept" (1972, 423). He characterizes it as having three main characteristics: it is "[1] incoherent and [2] inconsequential, [3] in conformity with the social and cultural position of those masses whose philosophy it is" (419). For common sense to be non-consecutively incoherent is for it to contain, in some sense, the possibility of contradiction. The commonsensical can hold both p and not-p and not be particularly bothered—perhaps not even notice. For common sense to be uncritically absorbed is for it to enter our consciousness un-interrogated, at a level beneath notice. Part of the difficulty, then, in any attempt to critically absorb common sense—assuming one wanted to do so—might be that the very nature of common sense resists a critical view, which is, at base, an articulate, propositional understanding. For something to be coherent and voiced is for it to no longer be commonsensical. In these respects, common sense should be understood as a kind of potentially propositional knowledge presently unresolved into claim-making activity. This characteristic is, I would argue, one of the central reasons theorists of race and ethnicity have called on a notion of common sense in thinking about racialization. Since all common sense is racialized common sense—though in differing ways depending on social relations, place, and time—understanding the presuppositional features of racial formation is important to seeing how to address what Du Bois calls the unconscious and subconscious reflexes of living things as they shape race.

A third characteristic of common sense is its adherence to the philosophy of what Gramsci calls the "masses of the people." There is a cycle in which common sense conforms to the conceptions of most everyone and in turn shapes taken-for-granted understanding. Gramsci says that the philosophy of common sense "is the 'philosophy of non-philosophers'" (1972, 419): the conception of the world that is uncritically absorbed by the various social and cultural environments in which the moral individuality of the average person is developed. Recall Bourdieu's characterization of the habitus as going without saying because it comes without saying. As I discuss below, Hall argues in this vein that common sense is the "terrain of conceptions and categories on which the practical consciousness of the masses of the people is actually formed" (1986, 431). But it is important that for Gramsci, common sense is not a single unique conception, identical in time and space. It is "the 'folklore' of philosophy, and, like folklore, it takes countless different forms" (Gramsci 1972, 419). Common sense conforms to most people's basic understandings of their world—that's what it is to be commonsensical—and also causes people's everyday, unconsidered conceptions. At the same time, common sense is multiple and mutable—it exceeds, and in its excess offers political possibilities for transforming ourselves and the social relations we shape.

Gramsci situates the possibility of change in terms of what he calls "good sense"—the elements of our unconsidered assumptions that are "the healthy nucleus" of common sense, "which deserves to be made more unitary and coherent" (328). Good sense is, in some way, the ground from which common sense is changed. Common sense is not, in other words, simply a mass of undifferentiated "bad stuff." It contains connections to what has come before us in whatever cultures we inhabit. We build on the "fragmentary collection of ideas and opinions" (328) to create a conscious direction in political activity and social change.

Gramsci argues that we always partake in some common sense, and that interrogating our unspoken conception of the world is to bring some of that conception to the foreground. Looking at common sense, in his words, "means therefore to make it a coherent unity. . . . The starting point of critical elaboration is the consciousness of what one really is, and is 'knowing thyself' as a product of the historical process to date which has deposited in you an infinity of traces, without leaving an inventory" (324). "Making an inventory" articulates a process of forming both coherence and expressiveness out of un-interrogated assumptions. That a movement beyond common sense is, for Gramsci, a movement into articulate, word-based conception indicates that normally common sense is implicitly understood. We see the implicit quality of commonsense (un)consciousness in the fact that historical processes result in a sedimented collection of an "infinity of traces" without leaving an account of those traces—"without leaving an inventory." And yet, as Gramsci indicates, what stands as common sense to us is deeply important to our lived experience.

We are influenced by common sense in all sorts of wordless ways. Many of those influences are actually harmful; they prevent people from taking action and reduce them to a state of passivity. Contradictory consciousness is both practical activity (implicit) and inherited conception (superficially explicit but actually less than explicit). Both sides of that consciousness seem to be commonsense aspects of a person's being. For Gramsci, common sense is both inchoate and inarticulate. It is not, however, inarticulable. Gramsci holds that what stands as common sense is at least potentially propositional; it is as-yet inarticulate and nonverbal.

One way the commonsensical is important to our experience is through its relation to ideology.[1] The ideological dimensions of race and ethnicity are, like everything ideological, situated in webs of meaning and understanding; the discourse of race is historically moored in particular ways, and takes meaning from the place it attaches and interweaves with broader social connotations and implications. Thus history influences the lines along which ideology is likely to develop. The sedimentation of such lines—or fields, in Hall's terms—is the terrain of common sense; common sense bears on what is possible and likely in ideological and therefore hegemonic formations. Common sense's relationship to ideology might be analogized with the way a grouping of children's building blocks—perhaps consisting of partially formed and also completed structures, random blocks, and so on— relates to a briefly reorganized and better structured grouping. The materials remain the same, whether they are deployed in the current formation or left to the side, and they can be taken out of formation and reused in a kind of bricolage. At the same time, there will be formations that any builders using those particular materials are more comfortable creating—formations that accord with what has been made before, for example. Such comfort will be the effect of particular ideologies. The collective and social nature of ideological formation also contributes to a complex and "inter-discursive" manifestation of the self in an ideological field. The stakes here should be clear: to the extent that race is a system of social relations held as unyielding and unquestionable through commonsense assumptions, we will need to transform common sense in order to meaningfully change the social world.

David Lionel Smith's discussion of common sense in relation to racial formation and culture is useful on this count. He writes: "Race is a commonsense notion. It falls apart under rational scrutiny, yet it is exceedingly difficult for us to attack." Further, commonsense notions of particular racialized identity, while demonstrably harmful in many ways, provide also a "sense of identity, community, and history" (Smith 1997, 182). This disjunctive and

---

1. Current work on ideology must be situated in the context of relatively early work at the Birmingham Centre for Contemporary Cultural Studies (CCCS). The CCCS arose out of the work of Richard Hoggart, Raymond Williams, and E. P. Thompson on culture and class; in the late 1950s and early 1960s, under Stuart Hall's directorship, it developed into a institution very much influenced by Gramsci. The writing of this time emanating from the CCCS is clearly engaged with Althusser's reading of Marx and Engels in *The German Ideology*. In Stuart Hall's work, however, Gramsci becomes a fruitful thinker precisely in the places where his notion of ideology differs from the later Althusser. Hall wants to retain a polyvalent voicing of ideology, one that intrinsically holds contradiction and liberatory potential in its makeup.

contradictory quality in part gives rise to the "self-vindicating character of common sense [that] gives notions like race a powerful durability" (Smith 1997, 182). Smith argues that because racial categories inform our consciousness, we cannot easily dismiss them. "The challenge," he says, "is to understand what race is, how it functions, and ultimately to theorize how we might endeavor within a culture bound by race to subvert the subordinating strictures that race was designed to perpetuate" (181). These are commonsense understandings that twist, constrain, and prevent accounts of social and cultural expressions of race. How might these same implicit frameworks give rise to the potential for heterodox or resistant commonsense knowledge as it relates to racial formation? Following my argument in chapter 1, I would also push Smith to consider how race as a commonsense notion might be transformed without bringing it under rational scrutiny. In other words, how can transformed implicit understanding matter to challenging racialized oppression?

EPISTEMOLOGIES OF IGNORANCE

To begin to answer this question, I turn next to a consideration of what an epistemological account of common sense might be. I also want to enrich these accounts of racial formation and common sense by talking explicitly about gender—another naturalized commonsense category and one that co-constitutes racial categories. Charles Mills's analysis of what he calls "the Racial Contract" offers an account of those formal and informal agreements that stabilize and regulate racial formation. An important piece of his account is the claim that the theory of the Racial Contract explains how "society was created or crucially transformed, how individuals in that society were reconstituted, how the state was established, and how a particular moral code and a certain moral psychology were brought into existence." Further, Mills sees the Racial Contract as "epistemological, prescribing norms for cognition to which signatories must adhere" (1997, 10). Mills characterizes this epistemological dimension as an inverted epistemology, an "epistemology of ignorance": "a particular pattern of localized and global cognitive dysfunctions (which are psychologically and socially functional), producing the ironic outcome that whites will in general be unable to understand the world they themselves have made" (18). This cognitive model, as Mills presents it, limits what individual white people know and how they know it. This limit on what an individual "can" know is supported and enabled by a network of other norms and practices; I see the functioning of an epistemology of ignorance to be very much connected to common sense and in many ways to map the epistemology of common sense.

Feminist theorists have recently extended Mills's explication of epistemologies of ignorance to account for structural limits on what is and can be known under current social conditions. They have also endeavored to think seriously about how to create and ground resistant epistemologies. Nancy Tuana taxonomizes epistemologies of ignorance, first in an article on how knowledge about women's genitalia and orgasm is ignored, dismissed, and misrepresented, and then in a piece on the women's health movement in the United States. Tuana categorizes ignorance into six interrelated categories: "knowing we do not know, and do not care to know" (as, for example, about a male hormonal contraceptive) (2006, 3–6); "we do not even know that we do not know," because other current interests or knowledge block the thing we might know (as, for example, the structure of the clitoris) (6–8); "they do not want us to know" (as with health risks of oral contraceptives, which pharmaceutical companies knew about but did not tell women) (9–10); "willful ignorance" as a systematic form of denial (11–13); "ignorance produced by the construction of epistemically disadvantaged identities" (as when people who claim abuse are diagnosed with false memory syndrome) (13–15); and what Tuana calls "loving ignorance," which she characterizes as involving "the realization that although much experience can be shared there will always be experience that cannot. . . . Loving ignorance is thus a recognition that there are modalities of being that exceed our own and cannot be fully comprehended" (16). These classifications of epistemologies of ignorance offer something to an epistemology of common sense. The mechanisms through which the commonsensical remains implicit, unspoken, or unspeakable may be similar to the mechanisms that produce and maintain these six "types" of ignorance-as-epistemic-practice. That is, when something stands as commonsensical, in Gramsci's terms, it expresses several facets of Tuana's classification. Common sense is formed at the fulcrum of what we care to know, what we cannot know under current conditions, what we refuse to know, and what we would have to transform ourselves in order to know. When we have commonsense knowledge, we do seem to know something, frequently even in a strong sense of the term "know"—but this knowledge is frequently a product of and productive of inequitable social worlds. As a norm, an epistemology of ignorance perpetuates the common sense it describes.

It is instructive, then, to examine some mechanisms for feminist transformation of ignorance alongside feminist cautions against what Cynthia Townley calls "epistemophilia," or the belief that more knowledge is ontologically good. Indeed, Townley's account speaks against Gramsci's call to systematize commonsense understanding into explicitness, which he identifies as the project of philosophy. Townley critiques the epistemic goal of maximizing true belief or knowledge, arguing that "epistemically responsible agency requires that epistemophilia's exclusive ascription of value to increasing knowledge be replaced by a cluster of values ensuring that the conditions for epistemic cooperation are maintained and that agents can develop and maintain the skills for contributing to a thriving epistemic community" (2006, 42–43). I would extend Townley's argument; just as having "more" knowledge should not be our prime epistemic goal, speakable knowledge should not define our knowing. The epistemic practices affiliated with commonsense apprehension of social worlds include practices, affects, and currently unspeakable knowledges. Transforming common sense may involve a strong commitment to what Dawn Rae Davis calls "a feminist ethic of love," one that relies on alterity and a corollary recognition that "what knowledge discloses is simultaneously an effect of what it inevitably conceals." Such an orientation is "not a will not to know, as in the condition of ignorance, but an ability to engage with what escapes propositions and representations" (Davis 2002, 155). These theorists' attention to epistemologies of ignorance, the ability of not-knowing, and what Joy James (2000) and Toni Morrison (1989, 1992) theorize as "discredited knowledge," points toward a concern with implicit understanding's relevance to gender and sex.

Reforming and overturning commonsense understandings about gender has been the terrain of so much feminist political work that I would not be able to schematize it all. To take a few examples, I am thinking of transformations in commonsense understandings of whether women had the intellectual capacities to be granted the right to vote, whether women are capable of doing construction work, or what constitutes sexual harassment in the workplace. I pick these examples because it is now relatively commonsensical that women do have the capacities to vote and to build things, and that certain behaviors in the workplace now understood as harassment would not have been thirty years ago. Even these examples, of course, are not uniformly commonsensical, and all three have different "results" if we complicate the category of "women" and think of "women of color" or "disabled women" or "white women."

I concluded the prior section with David Lionel Smith's call for subversion of "the subordinating strictures that race was designed to perpetuate." In this section, I've offered some epistemological resources for understanding the function of these implicit and explicit strictures, extending Charles Mills's account of racial epistemologies of ignorance into a consideration of gendered commonsense epistemologies. Wahneema Lubiano's discussion of culture as the ground for contradictory, potentially liberatory, common sense is helpful here. Lubiano also helps to situate racialized common sense in terms of cultural production.

COMMON SENSE AND STRUGGLE

Wahneema Lubiano articulates a powerful conception of the movement of common sense through culture in ideologically inflected formations of race, ethnicity, and gender. I discuss Lubiano to fill out the relationship between culture and common sense, and also because of the liberatory potential her work opens in relating to culture. Lubiano's oeuvre consistently and lucidly unpacks the cultural production of ideology; this is a partial reading of her theoretical framework, offering my account of implicit understanding to her articulation of ideology and race, particularly in terms of the formation of common sense.

In "Black Nationalism and Black Common Sense," Lubiano argues that black nationalism describes a wide range of activities and articulations, which manifest a critique of past and present U.S. racism and a method for the state to enact, perpetuate, and extend its racist work. Both these functions, and many more, are predicated on the relation between ideology and common sense, as Gramsci uses those terms. Lubiano claims that black nationalism functions as: a narrative of the past; an articulation of diverse presents; an explanation of what is "good and beautiful, as style"; a "rallying cry"; and "a critical analysis—and as an ongoing ever-renewed critique of black existence against white racial domination" (1997a, 233). In such a manifestation, black nationalism can be seen to provide crucial grounds for liberatory work. It is, Lubiano argues, of "inestimable ideological—commonsensical—importance given the reality that U.S. blacks" control none of the standard markers of nationhood (233). This is why she sees culture, and the common sense that arises out of culturally informed ideology, as the central terrain of struggle. Black nationalism functions as a contradictory common sense, where common sense is defined as "ideology lived and articulated in everyday understandings of the world and one's place in it" (232).

Lubiano sees liberatory potential in narratives of black nationalism; its "work as counter narrative is aestheticized in popular culture" (237). Narratives deploying tropes of black nationalism can turn against, and thereby shift, racist imaginings in fruitful ways; this kind of deployment can function as defense. It is a kind of resistant common sense and a corollary resistant epistemology, in which things are reclaimed as knowledge and practice that, in Tuana's terms, "they do not want us to know." Among other things, black identity, for example, is a "sign for [black American] specificity and aestheticizing [black American] resistance to racist trauma" (Lubiano 1997a, 238). Lubiano also explores, however, how black nationalism could also function "horribly, in 'new world order' terms" (238), as a state-led mobilization of blackness for the government's "repressive work and its policing of civil society" (245). She highlights, here, the danger of commonsense conceptions: that they can and often do function as deeply conservative. When common sense functions in these ways, it manifests many of the characteristics of an epistemology of ignorance about the twined threads that produce race and gender.

In discussing the possible virtues of the framework of "multiculturalism," another potentially heterodox racial formation, Lubiano is more specific about the potential dangers in naturalized narratives that benefit the state: "To put it bluntly, Black people who consciously think of themselves as part of a Black group often think of themselves as oppositional at the very same time as they are internalizing precisely the state's most effective narratives, narratives that are the medium by which the state dominates the group in ways the group does not recognize" (1992, 73). Such narratives manifest on the level of popular culture; they form a common sense that functions in the service of state interest—what Gramsci describes as its uncritical absorption and its resistance to critique.

For example, Lubiano analyzes the racialized and gendered common sense manifest in a picture of a returned soldier hugging his daughter, published as a full-page "welcome home" to soldiers who had fought in the first Gulf War. She unpacks a backstory of the picture, including black participation in early U.S. frontier making and genocide, current military actions, and by extension imperialist aspirations toward the world. Most significant, though, is the discussion Lubiano reports when she showed this picture to a group of women and talked with them about it. She says:

What came out in discussion is how incredibly interesting and attractive that photograph's representation of the black male soldier was among the women . . . for two different but overlapping reasons: (1) not because of his military status, but because they were aware of the racism in the U.S. that has produced the military as an attractive economic labor site for black people . . . and (2) because he is standing with his arms around his daughter. That photo and that pose evoke the "black family" in all of its distorted and pathos-inflected narrative glory. (Lubiano 1998, 447)

The photo thus mobilizes a common sense braiding racial understandings (both explicit and affective) and gendered common senses. The soldier is pictured hugging his female child, wedding ring prominently visible on the hand holding a U.S. flag. The image thus calls up and dispels the equally gendered picture of the single black mother on welfare; this black man serves his country, loves his daughter, and stays with his wife. As Lubiano puts it: "This is the U.S. state at its ugliest and most subtle: the Gulf War and the military's exploitation of a racially, economically, and politically oppressed group is costumed into a black father's doing his duty for his country and his daughter" (447–48). Here I would extend Lubiano's reading of this image to push Tuana's definitions, and even Gramsci's account of common sense. Lubiano shows, in this example, how resistant and regressive common senses can co-exist and co-constitute each other and how an understanding can be consciously known but affectively commonsensical. The women with whom Lubiano analyzes this image have a fraught positive response to the picture. This arises not in approbation of black men's military service but in condemnation of the social conditions that produce disproportionate representation of people of color in military service. Common sense both partakes in and exceeds epistemologies of ignorance, as is particularly clear when we look to examples in popular culture.

CULTURE, IDEOLOGY, AND MAKING SENSE

Following the work of cultural studies theorists like Hall and Lubiano, I see culture as the ground for common sense. As Bannerji argues, the concept of common sense "is useful for expanding the meaning of racism from something that is articulate, aggressive, and blatant, or a clearly thought out ideological position . . . to the level of everyday life and popular culture" (1995,

134–35). Pop culture across many media is always related to an economy of pleasure, politics, and policing, and provides a key aspect of the ground on which common senses form. What is commonsensical does not have to be articulated as, for example, "black nationalism"; it can remain implicit, inchoate, or unarticulated. The commonsensical merely has to function relatively smoothly for that person, and such functioning is supported by cultural artifacts that reinforce particular assumptions. This is one of the ways that ideological ideas stand as common sense. There is a recursive movement between artifacts, feelings, practices, and commonsense stances that stabilizes an ideological formation. While the "work" of cultural production and consumption is thus mostly affective, presuppositional, and bodily, its effects ripple out to expand and give weight to more formalized beliefs and propositions about the world.

Post-Gramscian conceptions of common sense rely on a particular style of thinking about "ideology" as containing a great deal of contradiction and possibility. Commonsense ideology's work is always happening in relation to the state; for example, writes Lubiano, state power does its work by virtue of its invisibility and because it is embedded in the public's understanding of everyday occurrences and beliefs. Photographs and other salient narratives are the means by which sense is made in and of the world; they also provide the means by which those who hold power (or influence the maintenance of power) make or attempt to make sense of the world for others. Such narratives are so naturalized, so pushed by the momentum of their ubiquity, that they first seem to be reality and then become reality. That dynamic is the work of ideology (Lubiano 1992, 329). We can think of ideology in a more or less constraining way, such that what is "given" to us in ideology is inescapable, dominating and determining our subject positions. The cartoon version of a strict notion of ideology takes us to be puppets of our particular, always ideological, social formation.

But we can also think of ideological formation as arising from a contradictory, multiply determined, shifting common sense—in Gramsci's terms—such that the "ingredients" for heterodox thinking are as present in the ideological soup as the elements making up orthodox social and subject formations. This layered and contradictory notion of common sense and ideology offers a way to acknowledge the power of state deployment of racist educational systems, for example, while allowing that those systems do not always successfully interpellate their subjects. Lubiano's work gives a useful example of how one might situate lived ideology in the realm of the cultural. If she is right, much of the terrain of common sense is given to us in the cultural forms of which we partake; the movies, magazines, and pop music we watch, read, and hear might be seen to inform our understanding of the world on deep levels. The "message" of any given movie is part of a larger "message"—an ideological formation that rests on, for example, harmful commonsense understandings of blackness, masculinity, class, and so on. Entertainment fills in critical inquiry and renders as spectacular pleasure much of the discomfort the viewer should arguably experience. When a movie or a song functions in the way Lubiano describes, it both draws on and creates a set of unarticulated assumptions required to participate in the viewing or hearing. Commonsense understandings of race are complexly related to commonsense understandings of gender; they co-constitute each other.

In such a context, it is fruitful to think of what stands as common sense to us in terms of its tacit, implicit, or unspoken character. Although Gramsci is particularly interested in the movement of articulation in forming and transforming common sense, I would argue for a more holistic conception of the multivalent facets of implicit understanding at play in stabilizing common sense as a cultural and ideological formation. Consider, for example, the visceral and emotional aspects of racism and gender panic expressed in the 1995 murder by inaction of Tyra Hunter, a black woman of trans experience who died after emergency response workers denied her treatment. Reportedly, they arrived to the scene of a car accident, finding Hunter unconscious and badly injured. As they began treatment, one of them discovered that her body was shaped in ways they did not associate with women, and, as Richard Juang depicts the scene, stopped treatment, saying, "This bitch ain't no girl. . . . It's a nigger, he got a dick" (2006, 712). This scene constellates a dire and extreme variation of the oppressive effects of race, gender, and other social relations held as common sense, but it emphasizes rather than distorts these effects. The EMT's response expresses a kind of inchoate common sense framed in the disjunction between the genitals he expected to see and what he saw, a shift marked in language through a transition from "bitch" to "girl" to an "it," "a nigger" with "a dick." Racism, sexism, and transphobia twine together and reveal the work of disrupted assumption and supposition.

Equally, it seems that there is a somatic and affective aspect to this scene. As Richard Shusterman describes some of the somatic ingredients in this sort of phobic response: "Much ethnic and racial hostility is not the product of logical thought but of deep prejudices that are somatically expressed or embodied in vague but disagreeable feelings that typically lie beneath the level of explicit consciousness. Such prejudices and feelings thus resist correction by mere discursive arguments for tolerance, which can be accepted on the rational level without changing the visceral grip of the prejudice" (2008, 25). I agree with Shusterman on this count, though, as I note above, I believe he ought to better distinguish feeling and prejudice without collapsing both into somatic response. While each of these aspects of what the EMT expressed in his racist and transphobic refusal to treat Hunter were present, they are separable. In particular, it is important to give a clear sense of how the feeling and bodily responses expressed here connected with the potentially propositional common sense Gramsci discusses.

So: where does understanding common sense as implicit get us in thinking about "race" and "gender"? I think it opens up at least three avenues. First, it addresses the scare quotes Paul Gilroy, for one, puts around the term "race"—and it implies a similar distanciation we ought to hear always around the term "gender." There is a distance imposed between the reader or hearer and the term in the act of quotation that relies on particular common senses; the mechanism of quotation functions as a trope to both call up and reject stabilizations of race. That trope needs an understanding to swerve toward, and it pushes against a network of assumptions and profoundly unacknowledged (un-"known") understandings. Naming "race" calcifies the terms of common sense, at least momentarily. It is possible to understand "race," within quotation marks, as both materially real, having actual, measurable effects on lives, and as not "there"—as a fiction that exists only in particular social spaces, but through which material effects are realized. How does "that long-lived trope" (Gilroy 2000, 48) maintain coherency in the face of the deep obsolescence of phenotypic typing? In part through the shallow, superficial, great power of unspoken commonsense understandings of what race is. So I would argue that having an articulation of race as implicit knowledge helps to describe the mechanism of "race" in its continued creation and development in this world.

Similarly, looking at how commonsense formations are always both gendered and racialized allows for a more nuanced account of what it would be to contest ideological formations. When Lubiano reads the photograph of the returned Gulf War soldier, she unwinds both the visual-discursive construction of his masculinity, the gendering his pictured daughter signals, and how those commonsense cues connect to broader understandings of black women in the United States. Taking common sense as a theoretical framework allows

Lubiano to show gender as both discursively created and materially real. And addressing the dual nature of this common sense reconfigures some of the facets of what Tuana taxonomizes as part of epistemologies of ignorance. The coproduction of racialized and gendered common sense that caused Hunter's death show how crucial it is to have first-pass somatic, affective, and presuppositional responses less structured by racism, sexism, and trans-hating.

Second, thinking through gender and racial formation as partially nonpropositional provides an account of how consent to hegemonic reproduction of these systems is itself materially but not necessarily discursively propagated. That is, if such an account can be said to help descriptively by giving a narrative of the ingredients of racial formation and racism, it is also useful in unpacking the methods by which those "ingredients" are promulgated. I have not discussed the transmission of common sense from one person to another or through culture; I agree with Gramsci (and, to some extent, Althusser) that much of that transmission happens in the realm of the state-modulated social realm—in churches and schools, among other places. But the content of that transmission, even in the text-based moments of those spaces, is not limited to a particular text. Rather, it inheres in the structures and in the interstices, in the explicit and in the implicit; clearly identifying the nonpropositional helps me think about "where" some of the most difficult prejudice "lives" when it is not visible in the world. That inexplicit manifestation is one of the markers of "difficulty." A conception that includes the implicit contents of racial and gender formation is more complete than one based on mostly propositional formulations.

Let me emphasize that it is not necessary to agree with Gramsci that the only use of common sense is in its resolution into coherency—and thus philosophy, in Gramsci's sense. It is possible to retain the argument he gives for common sense's qualities without reproducing his particular teleology for that conception. Gramsci's argument for what common sense would have to do in order to be an effective political philosophy clearly elucidates its nature as not primarily propositional. It is important, though, that common sense, as an always socially inflected necessary ingredient in understanding one's world, might usefully retain some of the very incoherence and inconsistency that also causes it to be problematic. This is the aspect of working with common sense that might maintain what Dawn Rae Davis theorizes as an attention to alterity as epistemic good.

Finally, it seems to me that understanding common sense in terms of implicit understanding provides openings for changing that understanding

in liberatory ways. Perhaps the fact that there are different senses of the common—different frameworks of nonpropositional understanding, different
situated knowledges, different embodiednesses, and so on—is precisely the
potential of common sense. That inchoateness, which can never be whole
even if that is its aim, shows what it is to be ruptured and what it is to require liberatory rupture. And part of common sense is the kernels of good
sense—the useful aspects of one's assumptions that Gramsci argues should
be rendered more coherent. Further, if the nonpropositional is what changes
in a move from racist understanding of the world to a less, or non-, racist
stance, we need to have access to how to actively change that understanding.
We need, at least, to be able to address the inarticulate but effective ways that
ideology might be structured. Charles Mills addresses this need: "Perhaps
even more important than ideologies at the explicit and articulated level (for
example, libertarianism, biological determinism) are ideologies in the more
primeval sense of underlying patterns and matrices of belief, or ideology as
'common sense.' . . . The latter may well be more influential and efficacious
than the former simply by virtue of their ability to set the terms of the debate,
to limit the options deemed worthy of consideration" (1998, 34). It is critical to think of commonsense understandings of race and gender in terms of
how what is tacit, nonpropositional, or implicit informs those understandings. If propositionality is the only option deemed worthy of consideration
in thinking about such systems of power, then deeply significant aspects of
people's experience, potentially liberatory spaces, and key parts of racial and
gender formation are passed over in silence.

THREE

AN AESTHETICS OF SENSUOUSNESS

If common sense is a key aspect of oppressive social relations, as the prior chapter argues, transforming social relations will involve changes at the level of common sense. Susan Babbitt speaks to this with the language of dreaming impossible dreams—working for things that exceed what is considered possible under current conditions. Robin D. G. Kelley calls this the work of freedom dreaming in social movements. Along with giving histories of black radical social movements in the United States, Kelley calls on the radical imaginary enacted in Afrodiasporic surrealism. Indeed, surrealism gives Kelley many of his central definitions and examples of freedom dreaming: "The surrealists not only taught me that any serious motion toward freedom must begin in the mind, but they have also given us some of the most imaginative, expansive, and playful dreams of a new world I have ever known." Kelley continues: "Contrary to popular belief, surrealism is not an aesthetic doctrine but an international revolutionary movement concerned with the emancipation of thought" (2002, 5). Kelley's discussion of surrealism and freedom, despite his repudiation of it as aesthetic doctrine, is deeply connected to, and shows us something important about, aesthetics and emancipation.

Thinkers from Marx to Kelley show us how aesthetics is connected to implicit understanding and political transformation. Susan Buck-Morss writes:

> Whether camera image or easel painting, whether filmic montage or architectural design, what matters is that the image provide a sensual, cognitive experience that is capable of resisting abusive power's self-justification. . . . The original field of aesthetics is not art but reality—corporeal, material nature. Hence, "Aesthetics is born as a discourse of the body." It is a form of cognition

achieved through taste, touch, hearing, seeing, smell—the whole
corporeal sensorium. (2000, 101)

Theories like Buck-Morss's that politically situate aesthetic experience value
aesthetics precisely because, as a theoretical field, it has accounted for a form
of cognition intimately involving our "whole corporeal sensorium." Fred
Moten's rich and complex work on an aesthetics of the black radical tradition is motivated in part by aesthetic amplification of what he describes as
"revolutionary tone," "recently muted in black discourse." He aims to am-
plify a politics in part grounded in "the socialization of the ensemble of the
senses, the sensualization of the ensemble of the social" (Moten 2003, 229). I
read Moten's engagement with aesthetics in relation to the Marxist aesthetic
tradition I explore below, taking up the notion of what it is to sensualize
the ensemble of the social in chapter 6. As I will argue in this chapter, the
space of aesthetics both constellates the four kinds of implicit understanding I articulate in chapter 1 and provides a window into one way to shift
the commonsense understanding I discuss in chapter 2. Recall that the four
species of implicit understanding include a foundationally nonpropositional
knowledge, embodied understanding, potentially propositional knowledge
currently held as tacit or distal, and affective or emotional knowledge. All
four of these constitute the space of aesthetic experience, and the aesthetic
has the potential to transform all four. This is one reason surrealism gives
Kelley imaginative, expansive, and playful dreams of a new world. As Herbert Marcuse argues, the aesthetic dimension has the potential to rupture
a given reality. Aesthetics are practical, sensory, political, situated, and relational; the knowledge expressed in aesthetics is termed "sensuous knowledge," naming its mediating connection between our corporeal sensorium
and our relationally constructed cognitive schemas.

 In this chapter, then, I look to one of the canonical sites for accounts
of implicit understanding, drawing on the intellectual history of aesthetics
to show how embodied knowing has been positioned in certain lineages of
philosophy. At the same time, I am interested in contesting the construction
of these lineages, muddying the waters drawn from a supposedly common
well. I want to take up and situate Kelley's call for freedom dreaming in relation to aesthetics. I ask: What does the turn to the aesthetic give theorists
who are trying to think about the category of the human, about practices of
freedom, and about heterodox knowledges? The specific kind of knowledge
we learn by tapping into the aesthetic realm is often depicted as unifying

our rational and sensual faculties. The aesthetic dimension is articulated as a space in which to be fully human—which is to say, fully free. Below I will trouble these conceptions of harmony, full humanity, and full freedom. But freedom and humanity, both deeply contested terms, are at the center of accounts that look to aesthetics. Ultimately, I find that the turn to aesthetics offers many theorists a rich account of the political valence of implicit understanding. That is, the torquing to which these theorists subject traditional aesthetic theory allows aesthetics to offer a political, relational space in which implicit understanding is formed and re-formed.

Examining how these writers take up aesthetics and politics fills in the accounts of implicit understanding I offered in chapter 1—expanding the erotic, extending Bourdieu's understanding of the habitus, and tracing the contours of how tacit knowledge and common sense shift. In all, the theorists I examine in this chapter continue the work of chapter 2, politically situating implicit understanding in order to better understand political transformation. Since the Marxist humanist approach I outline here has been a key site for unfurling a rich account of implicit understanding's political import, it is particularly important to look at what racialized and gendered freight it carries with it. In other words, seeing the epistemic and political implications of arguments for the ruptural and revolutionary power of the aesthetic dimension enriches and grounds this strand of thinking. The form of understanding bodied forth through aesthetic experience is epistemic—we know the world otherwise through this sensuous knowledge, and that knowing is beyond, beneath, and other than rational, cognitive, propositional knowledge. Thus I attend to the epistemic dimension of aesthetic experience.

I begin with an explication of Avery Gordon's discussion of the concept of sensuous knowledge, unpacking her argument for its importance for social movements. Marcuse argues for the aesthetic dimension as a liberatory space; I lay out his account in order to show how aesthetics can be understood as implicitly political and politically transformative. I then turn to a consideration of aesthetics more classically conceived, beginning with early writing on the subject. These histories contribute something useful to how we might understand socially situated embodiment and a contextualized knowledge. They also signal some of the ways conceptions of aesthetics and liberation are braided with potentially troubling conceptions of the human, of freedom, and of the telos appropriate to subjects who count as free and human. Throughout, I focus on Marxist aestheticians, whose writings offer both hope for the place of implicit, aesthetic understanding in political transformation and, often unintentionally, a warning: in the case of thinking about aesthetics, we see the effects of yoking the specificities of embodiment, classifications of "the human," and conceptions of freedom to deeply racialized and human-exceptionalist universalities. I thus offer positive accounts of the liberatory potential of sensuous experience—most notably Karl Marx's understanding of sensuousness as a counter to alienation—and raise some worries that I think help point us to a more useable conception of aesthetics, freedom, and relationality.

IMAGINING RADICALLY OTHERWISE

Robin D. G. Kelley's work is compelling for its investigation into the idea that social movements "generate new knowledge, new theories, new questions." This new knowledge can itself be read in relation to aesthetics, as I'll explore below. It is not simply facts or stories, Kelly argues; the knowledge produced in social movements helps in the project of freedom dreaming, knowledge that "transports us to another place," that allows new imaginings to arise. According to Kelley, "We must remember that the conditions and the very existence of social movements enable participants to imagine something different, to realize that things need not always be this way" (2002, 9). Kelley reveals the co-creation of the black radical imagination with actual struggles for liberation—and what "liberation" means in these contexts is specific. It is also generalizable—Kelley calls on the principles of surrealism to articulate a "living, mutable, creative vision of a world where love, play, human dignity, an end to poverty and want, and imagination are the pillars of freedom" (158).

The co-constitution of freedom and humanity present in the aesthetic theories I'll present below are here in Kelley's work too. He calls on "all of us who believe freedom is worth pursuing" to heed Grace Lee Boggs's evocation of the possibility of collectively creating a vision of the future that will "enlarge the humanity of all of us." Indeed, he concludes his chapter on the movement for reparations with Boggs's words:

> When people come together voluntarily to create their own vision, they begin wishing it to come into being with such passion that they begin creating an active path leading to it from the present. The spirit and the way to make the spirit live coalesce.

Instead of seeing ourselves only as victims, we begin to see ourselves as part of a continuing struggle of human beings, not only
to survive but to evolve into more human human beings. (Boggs
quoted in Kelley 2002, 133–34)

Kelley also closes his book with an echo of Boggs. He writes: "Struggle
is par for the course when our dreams go into action. But unless we have the
space to imagine and a vision of what it means to fully realize our humanity, all the protests and demonstrations in the world won't bring about our
liberation" (198). These calls for the space and vision to fully realize one's
humanity speak to the specific legacy of U.S. chattel slavery and the yoking
together of racial classification, a constitutive failure to achieve the status of
human, and something more than the mere withholding of freedom. In this
context, aesthetic experience, always politically situated, offers contingent
freedoms and contingent humanities. Struggle thus becomes a way of knowing newly and knowing otherwise—knowing, deep in the bones, that the
world does not have to be this way, that it can be changed. Without space
and vision, this sort of knowing is inaccessible.

In her book *Ghostly Matters*, the sociologist Avery Gordon offers a
rich consideration of how history haunts the present, how the past can show
up to us in affective, unspeakable modes, and thus how our present actions
always express contingent freedoms. In this context, she situates sensuous
knowledge as "receptive, close, perceptual, embodied, incarnate. It tells
and it transports at the same time. Sensuous knowledge is commanding: it
can spiral you out of your bounds. . . . Sensuous knowledge always involves
knowing and doing. Everything is in the experience with sensuous knowledge." For Gordon, sensuous knowledge has to do with the senses, and with
how we encounter what we sense. Our incarnate knowledge, rendered sensuous, opens possibilities for embodied transformation. It is a "different kind
of materialism, neither idealistic nor alienated, but an active practice or passion" (Gordon 1997, 205). Gordon's understanding of sensuous knowledge
involves pleasures and pains, sensations we can name and ones we have no
language for, and ways of being constrained or freed in the world. Her articulation is closest to my own understanding of this sort of knowledge as an
important nonpropositional resource for transformation.

I see Gordon's call for a sensuous knowledge as part of a Marxist tradition of aesthetics. We are offered in this tradition a nonbinary relation between mind and body, a space of unfixed play, and an antidote for collective

alienation. Even in early, non-Marxist articulations of aesthetics and sensuous knowledge, as I will discuss more below, I find Baumgarten, Kant, and Schiller articulating a socially situated embodiment. Though their accounts do, in general, posit a strong separation between mind and body, and reason and practice—a separation bridged on the ground of the aesthetic—the space of sensuousness itself clearly happens in at least these two registers, as though they were already intermeshed. Marx deepens and grounds sensuousness, articulating it as an alternative to alienation and a space of a different kind of freedom. As I will argue, for Marx and those who follow him in thinking about sensuous understanding, paying attention to social-sensuous praxis opens both unexpected oppositions to the constraints of life under capital and an unalienated objectification. Far from being an aesthetic theory having to do only with art, this theory of the significance of the sensuous forwards a complex account of the importance of implicit understanding to political transformation.

Sensuousness is central to Gordon's account of what it might be to "renarrativize the world"—to have a diagnostic and utopian account of how the world in fact is and how it could be, which is her reframing of Herbert Marcuse's thinking on the aesthetic dimension of what is and what could be. For Gordon, these diagnostics—reasoned ways of "facing up to what's killing us"—are inseparable from seeing the possibilities for reality to be otherwise: "Reimagining the world as it is always involves imagining how it could be otherwise. Knowledge for social movements must move us; it must be sensual and magical" (2004, 62). The language of aesthetic theory helps us think about the sites of imagining beyond current conditions and about the power of this radical imagination to move us. It also gives us some traction to talk about sensuous imagining as a catalyst for political transformation. Through the invested renarrativization Gordon imagines, it is possible to have an account that accords with the world as it now exists, diagnostically, but also to understand and imagine beyond this world. It is then possible to know in such a way that we are moved, and through this movement to change the world. This is the epistemic work of Marxist aesthetics.

Herbert Marcuse articulates an aesthetics aimed at creating new ways of understanding, and thus of shifting, material conditions: aesthetics as the grounds for political transformation. He argues that art can imagine, and so create, a new reality within the reality it inhabits, functioning as both indictment and as celebration—all through its capacity to "speak another language." On my reading of him, this other language is related to a nonpropositional but epistemic formation very much like Pierre Bourdieu's habitus. There is a great deal of Marcuse's work on and related to the aesthetic that I am not going to address here. Rather, I am teasing out the strand of his theory involved in this lineage of theorizing sensuousness. Marcuse also attends specifically to the pleasure involved in sensuousness, and to sensuousness as an affirmative, erotic relation. His work offers an account of the aesthetic as opening a space for radical change, as in the space of the play drive, within and despite the constraints of conditions under capital; in this way Marcuse offers another facet to Lorde's account of the erotic.

For Marcuse, the aesthetic speaks against objective conditions of domination in part through what he calls the "aesthetic form." In emphasizing the function of a form over the content it presents, Marcuse argues against a vulgar, orthodox Marxist aesthetics. There is no place in his theory for Stalinist realism. The power of a work of art cannot be assessed in terms of existing social and political relations—or even in terms of whether it reads as a work of art in conventional terms. That is, Marcuse is not primarily interested in the specific leverage a really good poster might exert in a given political struggle. Rather, he is interested in the aesthetic form as a space where given social relations are acknowledged, negated, and transcended—all in the realm of sensuous knowledge. This sort of art expresses "a truth, an experience, a necessity which, although not in the domain of radical praxis, are nevertheless essential components of revolution" (Marcuse 1978, 1). This truth/experience/necessity manifests in the aesthetic form, which Marcuse sees as holding the political potential of art.

While dwelling primarily with and in *The Aesthetic Dimension,* I want to impose a little distance between the idea of the aesthetic form and the idea of the work of art—even though Marcuse often focuses on the work itself. His account is important for articulating the aesthetic dimension as a space that might manifest and be important to the experience of art, but is not constrained to it. More might appear as or in the aesthetic dimension than what we conceptualize as artwork. The aesthetic form is that which subverts our perception and understanding of reality as it appears to us, which Marcuse understands as a prevailing reality principle structured by systems of (predominantly capitalist) domination. Marcuse presents three characteristics of the aesthetic form: (1) it manifests an estrangement from the given social reality; (2) it has as its end another reason, system of morality, and sensibility; and (3) it has the capacity to change people's consciousness and drives. These characteristics turn out to be intimately related to sensuous knowledge.

First, then, the aesthetic form works as indictment and estrangement. Marcuse writes that it "creates the realm in which the subversion of experience proper to art becomes possible: the world formed by art is recognized as a reality which is suppressed and distorted in the given reality" (1978, 6). That is, art opens another reality, one in which the possibilities for real liberation are not only possible but actual, created in the sphere of the artwork. The aesthetic form subverts the experience of everyday repressive reality through such imagination. It estranges its viewers or readers from the reality they experience as ubiquitous; this is art functioning as indictment.

Authentic art, as an expression of the aesthetic form, is in this sense "committed to that perception of the world which alienates individuals from their functional existence and performance in society." Being alienated from our functional existence, in Marcuse's terms, emancipates the features of our lives repressed by living as though we were our functions: our sensibilities, imaginations, and reason. To the degree that our subjectivity (and objectivity) are constituted by what Marcuse calls an "unfree society," these "repressed and distorted potentialities can be represented only in an estranging form." Thus Marcuse argues that "only as estrangement does art fulfill a *cognitive* function: it communicates truths not communicable in any other language; *it contradicts*" (10). That is, the "language" of the aesthetic dimension is precisely not cognitive and not reducible to rational or logical form— it communicates truths through taking us out of that mode and estranging us from our constraint, plunging us through the artwork into a new world.

Marcuse takes up art's cognitive function to name it as something that contradicts the given reality without functioning within its logic; as estrangement, art contradicts without positing the reality it negates. Through this contradiction and subversion of dominant consciousness, the aesthetic contains a truth that works against the mystified objective conditions of oppressive social formations. The estrangement of art is an estrangement from the given, unfree reality. At the same time, this estrangement shows a new reality, also present but currently suppressed: "The truth of art lies in this: that the world really is as it appears in the work of art" (xii). Marcuse's attention to the work of demystification can be read as a kind of magical realism; because of the alienating structures of capitalist production, within the world as it conventionally appears the realist cannot imagine another world. Tuning into the world of the aesthetic dimension, a new realism comes forth.

The second way Marcuse characterizes the aesthetic form is as ending in a new system of reason, sensibility, and morality (7). The aesthetic form transcends the given social conditions; it is radical both in its indictment and estrangement, and in its invocation of something new. Marcuse refers to this as the "beautiful image (*schöner Schein*) of liberation" (6). The quality of estrangement comes about through art's emancipation from a given reality's mode of being; the quality of invocation arises from what Marcuse describes as art's "overwhelming presence." The given reality is sublimated, and even its most destructive features present a rebuttal to the enervating forces of current social conditions. Through the aesthetic's transcendence of the given—unfree—reality, it births a rebellious subjectivity:

> The aesthetic form intensifies the experience of another world than that available to us: the world demystified. In this space, the intensification of perception can go as far as to distort things so that the unspeakable is spoken, the otherwise invisible becomes visible, and the unbearable explodes. Thus the aesthetic transformation turns into indictment—but also into a celebration of that which resists injustice and terror, and of that which can still be saved. (45)

The aesthetic form opens not only a negation of the given reality but also an affirmation of that which resists. Social movement praxis can be aesthetic in this sense as well. I take it that for Marcuse, what is unspeakable, otherwise invisible, and unbearable under given conditions of unfreedom are both affirmations of what could be otherwise and rejections of current injustice. It is important to ask why a demystified world should result in a better, more livable world—why the other world formed in the space of the aesthetic is a world to aspire to. For Marcuse, the answer to this question is almost axiomatic. Marcuse takes it that at root, people strive for freedom, wholeness, joy, fulfillment. This is his version of a human nature—one that departs from Marx's language of self-making as natural to human fulfillment, which I will discuss below. Kelley's invocation of love, play, human dignity, an end to want, and imagination echoes some of Marcuse's account.

Finally, Marcuse argues that the aesthetic form has the capacity to change our way of being in the world—what he calls our consciousness and drives. His discussion of this characteristic of the aesthetic form's inner logic returns to the notion of instinctual drives, which resonate with but do not recapitulate Freud's understanding of drives. Marcuse unpacks the ground of transformed consciousness through a discussion of species-being, oppositional movements, and the sensuousness of memory. Like Marx, Marcuse sees a connection between the space of the sensuous aesthetic and the potential of people to manifest as "species beings" capable of creating and living in a "community of freedom." Marcuse frames this possibility as "the subjective basis of a classless society" (17). The realization of people's potential to manifest species-being requires a transformation of our drives and needs toward the ends of solidarity, community, and play.

Marcuse sees an instantiation of the fulfillment of the aesthetic form in oppositional movements, arguing that they are spaces where the beautiful images of liberation evoked in the aesthetic form have become "aspects of the real." These manifestations are incomplete—damaged and broken by currently existing reality—but they mark a site of potential. This potential "appears today in the protest against the entire capitalist and state-socialist organization of work (the assembly line, Taylor system, hierarchy), in the struggle to end patriarchy, to reconstruct the destroyed life environment, and to develop and nurture a new morality and a new sensibility" (28).[1] In these movements, Marcuse identifies the kind of indictment and the kind of affirmation important to him in the aesthetic form: there is a rejection—or a critique—of everything currently existing, and a struggle for a transformed way of being in the world. Insofar as the images of the Beautiful—which are the images of liberation—are instantiated in these spaces, they move out of the imagination and into non-estranged reality. This notion is central to my reading of Marcuse: it highlights the play between a kind of ultimate liberation realized in the ruptural experience of the aesthetic form and a gradual, partial movement toward expression of transformed consciousness.

Above, I mentioned that aesthetic indictment of the given reality opens the space for the affirming aspects of the aesthetic form. Marcuse thinks this process liberates our impulse toward freedom and what he calls the potential for happiness. This is how he returns us squarely to the terrain of sensuous knowledge, now through the space of a present read as sensuous memory. The artwork is experienced in the present, sensibly, and as aesthetic form it shows a doubled present—indictment and celebration. But Marcuse argues that in order for the aesthetic form to speak its present rupturally, in a mode that can create new futures, it must reveal that present as already past. The aesthetic experience embeds the experience of rupture as memory. In his words, the mimesis integral to the artwork "translates reality into memory. In this remembrance, art has recognized what is and what could be, within

---

1. And, following Donna Haraway, Anna Tsing, and others, I would add protest against human exceptionalism.

and beyond the social conditions. Art has rescued this knowledge from the sphere of abstract concept and embedded it in the realm of sensuousness" (68). The realm of sensuousness is explicitly erotic and connected to the ideal of reconstructing nature and society. Marcuse names this ideal the Beautiful, again in direct critique of instrumentalist or social realist aesthetics. For him, the Beautiful pertains to the "domain of Eros" and "represents the pleasure principle. Thus, it rebels against the prevailing reality principle of domination" (62).

Sensuous knowledge is crucial, then, to the aesthetic form altogether; when the aesthetic form is "working," it manifests in the realm of sensuous knowledge. Marcuse stitches together the sensual and rational impulses, something like Schiller's irreconcilable play drive and Marx's understanding of the non-alienated sensuous, through an account of the aesthetic form; I discuss both in more detail below. Its autonomy manifests in the space of sensuous knowledge, where art presents the present as past and reality as mimetic memory. The Beautiful shows up in the aesthetic form (and the artwork is beautiful) to the degree that it manifests a non-repressive order, thus holding the potential for an ontological catharsis. The catharsis, like the time of the artwork, is not reconcilable, not fixed.

Still, insofar as a ruptural memory cannot escape a nostalgic mode (a past we want to project into the present), it participates in creating these frames of meaning. As Sue Campbell (1997) argues, the frames of meaning we have matter for how and whether we can feel in non-sanctioned ways. Often our heterodox, germinal, newly unfurling worlds are precisely unsanctioned and unframed. The trouble with nostalgia is that it offers a too-sanctioned, too-available frame of meaning for our felt sense of the world, folding what is not quite speakable into what is too easily said. So when we reach for some new world—as many social movements articulate themselves as doing—we are reaching toward a future that is not predetermined, but radically indeterminate and therefore possible. Even accounts that refer back to a better time have to articulate that time in relation to a contingent present. This is the importance of Marcuse's argument for a paradoxically ruptural memory production that attempts to evade these structures of nostalgia.

AESTHETICS, FREEDOM, AND HUMANITY

Although Gordon and Marcuse may seem to move their theory of aesthetics far from a commonsense conception of the work and content of art, their accounts are thematically and substantially very connected to histories of aesthetics. I situate their work within this history in order to think about the problems and potential of aesthetic theory's conventional and revolutionary accounts of how we experience politics. While Alexander Gottlieb Baumgarten is generally understood to be the first philosopher to use the term "aesthetics," in the modern sense, in his 1735 text *Reflections on Poetry*, Immanuel Kant's and Friedrich Schiller's interpretations of his work have been perhaps more important. Baumgarten is significant, though, for his insistence that there is a form of knowing associated with the senses, and that this knowledge can be honed and applied, just as reason is.[2] This is the domain of the aesthetic. In his third critique—the *Critique of Judgment*— Kant expands Baumgarten's understanding of the aesthetic, describing the aesthetic power of judgment as something that recognizes and affirms a sense of the beautiful. Unlike pure and practical reason, which can be understood to reference a priori, universal truths of reason and morality, aesthetic judgments are fundamentally subjective. Because the pleasure or displeasure arising in judgment is not susceptible to reason, this faculty cannot be said to give rise to knowledge. It is nonconceptual. The feelings of pleasure and displeasure associated with objects in the world are nonetheless universalizable, in that they are commonly held.[3] The faculty of feeling, the aesthetic power of judgment, arises only in relation to a community of others and within that community takes on a universal communicability. Marx and Marcuse both draw on the importance of a communally made judgment in this sense.

Two important categories attach to this ideal of aesthetic judgment within a universalizable commonality: "purposiveness without purpose"

2. Aesthetics, then, will address the perfection of a lower form of cognition than thought: the sensate, or sensuous. Referencing the ancient Greek (though Egyptian-born) Neoplatonist Plotinus, Baumgarten hones a distinction between intelligible and sensible things: "*Things known* are to be known by the superior faculty as the object of logic; *things perceived* [are to be known by the inferior faculty, as the object] of the science of perception, or **aesthetic**" (Baumgarten 1954, 78; translator's interjection). The aesthetic thus treats sensate knowledge, or objects of sensuous perception. Baumgarten looks for a way of working with the "lower faculties" that would allow for a kind of rigor normally associated with reason and the "higher faculties." He recommends that philosophers "inquire also into those devices by which they might improve the lower faculties of knowing, and sharpen them, and apply them more happily for the benefit of the whole world."

3. The power of judgment, manifest in the aesthetic experience, takes the generalizable form of *sensus communis*—a "faculty for judging that in its reflection takes account (*a priori*) of everyone else's way of representing in thought, in order as it were to hold its judgment up to human reason as a whole" (Kant 2000, 173). Although the power of judgment is thus primarily subjective, it also turns out to be sufficiently communicable that "the feeling in the judgment of taste is expected of everyone as if it were a duty" (176).

and "lawfulness without law." Because the aesthetic faculty is nonconceptual, and because articulated ends or functions signify the imputation of a concept to a thing, what we judge beautiful cannot be so judged according to an end or purpose it fulfills (or fails to fulfill) (Kant 2000, 114). The beauty of a flower has, for Kant, nothing to do with its function as part of a reproductive organ—Kant terms flowers, along with some birds and marine crustaceans, "free natural beauties." They are purposive aside from or without conceptually designated purpose. The judgment of taste cannot be restricted by the conceptual designations of reason if it is to remain a free judgment. At the same time, the lawfulness by which everyone is expected to agree that a given thing is beautiful is lawfulness without law—it is expected of everyone as if it were a duty, but not as a duty.[4] As aesthetic judgment is the mediating factor between morality and reason, it can be read to function as the space of free play—the manifestation of beauty.

In his *On the Aesthetic Education of Man, in a Series of Letters*, Friedrich Schiller further refines these categories, arguing for a harmony between what he calls the "sensuous drive" and the "formal drive." In Schiller's terms, the sensuous drive "proceeds from the physical existence of man, or his sensuous nature." It is the embodied situation we find ourselves in, which situates us in time and matter, and which ensures our "potentialities" while limiting their expression. The second drive, the formal, has to do with rationality, objectivity, and constancy over time.[5] The conscious unity of these two drives is the condition for a free disposition, which Schiller names the aesthetic condition (1967, 141). Schiller articulates this condition as a third drive: the play drive, which expresses the possibility of harmony between the other two drives.[6] The play drive is figured as something that makes both of

4. Thus only a lawfulness without law and a subjective correspondence of the imagination to the understanding without an objective one—where the representation is related to a determinate concept of an object—are consistent with the free lawfulness of the understanding (which is also called purposiveness without an end) and the peculiarity of a judgment of taste (Kant 2000, 125).

5. These two drives are explicitly gendered, and in the direction you might expect—the sensuous is characterized as passive, material, and in one instance as "Sense herself," who must "resist the violence which the mind, by its usurping tactics, would fain inflict upon her." The masculine faculty of reason, however, is explicitly not granted total dominion over the sensuous—Schiller sees that sort of dominion as possible, but productive of mere uniformity. Rather, these two drives must be in harmony, each affecting the other appropriately: "Personality [reason] must keep the sensuous drive within its proper bounds, and receptivity, or Nature, must do the same with the formal drive" (Schiller 1967, 93).

6. Schiller's example here is illuminating: When we "embrace with passion" someone we know deserves our contempt, we feel ourselves too much under the sway of our sensuous nature. When we feel hostile toward someone we know deserves our high regard, we are "painfully aware of the compulsion of reason." But when someone has "at the same time engaged our affection and won our esteem,

the other drives "contingent"—the faults of each separable drive are liberated and transmuted. According to Schiller, "It will therefore, just because it makes both contingent and because with all constraint all contingency too disappears, abolish contingency in both, and, as a result, introduce form into matter and reality into form" (99). Rather than the formal and sensuous drives being smothered in the space of the play drive, they are brought into their own, in harmony with each other.

Schiller's strong claim here is that we only play when we are expressing ourselves most fully, and only express our fullest human potential when we play. He names the expression of this potential the aesthetic condition, which implies the "development of the whole complex of our sensual and spiritual powers in the greatest possible harmony" (143). For Schiller, the aesthetic condition is radically indeterminate, and it is precisely in its indeterminacy that he sees radical freedom. He thinks that people are deprived of freedom when they enter into any determinate realm (the sensual, for example, or the realm of reasoned thought). It is only restored to us "each time anew through the life of the aesthetic" (147)—play opens a space between any determinate condition. The aesthetic condition, then, names a space of open, non-alienated play in which sensual and reasoned knowledge act in concert. The aesthetic is not subject to or produced by force, and functions as both precondition for and automatic manifestation of what it is to be fully human.

Aesthetics, then, as developed in the German enlightenment tradition, is connected to a conception of judgment and taste. Entering into the space of play, and the realm of the human, is connected to partaking in a commonly held understanding of what is beautiful. If we turn to another branch in the history of philosophy, we can deepen this conception of common sense as it relates to political transformation. Gadamer examines this history, tracing the concept of common sense back to Giambattista Vico, and before him to Aristotle and the Stoics. Gadamer credits Vico with conceiving of common sense, or sensus communis, as not only "that general faculty in all men but the sense that founds community" (1989, 21). He frames Vico's notion of common sense as "the sense of what is right and of the common good that is to be found in all men; moreover, it is a sense that is acquired through living in the community and is determined by its structures and aims" (22). For Gadamer, this alternative conception of sensus communis offers more to aesthetics than Kant's and Schiller's conceptions because it provides a kind

---

then both the compulsion of feeling and the compulsion of reason disappear and we begin to love him, i.e., we begin to play with both our affection and our esteem" (97).

of truth beyond "the possibilities of rational proof and instruction," which he argues "do not fully exhaust the sphere of knowledge" (23).

I've spent this time with this influential formation in part to highlight how sensual and rational knowledges are imbricated, for Baumgarten, Kant, and Schiller, in the aesthetic dimension. Much of their accounts I find highly useable, even aside from their place at one beginning of the history I am tracing. Baumgarten's return to the sensate in order to give it a place—however imperfectly—at the epistemic table marks a first toehold for any attempt to think about knowing otherwise. Kant's ambivalent articulation of the aesthetic as an intermediary between pure and practical reason extends this initial "place" for the aesthetic. He opens the door for thinking about the aesthetic as expressing a kind of freedom that Schiller then takes up and deepens. And I find Schiller's argument for a play drive compelling and pleasing. Gadamer's call to return to Vico's conception of sensus communis, and ultimately to Aristotle and the Stoics, offers an important resource for implicit and nonpropositional knowledge. But, as I unpack below, I have deep worries about the repeated appeal to a harmonious aesthetic ideal. And the persistent links between a conception of freedom and an account of the human articulated in these aesthetic theories should trouble us.

First, remember the philosophical account of personhood as a racialized category—some people have been defined as eligible to be persons and achieve full humanity and some have not. For example, the "community" Kant, and perhaps Vico, have in mind for thinking about sensus communis is importantly limited to those who partake in full human reason—the "white brunette" race, in Kant's terms (see Eze 1997; Goldberg 1993; Bernasconi 2001). The close link between reason, whiteness, and what it is to be human— or the extent to which those three attributes end up being coterminous— should give us pause.

Saidiya Hartman's account of the reconfiguration of the plantation system in the antebellum United States is instructive here. She offers an antidote to Schiller's and Kant's universalized (but in fact specific) understandings of freedom and humanity in her attention to contingent freedoms and personhoods. Perhaps more important, Hartman looks at the "disavowed transactions between slavery and freedom as modes of production and subjection" (1997, 13).[7] The freedom the newly emancipated entered

7. As Hartman writes, further, the "abolition of chattel slavery [in the United States] and the emergence of man, however laudable, long awaited, and cherished, fail to yield such absolute distinctions; instead fleeting, disabled, and short-lived practices stand for freedom and its failure" (13).

was determined by relations of power that, on Hartman's view, served to re-subordinate them in capitalist exchange relations. "In short," she writes, "the advent of freedom marked the transition from the pained and minimally sensate existence of the slave to the burdened individuality of the responsible and encumbered freeperson" (116–17). Hartman delineates the way that rights discourse, as the terrain of putative freedom, is constituted through complex modes of expropriation and subjection defined against and requiring (as in Kant) those others who can never attain humanity. Black personhood, even before emancipation, occupied an ambivalent position "in which all of the burdens and few of the entitlements came to characterize this humanity"—an ambivalence carried forward into emancipation (117).

The "burdened individuality" Hartman describes is also centrally about capitalist appropriation and incorporation of those who are freed to labor. The coproduction of equal rights and black subjugation produced and held contradictory characteristics in place—the freed as "sovereign, indivisible, and self-possessed and as fungible and individuated subjects whose capacities could be quantified, measured, exchanged, and alienated" (117). This burdened individuality is foundationally tied to liberal discourses of freedom and agency as the terrain of single, autonomous actors. It masks the embodied, specific experience of how access to abstract human rights is torqued in the concrete production of blackness as "disciplined, regulated, and disciplined," the freed as free to labor, and rights as a burden to live up to (121). Finally, Hartman observes the "entanglements of slavery and freedom," arguing that the continued production of racial subjection, along with the specific forms of laboring, clearly show the "continuities of slavery and freedom as modes of domination, exploitation, and subjection" (172).

Situating accounts of freedom and the human alongside accounts of these fraught histories—of aesthetics, of chattel slavery, of capitalism—reveals something important: that Robin D. G. Kelley's call for struggle to fully realize our humanity, and for the space to imagine that realization as a precondition for liberation, is—of course—a call without guarantees, to echo Stuart Hall. It all too easily carries an unspoken genealogy of thinking that connects whiteness, reason, and humanity in mutually constituting and limiting relationships; the humanity-defining freedom of aesthetic play has often also limned the boundaries of white European rationality, even as it moves outside the traditional epistemic bounds defining that sensus communis. I am interested in continuing to situate this call within a history of the aesthetic because there is something here in addition to the production of the burdened individuality Hartman articulates. The freedom and humanity evoked by later proponents of aesthetics are foundationally tied to an implicit aspect of aesthetics altogether: the importance of the senses, understood as sensuous knowledge. The accounts I've offered retain sharp distinctions between rational, affective, and sensual knowledges—even in the act of asserting that the distinctive power of aesthetic sensuousness lies in its capacity to bring these faculties together in harmony. We can read the calls for aesthetic understanding as a site of this kind of harmony as a classificatory method with unpleasant implications: if the space of play (the aesthetic dimension) synchronizes reason with passion, each of those categories hardens into conventional hierarchies of knowledge. I look for an account of sensuousness that would assert a synchronicity without thereby positing irreducible distinctions and separability. And so I turn to Karl Marx's theory of non-alienated experience. What we get from aesthetics is a socially situated embodiment, deeply contingent, realistic, and imaginative. It is precisely at the moment Hartman isolates as the production of burdened individuality that Marx sees potential for sensuous knowledge to work against the alienated experience of newly expropriated labor; the aesthetic works to counter the isolated, individuated actors who have been freed to labor.

SOCIAL-HUMAN SENSUOUS PRAXIS

I see Karl Marx's understanding of the place of sensuousness to have much in common with Schiller's account of the virtues of play.[8] Marx talks explicitly about sensuousness primarily in his early work, though there are ways that it shows up in the *Grundrisse* and *Capital*. I will focus on the *Economic and Philosophical Manuscripts of 1844* and the "Theses on Feuerbach." Marx's (and Engels's) explicit work on aesthetics is notoriously patchy. Because of this, I am reading Marx as both a historical and intellectual hinge between the kind of sensuous aesthetics we find Baumgarten and Schiller articulating and the ruptural, liberatory aesthetic and sensuous knowledge Gordon and Marcuse present. I forward the claim that we can read Marx's understanding of sensuousness as an important piece of his philosophy, in part through seeing homologies and cognates between his presentation

---

8. As, for example, when Marx writes, "It is true that thought and being are *distinct,* but at the same time they are in *unity* with one another" (1975, 351).

and the ideas of thinkers more overtly naming their concerns as aesthetic—though in practice those accounts are as much about sensuous knowledge, non-purposiveness, and freedom as they are about any particular artwork. Though he does not explicitly use the language of play, sensuousness turns out to be a cornerstone in the early Marx's theory of estrangement and of non-alienated social relations—it is the counter to the state of alienated labor under conditions of capital.

It seems to me that Marx cares about sensuousness because he cares about praxis. His discussion of sensuousness involves a complex account of the connection between theory and embodied practice, the social, materialism, humanness, objectivity (and objectification), and the senses. In the "Theses," Marx characterizes a new materialism as being about a social humanity, where human activity is objective activity—"practical, human sensuous activity" (1975, 421). Each of the terms in this characterization ("objective," "praxis," "social," and "human-sensuous") need some detailed discussion in order to give a picture of how Marx understands sensuous knowledge.

Reading somewhat narrowly, let me try to unpack these terms within the context of the *Economic and Philosophical Manuscripts*, though there are clearly other places where his understanding of objectivity, for example, is considerably deepened. Marx's discussion of objectification traces a movement from the problematic of estranged labor products to a kind of liberatory, relational, sensuous, and social objectification. But it begins with labor: labor's production of things as commodities and of the worker's own labor power as a commodity. In this process, labor produces an object, which Marx frames as congealed labor—the "objectification of labor." According to Marx, "In the conditions dealt with by political economy this realization of labor appears as loss of reality for the workers, objectification as loss of and bondage to the object, appropriation as estrangement, as alienation" (1975, 324). In this process, the very thing that could signal play, creation, and a kind of contingent freedom instead, under conditions of capital, becomes self-alienating. The product of labor appears as estrangement, and this appearance means that the "more the worker exerts himself in his work, the more powerful the alien, objective world becomes which he brings into being over against himself, the poorer he and his inner world become, and the less they belong to him" (324). And this impoverishment is not only individual.

Marx argues that intentional work distinguishes us as persons: it is our being, or our life activity. Thus the capacity to approach things with an intention is a defining characteristic of our being: "The whole character of a species, its species-character, resides in the nature of its life activity, and free conscious activity constitutes the species-character of man.... The practical creation of an *objective world,* the *fashioning* of inorganic nature, is proof that man is a conscious species-being" (328–29). The estrangement of the worker/creator from the product of her labor is an estrangement from her species-being and from the sociality of others. This latter estrangement ("the estrangement of man from man") is hypostatized as the relation between the capitalist and the worker. This is a form of deeply alienated objectification, which also negates the potential of work to be freely creative (and thus freely creative of our species-being). We might wonder about the degree to which Marx is able to value activity that is not directed toward an end; if the exercise of intentionality defines the possibility of freedom, does that freedom allow for the undetermined play Schiller values? Or does all activity need to be directed toward some end? Perhaps more important, the proof "that man is a conscious species-being" has necessarily to do with a fabrication and fashioning of nature we might emphatically reject as models for being: nature, here, is understood as simply and only for the use of the human, and this kind of exploitation, indeed, may define species-being. It may be that this form of self-making is particularly prevalent in the context of capitalist relations.

Below the products and relations of capitalist labor, then, is there a potentially freeing sense to the idea of "objective activity"? Marx answers this question from a few different angles, beginning with a definition of what an objective being is and is not: "A being which has no object outside itself is not an objective being. A being which is not itself an object for some third being has no being for its object, i.e., it is not objectively related. Its being is not objective" (1998, 390). In order to be something in the world, everything must be in relation to other things. A being without relations to other things would be a unique and purely theoretical construction. Thus to posit a state without relations between objects is to posit a kind of non-being. Having an object outside ourselves—a world—creates us as an object for that other, and thus creates an objective world. "Objective," then, names a kind of mutually constituting relation that we have with the world. It is a sensuous relation: "To be sensuous—i.e., to be real—is to be an object of sense, a sensuous object, and thus to have sensuous objects outside oneself, objects of one's sense perception. To be sensuous is to suffer (to be subjected to the actions of another)" (390). Most simply, this claim grounds theory in actual relations between objects of sense. More complexly, it makes a kind of ethical-ontological claim: to be sensuous is to be in relation with others, to whom we are responsible and who can affect us. To be sensuous is to suffer: to experience, to undergo, to be affected, to be in relation to.

The process of objectification is in part a process by which objects hold sway over us. We also have an appropriative, self-making relation to the objects we interact with, which Marx frames as expressing an integrated matrix of sensuous relations: "Man appropriates his integral essence in an integral way, as a total man. All his human relations to the world—seeing, hearing, smelling, tasting, feeling, thinking, contemplating, sensing, wanting, acting, loving—in short, all the organs of his individuality, like the organs which are directly communal in form, are in their objective approach or in their approach to the object the appropriation of that object" (1975, 351).

Appropriation of sensuous objects, and of the self as a sensuous object, is a human activity. It is integrated, which is to say that it incorporates and deploys our senses and our sensible world as a totality: the world and our place in it is, for Marx, a web of interconnections and points of relations. Interacting with it as a totality involves an appropriation in the sense that the world is actively brought into relation with the self, who is also appropriated in the act of objectification—though in that case there is a kind of self-relation. Further, there is a third term in any objective relation, in which a being is "an object for some third being." The appropriation involved in objectification supersedes the logic of private property, where objectification is a process of alienation and inhumanity of the self and its objects. In this case, appropriation is the opposite of estrangement—it is an integrated, sensuous relation with the social world that emancipates the senses from the logic of the "life of private property, labour and capitalization." This kind of objective appropriation situates us in intimate relation with the world and others in it.

Subjectively as well as objectively, sensuous perception situates us as social beings, as species-beings. According to Marx: "The eye has become a human eye, just as its object has become a social, human object, made by man for man. The senses have therefore become theoreticians in their immediate praxis. They relate to the thing for its own sake, but the thing itself is an objective human relation to itself and to man, and vice versa" (1975, 352). I am trying to be frank with the human-centrism and instrumentalism highlighted in this quote while at the same time reading Marx's framing of the term "human," here and throughout this discussion, to name a specific kind of sociality. This sociality might be able to extend to other species and perhaps to the world altogether. I am clearly reading against the grain of this proto-modernist, humanist account. Still, I think there is a way to read with and against Marx in this case, to loosen the hold of self-making and pur-posiveness toward a more complex understanding of the world's relations. Human-centrism has also been termed "human exceptionalism," which Donna Haraway defines as the "premise that humanity alone is not a spatial and temporal web of interspecies dependencies" (2008, 11).[9] As Anna Tsing argues, "Human exceptionalism blinds us" (4)—and Marcuse's and Marx's allegiances to a human self-making activity in which all is for the human are no exception. Tsing looks to roadside margins, to the outsides of and interlopers on capitalist human-world production, and to an interspecies re-sponsibility that crosses boundaries of "domestic" and "wild." She takes up fungi as an example of an interspecies actor in worlds that are important to, but not dependent on, the human sphere.

If we take seriously the idea that human nature is intimately rooted in interspecies relationships, we are forced to stop imagining "human spe-cies being, that is, the practices of being a species, as autonomously self-maintaining—and therefore constant across culture and history" (Tsing 4). Judith Butler describes "human life" such that "life" inscribes a relational-ity to living things that are not human. She argues that for "the human to be human, it must relate to what is nonhuman, to what is outside itself but continuous with itself by virtue of an interimplication in life" (Butler 2004, 12). Butler then holds up "livability" as a non-humanist ethical category per-taining both to humans and to nonhuman "living beings that exceed the human." Now, livability of nonhuman living beings gets us somewhere, and there is a way that even for Marx nonliving things are explicitly involved in any responsible account of the political and ethical world. For example, Marx's treatment of the commodity form and the objects to which it at-taches, or his description of the human-machine interface involved in indus-trial production, take seriously the way that, as Bruno Latour puts it, "things are not things." By extension, to follow Latour a bit further, if we distrib-ute our attention and analysis to "things, objects, machines, and the social" (among other things), and if we attribute power to those objects, we gain a different kind of livability. According to Latour: "It is true that by redis-tributing the action among all these mediators, we lose the reduced form of humanity, but we gain another form, which has to be called irreducible. The

9. I thank Donna Haraway for many conversations about human exceptionalism in Marx. My reading in what follows is in dialogue with her thinking on this question, discussed in *When Species Meet* (2008, 46, 323n2).

human is in the delegation itself, in the pass, in the sending, in the continuous exchange of forms" (1993, 138). This non-reductive approach to ethical-political relations opens a space for a different systematicity, not centered on the "human" simply conceived, but instead as a point in a field of interaction in which each point implies the whole.

To put Marx in conversation with Tsing, Butler, and Latour means to expand the human relation he describes, to understand any object in a social relation as itself affecting the human-as-object. That is, the relation Marx sketches is not only about the human appropriating the object into relation, but also about the object in question appropriating the human. Marx says that the "thing itself is an objective human relation to itself and to man, and vice versa" (1975 352), which is to say that the objects we humans perceive in some way affect us. Because "the thing itself" stands as the third term in an objective relation, in Marx's sense, to be in relation is to suffer—to be subjected to the actions of another. In this way, we can take seriously the idea that what it is to "be human" has as much to do with mushrooms (to use Tsing's example) as with self-referential self-making. While reading Marx from this margin may not rewrite his deep human exceptionalism, it does unseat the centrality of the human in his account. The eye may become a human eye and its object "a social, human object," but that object carries its own objective relation. Mushrooms relate to wheat, potatoes, skin, dry-rotting basements, sugarcane—they pull us into relations and we adapt a social-human world to them. This is a sensuous relation.

Within this context, the senses become theoreticians in their immediate praxis. Their relation to the thing itself reveals the interconnection of relations that make that thing itself. A sensuous uptake implies an integrated relational indexing of objects and the self so that they become a world. The senses are theoreticians in their praxis in that the act of perceiving with sociality in view entails a corollary view of relationality. Marx implies that this sort of sensory relation to the world allows people to maintain a non-alienated individuality—they do not lose themselves in objects even though recognizing themselves as constituted in and through the world. The process of sensuous perception as an expression of relationality situates one in relation to others, thus also placing the individual in relation to the world. The individuality picked out here is individual in light of the social, defined in relationality. And so the social also implies and maintains the individual. "Praxis" here points to the unity of a theory and practice of the social: the senses as relational stitch together a view of the world through a practice of being in it in a social-sensuous way. It is fair to say that for Marx (and indeed for Marcuse), this stitching together is for human ends in a humanist way—ends and ways that, if we retain their category of "the human," will pose deep problems for all the beings who fall outside the very narrow ethical relation involved in that term.

I read Marx to claim that sensuous knowledge, properly understood, has to do with more than the function of the senses and the capacities associated with them. Sensuous knowledge marks a material social relation; its objectivity is not alienated. Sensuous expression is connected to—perhaps a prerequisite for—non-alienated species-being. Self-objectification is "inexhaustible, vital, sensuous, concrete activity" (1975, 396). Sensuous knowledge and activity marks a reversal of the estrangement produced by capital and its kind of objectification. In this sense, the realm of sensuousness holds tremendous potential for working against the alienation of oppressive social relationships. There is a connection here with Schiller's notion of play. Sensuous knowledge is not unmediated; our senses must become something. They become theoreticians of immediate praxis, expressing something like a play drive—a working together of the senses, the embodied, with an understanding of relational connection.

I have dwelled on the early Marx's understanding of the sensuous in order to make a case for understanding sensuousness as a contingent, ontological-ethical relationality. His attention to it is imbued with a sense of the possibility for non-alienated sociality. Marcuse extends the kinds of commitments I see in Marx, arguing that the aesthetic dimension is ruptural of the given reality—an argument prefigured in Marx's attention to sensuous understanding as a force that might work against capitalist alienation. I have argued that we must hold in mind a critique of the enlightenment model implied in Marx's and Marcuse's (not to mention Baumgarten's, Kant's, and Schiller's) conceptions of freedom and humanity. Such a critique involves a resistance to human exceptionalism, a resistance to views of the world as solely a resource for human industry, and a resistance to easy nostalgia for pasts that really weren't so liberated. And always there must be an attempt to understand how even ruptural and liberatory modes of understanding encode the very structures of racist social relations. But although there are grounds for critique, these theorists show that there are also substantial reasons to pursue the connection between aesthetics and politics.

For the purposes of this project, the field of aesthetics offers a multi-layered, playful, sensuous account of the experience and transformation of implicit understanding. Because accounts of aesthetics attend to many layers of our experience, they produce a complex picture of implicit understanding in which the "pieces" of it are seamlessly already of a piece. The relational, political dimension of sensuous knowledge further places this form of understanding in a social world. And the potential for new freedom dreaming, for a sensuous apprehension of other worlds, signals the potential for what Marcuse thinks of as ruptural aesthetic experience of freedom. The aesthetic dimension as transformational opening is also a space for changing conceptions of who counts as human; within it, claims to the experience of aesthetics invokes a claim to the status of "human," even when such a claim constitutes a remaking of that very category. Aesthetic experience, as I have argued here, offers an important resource for political transformation. It does this through an immersive knowing that does not take the form of propositions, claims, and "S knows that p." Rather, the sensuous knowledge that Marxist aestheticians theorize as rupturing the given reality and countering alienation furnishes understanding that could not be gained any other way, and that is not reducible to our claim-making activity. Studying theory and examining empirical results are likely as important to the work of changing social relations as they are to any other work. But without the implicit knowledge signaled by this attention to new common senses—new sensus communis—work to build a new world within the shell of the old will be anemic and thin. As I will discuss in part 2, particularly in chapter 6, this sort of socially situated, embodied knowledge can function as impetus, sustenance, and imaginative motor for individual and collective change.

TWO

NAVIGATING TRANSFORMATIONS

FOUR

NEGATIVE AFFECT AND WHITENESS

I worry about the process by which things become popular. This orientation toward the hip, nourished equally in DIY culture and in academe, pursues the new and the obscure, preferring to be among the first to plumb a new well. This approach is also, I think, rooted in capitalist social relations of marketability and, by extension, cornering markets. On all these grounds, I ought to excise this chapter, written when talking about affect in general and shame in particular was less in vogue. On the contrary, though, I think we should read the recent and not-so-recent attention to affect as an important site for the propagation of thinking about implicit understanding and its political effects. In chapter 2, I focused on commonsense formations of race and gender. In this chapter I extend and ground some of that discussion by considering how feeling bad might be important to shifting our common-sense assumptions. The significance of the fourth kind of implicit under-standing I laid out in chapter 1, affective or emotional knowledge, is best explicated through looking at actual cases of affective transformation. Such transformations also have embodied, social characteristics legible through a conception of the habitus. I argue that accepting a certain kind of bad feel-ing can be important for producing meaningful solidarity across difference, particularly for individuals who benefit from racist social/political struc-tures. I am following the geographer Ruth Gilmore's definition of racism as "the state-sanctioned and/or legal production and exploitation of group-differentiated vulnerabilities to premature death, in distinct yet densely in-terconnected political geographies" (2007, 28); while individual thoughts, feelings, and actions connect to this definition of racism, it is not limited to those sorts of individualized feelings and attitudes. My core argument in this chapter, then: It is important and appropriate for white people to feel uncomfortable about our own and other people's individual racism. But this only takes us so far. Negative affect is a good thing when it is both an appropriate response to loathsome social relations and provides a spur or a method for transforming those social relations.

The constellation of bad feeling associated with racial thinking is complex and multiple. For people socially and self-identified as white[1] it might include guilt, anger, sadness, panic, shame, embarrassment, and other emotions not easy to name. In this chapter, I willfully mix philosophical accounts of affect with activist thinking on antiracist activism in order to talk about some of the sites at which complex negative affect manifests. Explicit bad feeling is an optic that helps illuminate the complex of unarticulated beliefs, feelings, inclinations, attitudes, emotions, first-pass responses, and so on that underlie and shape racialized understanding. I explore the paired constellation of guilt and shame and ask what these affects might tell us about the formation and transformation of whiteness. Remembering Sue Campbell's work (1997) on the relationship between feeling and public expression of feeling, it is also important to note that I am not sure these words—"guilt," "shame"—are the best names for the complex and frequently inarticulate feeling I call more broadly "negative affect." I follow the usage of these terms as they show up in theory and memoir, but I also hold in mind the fact that they are heuristics and approximations at best. It is important that unease and discomfort of the sorts I explore here are useful in working against racism primarily, and perhaps only, to the people for whom it is possible to experience little or no discomfort in relation to racism, and who are in fact beneficiaries of racist structures. I see potential for challenging white supremacist thinking when people self- and other-identified as white, and variously privileged, experience the particular discomfort of shame in response to racism. In other words, negative affects like this should be understood as both epistemically and politically salient.

---

1. At many points in this piece I name white people as "socially and self-identified." I mean this to mark the fact that there are many people who are identified by others as "white" who self-identify in other ways, for myriad reasons. It also marks, for me, the confluence of social identification with self-identification, and the ways that whiteness (along with other modalities of racial classification) has been maintained by individual people purposefully taking up the matrix of social realities that "whiteness" stabilizes. It seems important that whiteness is stabilized by individual investment in the category—in part because rebelling against the category has some effect on whiteness. At the same time, as I argue below, the system of whiteness is such that it cannot be undone or disavowed on an individual level alone—being identified as white by others is too powerful, and often too violent, for one's own reversal to have systemic effect. As I hope is clear throughout, I occupy the fraught position of someone socially and self-identified as white, who wishes to repudiate the racism encoded in the category itself. This chapter, and the one that follows it, is primarily directed at people who, like me, identify as white in more or less this way. I use the terms "we" and "our" to reference socially and self-identified white people most broadly, and white people attempting to engage in antiracist praxis more narrowly.

Shaming is an active, transitive practice; "whiteness" is an equally transitive location, but one that is densely reified, defended, and normalized. As I discuss in the next chapter, solidarity is likewise something that must be created, enacted—as something made, not found. I have been motivated in thinking about race and shaming, about the project of shaming whiteness, for two reasons. First, I notice in myself and in other white academics an affect in response to explicit foregrounding of "race" in classrooms and in theory that I think is best characterized by the word "shame." While this category—"white academics consciously responding to race"—is occupied by fewer people than I'd like, I find that thinking about shaming here, where I also dwell, is worthwhile. In part, this location names one nexus where theory all by itself is explicitly inadequate to affect practice. Being able to talk about race doesn't necessarily translate into radically egalitarian practice (though it might help in moving toward that goal). That failure of translation may be both a result and a cause of shame. Sometimes even making "race" visible in a given situation can be shaming.

Second, I am invested in listening to the explicit repudiation of white guilt echoing through much current activist writing challenging white supremacy. For reasons I explain below, I agree with these writers that white guilt is frequently a useless stance in antiracist projects. But it seems to me that there is something significant in the experience of negative affect in response to racism, and I offer shame as a more adequate name for one part of such negative affect that might, in a limited way, enable action. This is because the notion of shaming constellates interesting thinking on nonessential identity formation, racism, and the role of affect in calling whiteness out—and "calling out," here, means "calling to account," as well as showing how whiteness happens always both systemically and individually. I also attempt to recuperate white guilt somewhat, under the rubric of negative affect articulated through shame.

This chapter will trace responses to some of these motivations. In the first part, which centers around guilt and shame, I look at some problems associated with white guilt and offer an account of shame and racial (re)identification. I argue that while guilt should be understood as unproductive for antiracist action, there is some place for thinking about negative affect as potentially motivating—or at least being important in—such action. Negative affect, and shame in particular, are not all by themselves motivators for taking these routes. In chapter 5, I begin thinking about sympathy and solidarity as both related to guilt and shame, and as motivations for action.

I conclude this chapter with some worries about my own argument, and the current academic attention to shame, in relation to questions about intersectionality and the ways that multiple forms of oppression might be experienced at the site of shame.

Let me start with an example from a psychology book on shame and guilt: "Pat" sits at a table with a group of friends. One starts telling "very rude racist jokes." Pat says, "Although I realized this was inappropriate, I did not make the effort to tell the person and was eventually taken in by the jokes. I did not realize that a friend of mine who is black and with whom I participated in a 'racism workshop' was sitting at the table directly behind us and had heard every single word. When I noticed her, I felt the greatest shame" (Tangney and Dearing 2002, 84). At a superficial level, Pat symbolizes for me the socially and self-identified white person who isn't able to consistently follow through with his antiracist aspirations. He interests me in part because I recognize that most of us are not able, in fact, to completely live the worlds we aspire to create, regardless of the racial formation we inhabit.

Pat's shame highlights one strand of a range of socially and self-identified white people's diverse responses to racism—one's own and other people's. Individual and institutional racism often moves and manifests without emerging into conceptual consciousness; it takes the form of practices, avoidances, unspoken affective responses. It is connected to conceptual schemes (knowing that this "is inappropriate") without taking (or, sometimes, having) practical avenues for action ("I did not make the effort"). Significantly, white people's racism is often experienced as a source of shame only in relation to others identified by a white eye as objects of racism. And what it takes to count, in many white people's cognitive schemes, as being targeted by racism is significant. In Pat's case, shaming happens only through relationality, only in the presence of someone he identifies as capable of shaming him. Pat is more complicated than he may appear; his failure and the ways that the frameworks available to him have failed him are also complicated. The primary failure, as this chapter will argue, is an assumption that Pat could simply change his behavior and stop making mistakes—become a good, antiracist white person who says the right things at the right times and doesn't say or do anything to offend anyone. The idea that antiracist practice amounts to some form of self-censorship is unsatisfying to me. Rather, I want to look at some of the ways that Pat's shame points to an opening for a shift in his implicit frameworks of moving through the world—for crafting solidarity.

Shame highlights the intersection of inarticulate frameworks of understanding with systems of power, visible in the exercise of dominative privilege. While implicit understanding always moves in relation to power, racialized shame can reveal the implicit as it manifests in "unconscious" racism. Thinking about shame as mapping some part of an implicit ground of racial formation provides resources for more adequate theorizing of racial formation. Simultaneously, I'm interested in correcting a tendency in the literature on shame and affect to downplay the degree to which affects are racialized. Racialized shame experienced by white people might mark a boundary between different commonsense understandings of racial situations—in Pat's case, for example, between knowing that racist jokes are "inappropriate" and yet going along with them. Pat's shame reveals a kind of social common sense— "knowing how" to be racist, how to laugh at the "very rude racist jokes," even with discomfort. At the same time, Pat does not quite know how to not go along with the situation he finds himself in. He knows that he should not go along—he has a conceptual understanding that it is inappropriate to do so— but he has no socially habituated mode through which to oppose the racist habitus expressed in the jokes and his response to them.

Shame can make unspeakable things viscerally present—things that seem too horrible to talk about or that are so assumed that they "go without saying." The act of shaming, and the experience of shame, reveals also an aspect of implicit understanding that facilitates the assumption of harmful norms in ways that perpetuate them. Thinking and talking about race and ethnicity is a difficult, uncomfortable project. Taking antiracist action is, then, just as complex, dense, and multilayered: judgment and social sanction for action are tangled together. For many people, particularly white-identified people, attempting antiracist thinking and action evokes fear and discomfort. Importantly, there will be different kinds of fear and discomfort depending on how we are positioned on racialized, classed, and gendered scales. This affective response indicates one reason for thinking about race in relation to the implicit: the relation functions as an example of the political and personal significance of the implicit.

SEDGWICK ON SHAME

In order to begin to unpack what might, in fact, be useable in the bad feeling that appropriately arises in response to racism, I draw on Eve Kosofsky

Sedgwick's rich work on shame. Sedgwick reads queer performativity in particular and identity formation in general in relation to the affect of shame. She draws on the work of the U.S. psychologist Silvan Tomkins, who took shame as a prototypical affect in his schema, which attempted to think about affect as being just as significant as Freud's drives. Sedgwick thinks about shame in three ways. First, she argues that shame tells us something important about identity formation. Second, it reveals one site of queer politics and performativity, extendable into other political areas. Third, shame braids together hope (or desire) with failure, in ways that allow it to act as what Sedgwick calls a "switch point" in creating the conditions for political transformation. What might we learn about identity formation by attending to shame as an unease that is always intersubjective, always other? What might a story of shame as identity-constituting tell us about the racial formation of identity?

Sedgwick argues that shame expresses a failure of recognition, and in that failure a window onto how people's identities are formed in relation to others. Shame makes a double movement toward "painful individuation, toward uncontrollable relationality" (Sedgwick 2003, 37). Shame, Sedgwick argues, "floods into being as a moment, a disruptive moment, in a circuit of identity-constituting identificatory communication. Indeed, like a stigma, shame is itself a form of communication. Blazons of shame—the 'fallen face' with eyes down and head averted—and, to a lesser extent, the blush—are semaphores of trouble and at the same time of a desire to reconstitute the interpersonal bridge" (36). Shame disrupts smooth circuits of assumption and behavior through revealing disjunctures and unwieldy sites of relation. The identificatory communication disclosed in the experience of shame makes it, for Sedgwick, "integral to and residual in the processes by which identity itself is formed" (63), and therefore a useful site for thinking about identity politics.

The question of identity "arises most originarily and most relationally" at the place of shame. Sedgwick places this notion at the site of a developmental account of infant identity formation: when a baby attempts a circuit of mirrored expressions with a recognized caregiver's face and fails to be recognized, shame arises. She says:

> Lecturing on shame, I used to ask listeners to join in a thought experiment, visualizing an unwashed, half-insane man who would wander into the lecture hall, his speech increasingly accusatory and disjointed, and publicly urinate in the front of the room,

then wander out again. I pictured the excruciation of everyone else in the room: each looking down, wishing to be anywhere else yet conscious of the inexorable fate of being exactly there, inside the individual skin of which each was burningly aware; at the same time, though, unable to staunch the hemorrhage of painful identification with the misbehaving man. (37)

As I unpack in more detail below, there might be some homology between the experiences of attempting to make contact with others and failing—at any age—and the kind of situation Sedgwick describes. I am reading the pervading quality of this affect as one of its powers.

Sedgwick finds a "conceptual leverage" in shame, one particularly useful for political projects: in shame, we are affected, even when something shameful happens to someone else. She argues, "Bad treatment of someone else, bad treatment by someone else, someone else's embarrassment, stigma, debility, bad smell, or strange behavior, seemingly having nothing to do with me, can so readily flood me—assuming I'm a shame-prone person—with this sensation whose very suffusiveness seems to delineate my precise, individual outlines in the most isolating way imaginable" (37). Part of the conceptual leverage offered by this affect, then, is a way of thinking why it might matter to us when other people are treated shamefully, or behave shamefully, or show up in the world in some way that we read as shameful. The most interesting conceptual leverage shame offers us attaches to the question of how people who are not themselves the objects of social or material degradation come to see other people's subjection to those forces as relevant to their own lives. The middle-class examples Sedgwick offers might not be accidental.

Because identity is fluid, the moment of shame seems able to cathect and reify an already present pattern that manifests as a solid identity. It may also be particularly able to reveal the fluidity of identity formation—one has just been something one does not want to be. If Sedgwick is right to think that shame is a method of identification, can it also enable a kind of re-identification? Insofar as one feels shame, it seems that there is a movement on the identificatory level—shame reveals something deep inside us. Shame turns on an inter- and intra-subjective hinge, which is to say that I see myself in relation to others. I feel toward them—perhaps even when the feeling I manifest in relation to people who have shamed me or toward whom I feel shame is anger or resentment. Shame always relates to others. This seems to be the case regardless of whether there is an actual other person present at the moment of shame—shame marks one site in which we have been formed by the look and the presence of others. Shame is not dependent on the actual presence of others; it can arise even when we are alone.[2] As Susan Brison (2002) notes, the self is relational to its core; there is no self-formation that does not involve other agents.

GUILT, SHAME, AND WHITENESS

Why might it be a good thing for white people to be (a)shamed in racial situations? This question assumes that a negative affect is either called for or forced on players in the scene. That is, I am not looking for a way to "do" racism with no negativity. I am, rather, looking for some kinds of negative affect that might make race differently visible to white people while simultaneously de-centering whiteness.[3] At the same time, I do not think that white people who attempt antiracist action out of other affective states—aspiration for social relations that express dignity, hope, or love—should be forced to feel bad in order to "count" as doing good antiracist work. Rather, given the widespread refusal and avoidance of negative affects in many social spaces in North America in particular, and an implicit idea that the purpose of life is to be endlessly comfortable and at ease, it is worthwhile to encourage socially and self-identified white people to lean in to the sharp points of discomfort frequently attached to racism rather than cushioning ourselves from it. Understanding racism in Gilmore's terms—as group-differentiated vulnerability to premature death—will tend to bring a number of difficult-to-feel feelings into consciousness and experience. Speaking pragmatically, if those of us working on transforming the social relations that maintain multiple forms of oppression lack a way to "meet" negative affect as it arises in this political work, we will be missing a major practical tool. Alongside this

2. Jean-Paul Sartre's discussion of shame before the other is the locus classicus here (1992, 303, 348).

3. Clare Holzman (1995) offers an argument close to some of what I argue in what follows, approaching the questions of guilt and shame from a therapeutic perspective. Holzman argues for an understanding of the guilt and shame that arise in response to racism—especially one's own racism—as a normal reaction that can, with therapeutic intervention, appropriate conceptual framing, and strategies for working with guilt and shame, result in "increased freedom to think clearly and act effectively in resisting racism" (331). Though I encountered Holzman's short article late in the process of writing this chapter, I've found her thinking on this both reassuring and grounding for the suggestions I raise here.

lack, we'll replicate a significant philosophical gap in theorizing the import of affect to both epistemic and political theorizing.

Consider the negative affect of guilt and the specifically racialized feeling of "white guilt." As I will show, white guilt is a frequently cited candidate for appropriate white affect in relation to race—even (or maybe particularly) when we are asserting that such guilt is useless and perhaps extremely counterproductive.[4] As I will explore below, the attempt to call up a sense of guilt for being white does not address many people's sense that they are personally innocent of racial wrongdoing. Imagine a person socially and self-identified as white saying, "But I never did anything bad to any people of color. I don't even know any, so how could I have done so? Maybe my family owned slaves way back, but that wasn't me, I didn't do that." In this case we may have a hard time showing the way racism is involved in that person's life. And one thing we need to get at is why it matters personally to be the beneficiary of a systemic granting of white primacy in relation to a corollary exploitation and coarctation of the lives of people of color.[5]

White guilt has been trenchantly critiqued along a number of such axes, particularly by people organizing against white supremacist thinking and practice. Two significant tropes appear in white antiracist activist writings about coming to some kind of racial consciousness as white: In one, there is an expression of guilt about how one was in the past, now identified as having been racist. In another, the expression of guilt is identified as itself problematic. The activist-theorist Michelle O'Brien's generative thinking on white guilt in the context of antiracist organizing is useful here. For example, O'Brien writes of herself: "From my first antiracism workshops as a teenager, I've had it repeated[ly] asserted that white guilt was unhelpful

---

4. Sandra Lee Bartky discusses the uses of guilt in ways I understand as compatible with the discussion I give here of shame (see "In Defense of Guilt," in Bartky 2002).

5. This term is one I'm using to try out alternatives to the now-standard "white privilege." While I'm very grateful to the theorists who argue for the notion of white privilege, and while I see political utility for thinking about whiteness in this way—especially in terms of helping white people see how they benefit from a system that privileges them—I think that "privilege" also erases some of the consistent and brutal harm that goes along with the maintenance of whiteness. Who doesn't want to be privileged? "Primacy" perhaps names the sense of being put first, epistemologically as well as in line for credit at the bank, without the positive middle-class affective resonance of "privilege." I am naming both exploitation and coarctation here to evoke white primacy's dual role of taking the lives, labor, and affective work of people of color and also its capacity—primarily through racist social institutions—to narrow the range of possibilities and options available to many people of color globally (in the same way that cholesterol narrows one's arteries).

and racist. An accurate fact I've been correctly parroting since" (2002–3, 18). Laura McNeill (2004), reflecting on coming to antiracist praxis, writes:

> The hardest thing for me when I started to engage in anti-racist education and action was getting past feeling guilty. When I started to learn about my white privilege and understand the role white privilege plays in society, I felt guilty for being white. It took me a while to realize that feeling guilty does no one any good. It is through understanding the role that white privilege contributes to racism that I can move to acting in solidarity.

One thing I think is significant about McNeill's statement here is the move from a personal to a social and systemic understanding of antiracist work. This move is, as she articulates, made through creating new cognitive schemas—through both education and action. There is something about guilt that, as McNeill thinks about it, "does no one any good." Why might this be the case?

Typifications of white guilt as unusable for antiracist projects often assert that it usually shuts down action. William Aal writes: "We have found in our antiracist work that the first hurdle to get around is a paralysis of guilt and defensiveness. Most white people know very well their skin color is tied to social privileges—so they feel guilty and at the same time don't feel personally invested in change" (2001, 305). First, then, guilt is seen as immobilizing. Second, as Aal indicates, white guilt may prohibit or occlude any sense of personal investment in change. If the goal of raising individual people's consciousness about racial formation and racism is to make them allies or instigators of racial justice work, we should reject such immobilization. Rather, we should call for modes and approaches that open possibilities for action and change. As many people have noted, often feeling guilty for being white means that white people freeze up in response to racism; white guilt delineates a non-transitive inner space, a dead end.[6] The immobilization involved in white guilt indicates an over-personalization of racial situations. Repudiating personal investment in change is often also an attempt to disembed oneself from racist structures through a false claim of noninvolvement.

---

6. Also, as Lawrence Blum (2002) outlines, we may need more nuanced names for the expression or feeling of racial prejudice than simply "racism"—a term encompassing so many meanings that it holds sometimes a disparate and immobilizing charge.

Understanding the negative personal valence of being a beneficiary of systemic racism can, as many theorists have pointed out, restrict one's analysis to how bad one feels individually and personally. This restriction often has an individuating effect. O'Brien argues convincingly that white guilt abstracts and personalizes race, obscuring the complex realities of structural racism in service of making individual white people feel better about their actions (or nonactions, if they perceive themselves as not guilty) in relation to race. O'Brien writes, "Action out of guilt is first and foremost about trying to feel good about ourselves, searching out some way of getting off the hook." She sees white guilt as a "backlash strategy, a particular way of recentralizing white identity and white experience, reentrenching dynamics in the needs and preoccupations of white people" (2002–3, 21). On O'Brien's analysis, then, guilt both falsely telescopes racial situations into individual white people's affective terrain and, in that process, enacts precisely the granting of white primacy that antiracist action aims to avoid. In O'Brien's words:

> The signs of white guilt are clear. Often white people are searching for some individual activity they can do that they rationalize will ameliorate the structural violence of the situation, without actually being willing to address the overall complexities or the real lived realities of all of us within that violence. Often this is linked to an overvaluation of the effect of the actions of individual white people, believing a great deal hinges on every action. (19–20)

In thinking through O'Brien's work in this piece, I am trying to find a theoretical account that names the enmeshment of the individual with the systemic—one that is not about making people "feel better" personally, and that might open spaces for taking meaningful antiracist action. Below, I'll trace how shame might intervene on the level of the habitus.

O'Brien theorizes another dynamic of an experience of white guilt: that the confession of guilt can serve as both an avowal of one's self-extraction from racist structures and as a false end point of supposed antiracist action—what she calls "confession as a screen." In her words: "So long as guilt, and the confession, provide the frame of a self-critique, the crucial piece is never quite addressed. . . . The confession masks not further guilt, but the very possibility of honesty, openness and transformation. It precludes the very chance of ever recognizing what is happening in a real, grounded, substantive way" (22). The structure of white guilt, then, can be read as one that individuates race, occludes the structures that maintain racism systemically, and re-centers white people through validating their expression of past racism as in and of itself antiracist action.

Naomi Zack critiques the assertion of white guilt along somewhat similar lines. She argues that white guilt arises either from recognizing that one has been granted unearned personal benefits or from recognizing one's membership in a group "historically guilty of injustices against other groups." Zack's assessment of white guilt is that "neither the psychological guilt based on unearned advantages nor the moral guilt based on past injustice entails an awareness of contemporary white moral obligations arising from contemporary racism" (1999, 81). Like others, Zack takes white guilt to relate solely to the moral or ethical stance of individual white people. She suggests that it is important to attend instead to institutional racism, arguing that such attention relates to an idea of white responsibility. In many ways, however, Zack retains a kind of individuation in this notion of responsibility, arguing that white people are responsible for attending to "dimensions of constraint in nonwhite life that are held in place by customs and practices within institutions. . . . The responsibility of whites in these contexts is to become aware of what they do individually to enact and support the racist customs and practices that are still taken for granted in American life" (82). I would suggest that such awareness of one's individual actions is insufficient, and that a notion of responsibility would need to be more expansive than Zack here suggests.

The expansion I have in mind takes three forms, complexly related to critique correctly leveled at guilt in antiracist circles. First, white people need to do more than become aware of what we do individually to support taken-for-granted racist customs and practices; we need to take action. Second, we need to have a way of working with the negative affect that awareness of racism rightly carries. Third, we need to open routes for deep political transformation on both personal and systemic levels.

Becky Thompson argues that in cases where white women, in particular, are reluctant to see themselves as benefiting from power inequalities, "guilt becomes a safer response than taking responsibility for racial inequality" (1996, 106). There is reason for taking the safer response as one's own, and a reason for many white people's descriptions of feeling guilt as part of the process of becoming minimally aware of injustice perpetuated along racial lines. In her book *Blush*, Elspeth Probyn renders this process as a dialectic in which "avoiding shame can allow guilt to flourish. Guilt then becomes the default mode for living in a colonized land. Guilt, or fear of being found guilty, produces a situation where shame cannot be admitted" (2005, 46).

The fact that it is often white women who aspire to be antiracist activists and who experience both guilt and shame is notable. White antiracist women activists participate in matrices of historical inequity and betrayal, beginning at least with the white suffragette movement's sellout of any antiracist aspirations, and continuing with the second-wave feminist movement's wildly inadequate and frequently racist attention to racism. More generally, a big part of the choice to feel guilty rather than responsible is precisely the fact of it being a choice—whiteness frequently carries the "option" of choosing whether and how to think and actively respond to racial situations. But another significant part of the process of pursuing radically egalitarian racial politics is wrapped up in the kinds of re-identifications white people must enact in order to move toward different awarenesses of the world. Minnie Bruce Pratt reflects on her process of groping "toward an understanding of injustice done to others," through which she began to envision radical political change. Her account gives a window into why one might choose guilt over shame. She writes: "But I did not feel that my new understanding simply moved me into a place where I joined others to struggle with them against common injustices. Because I was implicated in the doing of some of these injustices, myself and my people, I felt in a struggle with myself, against myself. This breaking through did not feel like liberation but like destruction" (Pratt 1991, 53).

Coming to see the way racism has structured the material and social conditions of the present, and to perceive oneself in a lineage with the arbiters and beneficiaries of these conditions, can make one feel, as Pratt puts it, like a "disintegrating, rotting nothing" (57). I read this as an expression of shame. How can we patch together an identity that can, in Pratt's sense, struggle with others while also struggling against aspects of our selves? This is a question of why and how we might begin and continue work against a system that invites white ontological expansiveness, to use Elspeth Probyn's phrase, and simultaneously no responsibility for the effects our position have on others. How might white people do such work without arrogating back to ourselves epistemic, affective, and political primacy in the ways that I have been arguing expressions of guilt over whiteness do?

In the accounts I've highlighted here, I see the inutility of articulating as guilt what is in fact a complex matrix of feeling, inchoate and multiple. Among other things, to call the response people sometimes have to racism (and perhaps the thought of race *simpliciter*) "guilt" is hopelessly reductive. More than reducing a potentially rich and nuanced response to a relatively simple category, "guilt" carries with it some serious problems for a liberatory agenda. The most obvious of these is the ease with which guilt individuates white people's responsibilities for racial inequity—thereby making them feel no responsibility at all. White guilt's false telescoping of racial matters to white people's perspective—thereby centering whiteness as norm for white people—also brings up the freezing and inaction associated with inaccurately collapsing all the things that come up in response to racial thinking and acting into "guilt." There is power in what we name things, especially when those names are freighted with heavy loads of cultural expectation, as is the notion of guilt. In the attempt to think seriously and responsibly about appropriate negative affect around "race," we need more nuanced interpretive and emotive categories. Hence I return to a discussion of shame, drawing on Eve Sedgwick's articulation, discussed above. Shame is different from guilt in that it expresses a sense of connection that has been variously termed "empathy," "sympathy," and "feeling-with." It is this aspect of it that might produce political solidarity, and this is why I attend to shame as a kind of case study for the one part of the matrix of negative affect that might arise in response to racism. There are overlaps between guilt and shame, of course—in arguing for salient differences I am not trying to efface similarities and continuities. But reading back toward guilt from the point of view of shame might allow richer and more collective accounts of negative affect and racial formation.

INTERSUBJECTIVITY, FEELING BAD, AND HETERODOX WHITE RACIAL FORMATION

As I indicate above, because of shame's intersubjective manifestation, I see in it the potential to rearticulate some of how white people feel bad about race. If shame is in fact an always-relational, identificatory affect, white people's shame response to racism may mark and create a kind of responsible attention to racial formation as structural and systemic within the context of changing who and how we are in relation to race. Thinking about shame and racial formation offers a window into the more complex network of bad feelings appropriately associated with racism and racialized ontologies.[7] Most

7. I follow Shannon Sullivan in understanding racialization as an ontologizing process. Sullivan writes: "Ontology is not composed of eternal and unchanging characteristics, nor is it reducible

important, as I discuss in chapter 5, understanding the tangle of responses to our own, others', and systemic racism in terms of shame may also name one aspect of our response that might, in combination with other things, produce solidarity.

Shame is a paradigmatic example of discomfort. Shame rarely, if ever, feels good. Most of us want to avoid shame, in part because the experience of it holds few avenues of escape. Perhaps we cannot address the experience of shame by directly doing something in the world, or we think that we cannot change the thing that has happened to cause shame. Shame seems to stick to our skin, seep in through our pores, run along our veins. It feels as though it is part of our body and our being. At the same time, shame hums between people, arises constitutively in relation to real or imagined others. I am thinking here of the shame that arises in explicitly attempting and failing to identify with someone else—as when you say hello, or go over to someone, and are rebuffed in a shaming way. I am also thinking of the kind of shame that arises for some people who had, until the moment of feeling shame, been moving unself-consciously through the world—as when you are running for the bus, catch someone's eye, and perceive yourself as ridiculous, unwieldy, or disgusting. This aspect of shame marks its embodied situation within a schema of social relations—the bad feeling is felt in the body, often attaches to embodiment, and concerns how our bodily selves are positioned and "read" within a social world. It is one expression of what Bourdieu articulated as the habitus.

There is also the shame of being caught in doing something you yourself perceive to be shameful—as when Pat experiences shame in explicitly knowing the shame-worthiness of being taken up in racist jokes—and yet "going along"—a shame only manifest in relation to the presence of a black woman he identifies as a friend. These examples underscore not only shame's essentially intersubjective character; they also mark how affect and habitus are intertwined with currently unspoken but potentially propositional understanding. The experience of feeling the greatest shame, in Pat's experience, discloses multiple levels of tacit understandings around racialization—things

---

to conscious experience. Ontology is constituted instead by the historical, contextual, simultaneously malleable and stable, and only occasionally felt features of situated, located beings. To deny that race is ontological is to imply that race is a sort of veneer laid over a nonraced human core. But it is too simple to characterize race as imposed by a racist society upon a pre-racialized human being. Such an understanding of race inadequately acknowledges the ways in which the transactions between a raced world and those who live in it racially constitute the very being of those beings" (2006, 32).

that he might or might not be able to articulate without the feeling. Shame experiences rely significantly on the shamed person perceiving the other as a subject, as one capable of shaming. Shame thus opens a potential space for thinking adequately about a constitutive relation between self and other. Such a relation is interesting especially because the self and the other are each racialized in ways that shame's intersubjective, discomfited enactment highlights. As Probyn discusses in her account of whiteness and shame, the "viscerality of the feeling body shakes up our habitus, causing us to question at various levels its seemingly static nature" (2005, 64).

There is some warrant for thinking that racial identity is, for most people, constitutively marked by shame. This is perhaps most often visible in the stories about children of color becoming racialized through a contemptuous, shaming white gaze. But when white people understand themselves as white, it is frequently also in terms of re-identificatory shame. Probyn understands this in terms of Silvan Tomkins's framing of shame as an interest/shame pair, reading it in terms of the habitus. She writes:

> White-hot shame is in the habitus: the body expresses such interest and then registers that the interest cannot be fully followed through. This is not, however, a romanticization of shame that can be readily incorporated into already constituted political projects, nor is it a condemnation of a generalized white history. It's harder than that. It's not a shame that can be relieved by apology. Neither heroic nor scandalous, this white shame is deeply interested and interesting. (71)

For example, Becky Thompson quotes Mab Segrest's memory of "hiding under bushes across from her high school to watch 200 Alabama Highway Patrol troopers surround twelve Black children who were the first to 'integrate' the school." Segrest recalls having "a tremendous flash of empathy, of identification, with their vulnerability and their aloneness inside that circle of force. Their separation is mine" (quoted in Thompson 1996, 100). Segrest suggests here a realization of embeddedness within structures of racist violence, both maintained and challenged by the logics and actions of the state. This embeddedness is troubled; the separation that Segrest says is hers does not make her the same as the twelve children within the circle of state troopers. The separation is hers in the sense that it defines Segrest's identity. An important aspect of this story is also what it highlights about the experience of transformative sympathy (more about this below).

Thompson herself describes a formative experience of racialized shame. She writes that despite her mother's sometime opposition to expressions of racism, during her mother's second marriage "her opposition to racism was clouded by a complicity that left me feeling ashamed and confused." This complicity manifested in how she related to an African American woman hired to clean the house. Once, this woman cleaned the oven with a product not meant for ovens. In response to her mother's contemptuous, angry reaction, Thompson writes, "most of all I remember feeling shame: shame for being there, shame about my mother's attitude, and shame that this woman had to clean our house. Later, I came to understand what was modeled for me in this instance: white people may be opposed to racism on a structural level, while simultaneously upholding it in private contexts. This contradiction was certainly not open for discussion" (99).

More often, of course, the reverse contradiction is not up for discussion: white people assert personal, private opposition to racism while upholding the structural racism that benefits and constructs whiteness. Shame about either disjunction can be a site of realization of whiteness. Thompson's realization, like Pat's, is relational in troubled ways: it arises in relation to an already racialized other, and contributes to that racialization. This shame attaches to specifically gendered aspects of the situation: Thompson feels shame that this woman had to clean her house, a shame that picks out both the failure and expansion of white womanhood signaled by her mother's capacity to hire help for the housework. And the gendered character of the black woman is stabilized in part through her being "freed to work" in, presumably, her own household as well as Thompson's. This example, too, brings out an important disconnect between an understanding of systemic and "private" racism—a disjunction that manifests in both directions.

Ruth Frankenberg writes about multiple points of beginning to understand her whiteness, though always as contingent and historical, in multiple "mundane, daily" ways. She asks:

> *So. But what was the specific <u>emotional</u> work of being white for me, in that period?*
> Varied. Shame, pain. An inordinate, almost bodily discomfort, perhaps that of twisting and turning to try to get away from, to resist, what was. What is. (*And did not need to be. The injustice. The unnecessary injustice.*) What or who I was. (*And again, did not need to be. Yet, was, <u>is</u>.*) (Frankenberg 1996, 14)

Frankenberg highlights a nonessential, contingent, yet historically and materially stabilized racial formation. An important part of this formation is the sense in which the work of seeing herself as white was marked by many of the characteristics of shame. It is significant, again, that most of the examples I am giving of shame at the site of these imagined (and perhaps also actual) moments of first coming to racial consciousness are also sites of gendering—the women giving these accounts are formed, in these shame relations, as both white and women.

UNENUNCIATED SHAME

As I have discussed, thinking about shame is useful because of its inarticulate character. Shame is hard to enunciate because there is some shame attached to feeling shame, because it is an affect, and because it is broad, amorphous, and not clearly defined. There is an internal obstruction to expressing the feeling of shame, perhaps even to oneself, because to do so involves admitting that one has proceeded through the world in a way that oneself perceives as somehow wrong. Shame often arises in relation to a network of facts and relations that cumulatively produce an uneasy feeling without illuminating a path toward feeling better.

One of the unpleasant things about shame can also become, in very particular contexts, one of its virtues: one doesn't know what to do in response to feeling shame. Shame can provide a gap in practice; it can stop the conceptual habits we comfortably use to navigate the world. It has a disruptive function. I see some use, then, in shame's potential capacity to hold open, to not freeze, affective space. That virtue inheres in its unenunciated state; the unclarity around how to say "what it is," or what a person is, when they feel ashamed, might open possibilities for experiencing the shaming situation without stabilizing and freezing it, however briefly. This virtue inheres also in shame's relative lack of telos: the fact of not automatically knowing what to do with the feeling of shame opens the possibility for being—not just doing—something else. Probyn usefully reprises Bourdieu here, arguing that in shame "our habitus becomes reordered, shaken up, it admits other possibilities and in turn allows for more interest to be registered" (Probyn 2005, 72). What we do with the gap shame might open in practice is, of course, up for grabs—this shame is without guarantees. This is one of the reasons I see the strong need for shame to be unpacked in terms of some other networks of feeling and response—sympathy and solidarity in particular.

Shame is an affect, with all the nonpropositional content that term evokes, and an affect whose only appropriate response sometimes seems to be denial or rejection. Most of the time, in fact, shame signals the need for a change in the world, such that people who feel shame about themselves or their actions can either refuse the shaming gaze or stare back. Eli Clare theorizes this kind of refusal in a discussion of reclaiming derogatory names, turning them into signs of pride or modes of witnessing. In an essay titled "Freaks and Queers," Clare weaves a history of freak shows together with a meditation on current appropriations and reversals of terms like "cripple," "gimp," "queer," and "freak." The broader project of Clare's essay is to think about how pride and a politics of witnessing connect to refusing shame, particularly in disability-rights struggles.[8] "Shame" is one of the ways Clare names a socially produced self-hatred that is always political. He says: "I can feel slivers of shame, silence, and isolation still imbedded deep in my body. I hate these fragments. In the last decade I've stretched into the joy of being a gimp among gimps, learning anger and subversion, coming to recognize the grace in a gnarly hand, tremor, rolling limp, raspy breath, finding comfort and camaraderie with disabled people" (Clare 1999, 93–94).

In this context, shame flags sites for political transformation, and refusing shame is a first step toward changing things. Disability rights activists, particularly as people who reach to create something far beyond just rights, refuse shame in this way. Recent fat-positive feminist activism echoes this refusal.[9] As Sandra Bartky has argued in thinking about shame and gender, shame must be theorized in relation to oppression. She writes: "'Feeling inadequate' may color a person's entire emotional life. Under conditions of oppression, the oppressed must struggle not only against more visible disadvantages but against guilt and shame as well. . . . The experience of shame may tend to lend legitimacy to the structure of authority that occasions it, for the majesty of judgment is affirmed in its very capacity to injure" (Bartky 1990, 97). There are, without doubt, many situations in which refusing shame

---

8. Clare writes: "Both witness and pride strengthen identity, foster resistance, cultivate subversion. People who have lived in shame and isolation need all the pride we can muster, not to mire ourselves in a narrowly defined identity politics, but to sustain broad-based rebellion. And likewise, we need a witness to all our histories, both collective and personal. . . . Witness pairs grief and rage with remembrance. Pride pairs joy with a determination to be visible" (1999, 98–99).

9. See Stimson n.d.; Wann 1998; Shanker 2004; Frater 2005, among many others.

is necessary, and where such a refusal does the work that in other situations opening to shame might accomplish.

While some might dismiss shame as a productive route to liberatory change on these grounds, I hold out for the potential of affects like shame to get at and under conceptual frameworks and grids of intelligibility and to shift the terms on which life as usual proceeds. Always—and only when—situated alongside sharp, steady understanding of how multiple systems of oppression co-constitute subjectivities, appropriate negative affect can offer some leverage for reconstituting selves against the systems that constitute us. In some cases shame can offer this leverage through refusal: people ought to and do refuse the shame layered on them through manifesting crip pride, queer outrage, and working-class dignity. In other cases, people ought to and do accept various negative affects associated with being the beneficiaries of systems of oppression. There are, then, times and situations in which shame is appropriate, and in which it can illuminate commonsense habits. In other words, where people are avid practitioners of overt racism, or where they assert non-racist sensibility but persist in enacting racist scripts, I have hope for the possibilities of shifting their inarticulate frameworks, in part through affect. The people I have in mind for this kind of productive shame are those who Bartky argues have been posited as the abstract agent in much moral psychology. She writes:

> Moral psychology posits as universal an agent who is specific and quite privileged, an agent whose social location is such that he has the capacity not only to be judged but to judge, not only to be defined by others but to define them as well. This agent has escaped the characteristic sorts of psychological oppression on which modern hierarchies of class, race, and gender rely so heavily. The experience of shame can be salutary for such a person because he is not systematically impoverished by the moral economy he is compelled to inhabit. (Bartky 1990, 97)

My claim here is that white people occupy this position, however differently and unevenly, and that shame can have a salutary effect for this reason. Shame, in fact, marks some of the cracks and seams at the intersection of moral and political economies of oppression.

As a motivator of racialized redefinition, it is important that shame is also polymorphous. It attaches itself variously to the self and to things in the world. One can feel shame for or toward oneself, on behalf of or toward someone else, and for something as broad as the actions of the nation one lives in. And in each of these cases, or other shame-worthy sites, relations of scale break down; shame for one's nation can collapse into a seamless application to the self, and shame about the self can expand into an affect with effects on one's family network.[10] The shame one feels individually can have a similarly unsettled topography and a similarly protean relation of causes to effects—seemingly small events can produce pervasive shame. It may be difficult to delineate the bounds of shame; the effort to define what makes one feel shame may cause the feeling to expand and contract in ways that make it hard to "see" clearly.

Understanding particular kinds of racialized moments as shame situations is, here, a heuristic. That is, to think about the particular negative affect of racial situations as shame opens a space for something, if you think that shame has identificatory and re-identificatory potential. In a sense, though, shame is instrumental. I am thinking about shame as manifesting a kind of haunting, in Avery Gordon's terms. Gordon writes, "Being haunted draws us affectively, sometimes against our will and always a bit magically, into the structure of feeling of a reality we come to experience, not as cold knowledge, but as transformative recognition" (1997, 8). She investigates the ghost as a social figure, or as a figure that manifests social systems. Being haunted means that one exists in relation to a ghost that "has designs on us such that we must reckon with it graciously, attempting to offer it a hospitable memory *out of a concern for justice*" (64). Gordon is particularly interested in the aspect of haunting, manifesting for example in U.S. racism, that pulls people in the present into relation with unsettled facts of the past. A core claim here is that what matters is what you do with the ghost after the haunting.

In this sense, I understand certain sorts of shame as haunting. Shame might be its own poltergeist, rearranging the conceptual and affective furniture of our mental spaces without our permission but perhaps with our intent. Shame represents being thrown into the self you are that you also repudiate, a self you don't want to be. This implies a self you also are, a self you want to be. This is the aspect of haunting that is utopian, that implies a future. Out of a concern for justice we might respond to shame by changing our selves and our worlds. We might respond with solidarity. But it will be

---

10. I think, for example, of a character in the novel *The Assault* whose father was a Nazi collaborator in the Netherlands at the end of the war. This character, Fake, feels deep shame toward the narrator, whose family was killed as a result of Fake's father's actions. In his case, though, he responds to his own shame with rage toward the narrator (Mulisch 1985).

important to consider where we come by a concern for justice, and we must remember that—contra many academics who use conceptions of haunting flippantly—being haunted tends to be terrifying.

Because white supremacist thinking works to the benefit of individual white people, some change needs to happen to those individuals as part of a project of systemic change. White shame is an appropriate affective response to the degradations of current racist practice.[11] This will be seen to be the case particularly if it turns out that the experience of appropriate shame works toward changing the conditions that gave rise to shame. On one hand, then, it is important for people to change how they act toward particular racialized others; that is, it is appropriate to feel guilty when you have mistreated someone. What needs to happen, however, is also a very basic shift on the level of how and who we are, and this is not coextensive with or reducible to the things we do. And in fact there are often things that people do (or don't do) without having any sense of that doing (or not doing) as racist—and shame might enable a different optic for action. This might be a way of seeing in which racist situations are correctly perceived as shameful and in which partaking of the benefits accruing to whiteness in a systemically racist world is a source of shame.

Though it can feel core-deep, shame marks a nonessential relational self, one that by nature is malleable. Our selves manifest as coherent within a given situation—there is something that is held true by virtue of the facts and fictions that turn around that thing, or that self. While racist stances and acts are the stuff of racism, then, they do not imply fixed racist identities. Racist stances and acts indicate that one was racist, and they do pattern the limits and possibilities for future actions. But the fact that racialized shame reveals something you are does not hold those patterns and possibilities constant. Rather, shame reveals something you "were then," perhaps "are now," but also a self you refuse in the fact of feeling shamed. The experience of shame implies a repudiation of who one was then, and carries the sense that one also was not, inherently, that shamed self. In other words, the experience of shame in the face of racism—one's own or other people's—discloses both present racism and also potential for antiracist praxis, embedded in the desire to deny the racist self. Shame can be thought of as a moment of

---

11. Anger is another appropriate response. Audre Lorde famously writes, "Anger is an appropriate reaction to racist attitudes, as is fury when the actions arising from those attitudes do not change" (1984, 129).

contradiction in the multiple selves that we comprise, a confrontation between the self one has been and various selves one wants to have been.[12] All those identities are present in the self and available for identification. Pat, in the example I began with, manifests a self structured by powerful racist norms in his "going along with" his tablemate's racist jokes, and also a self that feels "the greatest shame"—a self manifesting at least the possibility for heterodox self-identification.

I attend here, carefully and hesitantly, to the aspect of shame that is profoundly hopeful. The depth of negativity associated with shame is in part a result of the positivity and potential signified to have failed in the fact of being ashamed. Shame expresses a kind of connection that is revealed to be desired in its failure to happen.[13] That is, someone (a)shamed feels that she has failed in some way. And yet, recognition of failure requires recognition of the possibility of success. The latter recognition may not come until after the onset of shame. I see shame as an expression of pained feeling-with and a failure of solidarity.

Perhaps the most important aspect of shame for a liberatory project is the sense that insofar as white people feel shame in racist situations, they manifest a self that has already shifted toward potentially less racist manifestations in the shaming. The fact of feeling shame indicates a site of potential re-identification in process. When white subjects experience negative affect in the face of racism, there is a possibility for choice: we can move away from the experience of shame in a direction that protects white primacy, or in a direction that foregrounds the fact of racism as intolerable. To be the sort of person who experiences negative affect around racism is already, it is true, to be the sort of person who may be prone to antiracist re-identification. If shame is always about the other, the feeling of shame indicates a particular view of the other in question: that other is viewed as capable of shaming, hence of seeing and being seen as a person. The experience of shame indicates an intersubjective relationship, where the actors involved are subjects in a strong sense.

There is, then, some use in simply renaming as "shame" experiences many situations that are now identified as "guilt" situations. Doing so might

12. I thank Kim Bird for suggesting shame as a point of confrontation between one's actual and ideal selves.

13. Probyn frames a similar point in this way: "Against the dynamics of guilt that underpin moral reproach, shame may provide us with a more positive ethos. Drawing on the deeply embodied experience of shame compels a different approach to envisioning social life: it highlights the connections and proximities of individuals to one another and as the basis on which political action ultimately rests" (2005, 77).

evade some of the individuating, escapist, and occluding tendencies that cluster around the label "guilt." There is something useful in the project of renaming our matrices of response. At the same time, separating guilt and shame is neither so easy nor so useful as these analytic maneuvers might indicate.[14] We need to hold together the critiques of white guilt, a potentially positive role for shaming whiteness, and an understanding that the way affect happens is multiple, complex, and in process. As Clare Holzman argues: "Guilt and shame are appropriate emotional responses to becoming aware of one's own racism, and can be major sources of motivation for change. However, in order for these emotions to be productive rather than immobilizing, many white women will need a training or therapy experience that provides a structure, a conceptual framework, and concrete strategies for dealing with guilt and shame constructively and keeping them at or returning them to the rational level" (1995, 329).

As I hope my discussion has made clear, I am not interested in engaging guilt and shame in order to bring them to or keep them at the level of the rational, but rather to think through what they show us that makes productive intercessions in the rational. At the same time, Holzman's caution here is vital: white women in particular require concrete strategies for dealing with guilt and shame constructively. Sedgwick says that shame can easily flood me assuming I'm a shame-prone person. As I discuss above, women are far more shame-prone than men, which is perhaps one reason for women's comparatively greater participation in and discussion of antiracist activism.[15] Sandra Bartky compellingly argues that "women typically are more shame-prone than men, that shame is not so much a particular feeling or emotion (though it involves specific feelings and emotions) as a pervasive affective attunement to the social environment, that women's shame is . . . a profound mode of disclosure of both self and situation" (1990, 85). The call I make for an attention to white shame is risky and multiply challenging, particularly along gendered lines of affective formation. Still, taking shame and guilt as foundationally gendered affects illuminates some of the deeper dynamics in antiracist activism.

14. This conviction is thanks to Barbara Epstein's nuanced reading and comments on early drafts of this chapter.

15. That is, it may be that there are in fact equal numbers of white women and white men doing antiracist activist work. As a field, however, there tend to be many more accounts of white women doing antiracist work than usual. It is only recently that there have been anthologies looking at white men's antiracist activism, and they cite a perceived need to attend to this as a gendered field. See, for example, Feagin and O'Brien 2003.

Guilt and shame are densely intertwined, neither transparently to be discarded, and neither transparently to be taken up as a personal/political project. But I find some potential in the complex of response of which guilt and shame each name overlapping parts. While shame on its own doesn't build a positive politics, it expresses and connects to some valuable sites for antiracist action. Further, understanding some experiences of whiteness through a shaming rather than a guilt-ridden optic may open more accurate understandings of racialized spaces. If Sedgwick is right to argue that shame marks an identificatory and re-identificatory affect, accurate understandings will involve both a sense of relationality and of a need to radically transform social spaces—the worlds we move through. Crucially, this form of transformation happens in terms of implicit understanding, particularly our socially situated, embodied, affective interaction with the world. In this world, now, maintaining white supremacist structures and systems requires forming and situating whiteness in particular bodies and people. This is a process of relational identification, which requires relational re-identification.

FIVE

ENACTING SOLIDARITY

Often people's racial, gendered commonsense understandings become palpable when they try to work in solidarity with others. As Gadamer suggests, it is something outside our horizon of presupposition—a text, a person—that puts our prejudgments into play. Minnie Bruce Pratt describes feeling that she could not simply move to a place where she "joined others to struggle with them against common injustices." Rather, working with others against injustice required her to struggle against aspects of herself and her history. And it seems that her realization of the need to struggle against her own history was only provoked by her attempts to work with others. Working with others in solidarity is a powerful ideal, though often equally difficult to enact. As I will lay out below, attempts to think about and work in solidarity show some of the subtle effects of calcified common sense and habituated modes of perception that happen on the level of implicit understanding. Because the practice of solidarity brings one's presuppositions, aspirations, and hopes into conversation and sometimes conflict with others' dreams and practices, it shows clearly the limits, the challenges, and the importance of commonsense, implicit understandings. While it is crucial to shift conceptual understanding in order to act in solidarity, much of the work of solidarity depends on more pervasive shifts in implicit understanding. To use Michael Polanyi's terms, the work of solidarity brings tacit, or distal, knowledge into the forefront and also produces new configurations of one's implicit knowledge. Solidarity involves different investments and commitments of the personal attention Polanyi theorizes as central to knowing.

In chapter 4 I argued that complex negative affect is an appropriate response to racialization, offering shame as an example of one such affect. I suggested that one aspect of its utility lay in the relational identification and transformation implied in the experience of shame, expressed in terms of experiences and transformations of the habitus. One form of relational re-identification might be created through the process of acting in solidarity with others. This is a space that might come out of, and produce, new possibilities for action. In this chapter, I argue that the grounds for white antiracist solidarity are partially interleaved with complex experiences of negative affect, shame among them. One important aspect of this negative affect is the knowledge-without-words revealed when white people feel bad in response to racial situations. This is a productive discomfort, which could open spaces for political antiracist transformation.

But the experience of discomfort needs to be paired with matrices of perception and habit that enable positive, sustainable action. To generalize: people who take political action solely out of feeling bad about themselves and their world are among the least effective of political actors, tending toward martyr complexes, assumed moral superiority, and insufficient compassion toward others less conscious of injustice. White people in particular need approaches that articulate an understanding of the shame-worthiness of our social position as white, with a sensibility that moves toward another political and social world out of a sense of joy and connection. That is, I am keeping in mind Michelle O'Brien's statement:

> Let's assume my complicity and participation in white supremacy is, to some extent for all white people, unavoidable. I don't get off scot-free, I never get to feel just good about myself, and that's not the fucking point. Being antiracist isn't the same as carefully avoiding ever doing or saying the wrong thing; it's about actually caring about real people and actually helping to make a different kind of world. (2002–3)

I am looking for accounts of why, if we can't just feel good, white people work against racism and against white primacy. More important, as O'Brien indicates, there has to be more to antiracist transformation than just avoiding doing or saying the wrong thing. Consider, then, examples in thinking about sympathy as ground for engaging in solidarity work. I take two theoretical touchstones for thinking about the roots of solidarity: philosophical work on sympathy, and people's accounts of how they came to work in a radical justice framework—particularly against racism.

Solidarity is an important optic through which to see the political stakes and effects of implicit understanding. Caring about people and helping make a different kind of world involves propositional, claim-making activity, for sure. But this activity only matters within the context of that caring and that work in the world. Why does it matter to do political solidarity work?[1] What sorts of claims are significant? The work of acting in solidarity foregrounds presuppositional and commonsense understandings—the potentially propositional aspects of understanding that emerge into consciousness at the point of provocation. Using Gadamer's terms, attempting to act in solidarity across power difference in particular provokes the space of a question, putting into play and up for risk the grounding horizon within which political actors move. Working in solidarity often arises from affective stakes—caring for someone, outrage about an injustice, or aspiration for a changed world. The feeling work of solidarity is productive and transformative, making new expressive resources, which then engender new sites for solidarity struggles. And the habitus expressed in social relations comes into play particularly when working across difference—of work site, class, ethnicity, citizenship, and so on. Solidarity is primarily a product of and productive of implicit understanding in all its manifestations, but particularly the aspects of the unspoken with political effects: habitus, presuppositions, and feelings. Addressing the implicit aspects of solidarity work is thus an important piece of the work itself; if we assume that solidarity can be pursued through propositional means, we'll both miss real opportunities for working meaningfully together and also fail to address the frictions and troubles that so often happen in nonpropositional strata of our work.

June Jordan's complex thinking about solidarity is useful here. She writes about solidarity across difference by reflecting on her vacation in the Bahamas:

> My "rights" and my "freedom" and my "desire" and a slew of other New World values; what would they sound like to this Black woman described on the card atop my hotel bureau as "Olive the Maid"? "Olive" is older than I am and I may smoke a cigarette while she changes the sheets on my bed. Whose rights? Whose freedom? Whose desire?
>
> And why should she give a shit about mine unless I do something, for real, about hers? (1985, 41)

The dynamics of rights, freedom, and desire at work between Jordan and "Olive" are crosscut with dynamics of differential experiences of racial

---

1. I follow Sally J. Scholz's useful understanding of political solidarity as having a "social justice content or aim; it opposes injustice, oppression, tyranny, and social vulnerabilities" (2008, 54).

formation, age, capital, and imperialism. More significant, the obvious trajectory of "solidarity" in this situation would be for Jordan—a black woman from the United States on vacation in the Bahamas—to stand in solidarity with "Olive"—a black woman working as a maid in a Sheraton British Colonial hotel. But what Jordan highlights is the sense in which she might also call for Olive to stand in solidarity with her in her own work for rights, freedom, and so on. Jordan is implying that there should be reason for Olive to care about Jordan's rights, freedom, and desire, as well as vice versa. Solidarity does not condescend.

One way she unpacks this notion is through thinking about the "report card" left on the hotel bureau, on which she is expected to rate Olive as "Excellent. Good. Average. [or] Poor." Jordan wonders: "How would 'Olive' rate me? What would it mean for us to seem 'good' to each other? What would that rating require?" (46). This question is important and suggestive: what is it for people working across difference to be good to—and for—each other? That is, in order for Jordan to stand in solidarity with Olive and whatever her struggles might be, and in order for Olive to stand in solidarity with June Jordan, they must be able to evaluate each other. The relationship they stand in is freighted with power dynamics that make the contents of any solidarity with each other, the activity of it, very different. More will be required of Jordan, in her position as U.S. citizen and tourist—a position complicated by her doubled situation of relative disadvantage and oppression as African American, a woman, a single parent, and more. There will be different things required of Jordan and Olive in order for them to rate each other as "good," but in Jordan's analysis Olive has as much right to rate her as vice versa. And this moves Olive from the position of subordinate maid to the position of a political equal: this at least becomes a relationship in which they could work for each other's good.

Jordan is trying to account for the realities of race, class, and gender without assuming that those realities automatically produce unity. What those realities say "about the contact between two individuals is less obvious and, like the weather, not predictable" (46). Solidarity can't, on Jordan's account, be naturalized or assumed. As she argues, "Partnership in misery does not necessarily provide for partnership for change: *When we get the monsters off our backs all of us may want to run in very different directions*" (47). The common identities imposed by a structure or a system do not necessarily map the real interests not encompassed by imposed commonalities. For example, the position of the "exploited worker" might create contingent alliances and commonalities, which would neither encompass the whole of an individual (what could?) nor last past the exploitative working conditions. In the situation where a third party "hostile to both of us, has worked it so that the two of us, like it or not, share a common enemy," Jordan asks, *"What happens beyond the idea of that enemy and beyond the consequences of that enemy?"* (47). She implies, then, that we have to rest solidarity on something more substantial than a common fight.[2]

At the same time, Jordan is not calling for a politics emerging from our identity—perhaps in part because she takes the identities we occupy to be significantly given by oppressive political contexts. The way we find the connections that give rise to solidarity will have to do with what good we can be to one another—as between Jordan and Olive. Jordan argues: "I am saying that the ultimate connection cannot be the enemy. The ultimate connection must be the need that we find between us. It is not only who you are, in other words, but what we can do for each other that will determine the connection" (47).

This position assumes a set of contingent relations determined by our needs. This connection is contingent insofar as those needs are dictated by constraints arising from a common enemy. It is a deeper connection insofar as it takes into account what happens beyond the idea of that enemy and beyond the consequences of that enemy. The solidarity Jordan envisions involves a complex set of relations, based ultimately on what good we might be to one another and how we might form ourselves in relation to those politics. We find need between us—the formation of solidarity is a relational and collaborative process.

This is a very different conception than that expressed in liberal politics of working for marginalized or disadvantaged others under the sign of solidarity. Richard Rorty offers a complex example of this mode, which I think is quite widespread. Rorty attempts to flesh out the claim that "we have a moral obligation to feel a sense of solidarity with all other human beings" (1989, 190). He argues that solidarity can best arise with others who we think have salient similarities to ourselves—who are "like us." Therefore, to extend solidarity to all other human beings, we ought to expand the circle of whom we identify as "us." As Rorty puts it: "Our sense of solidarity

2. In this, Jordan differs from influential theorists like Tommie Shelby, who argues that solidarity ought to be based on shared opposition to common oppression. Shelby writes: "As an alternative to conceptions of black solidarity that emphasize a shared identity among blacks (whether racial, ethnic, national, or cultural), I defend a conception of solidarity based strictly on the shared experience of racial oppression and a joint commitment to resist it. The practicality and scope of black solidarity depends on a diagnosis of the complex forces that constitute black oppression and on the extent to which blacks suffer specifically because of antiblack racism, past and present" (2005, 11–12).

is strongest when those with whom solidarity is expressed are thought of as 'one of us,' where 'us' means something smaller and more local than the human race. That is why 'because she is a human being' is a weak, unconvincing explanation of a generous action" (191).

There is, though, a method for attempting to expand the small and local solidarities that we experience with relative ease. This is to understand the ways we have similarities with others, to identify our tendencies to dichotomize our world into "us" and "them," and to attempt to create connections where they may not yet exist. According to Rorty:

> We should stay on the lookout for marginalized people—people whom we still instinctively think of as "they" rather than "us." We should try to notice our similarities with them. The right way to construe the slogan is as urging us to create a more expansive sense of solidarity than we presently have. The wrong way is to think of it as urging us to *recognize* such a solidarity, as something that exists antecedently to our recognition of it. (196)

There are useful aspects to Rorty's argument: it articulates an intuitive sense of how solidarity arises—naturally, and in response to others with whom one feels a sense of empathy. His idea that solidarity is contingently created—made—rather than discovered or recognized is a compelling one.

But there are also some problems with Rorty's model. First, it has the unfortunate rhetorical effect of centering a relatively privileged and dominant worldview as the "we" from which an expanded "us" is created. So, when Rorty writes that we should "stay on the lookout for marginalized people" I think he means "marginal" to indicate whoever is marginal to any given community or group. Because this is in fact a world in which "marginal" reads as "not white" or "not straight" or "not Anglo" (and so on), Rorty's imperative tends to re-center an orthodox subject. Extended beyond his account, this solidarity is in danger of becoming an attempt to see sameness where there is difference, or to annex and co-opt difference when it cannot be understood as a sameness, or to actively destroy difference under the sign of a post-enlightenment helping hand. The "we" who should stay on the lookout for marginalized people is too often a "we" who, because of social, economic, and affective structures, escapes the margin. This "we" has to actively look out, from a center to the margin, in an effort that simultaneously addresses and re-instantiates a conception of "they." The problem here is structural: expanding the sense of an "us" inscribes a center and a margin.

It is also most familiar to socially and politically dominant persons. Rorty's conception may turn out to be most efficacious for people who are actually positioned in dominant ways, but on these grounds I find it dissatisfying as a general model for solidarity work.

Second, Rorty's model assumes that the way to address a distinction between an "us" and an "other" is to nourish a sense of sameness. This, I will argue, cuts the feet out from under meaningful solidarity. Rorty's model collapses the distance between the actors involved in potential solidarity work in a troubling way. Through attempting to notice our similarities with those "we" perceive as other, real differences are either written over or seen as legitimate barriers to empathizing with them. When someone on the Rorty model attempts to see people they think of as different in terms of similarities and an "us," they highlight potential or actual similarities and efface potential or actual differences. An incapacity to perceive relevant sameness in an other or group of others then becomes either proof of un-recoupable difference (where that difference is a problem) or personal failure to perceive and act properly. A solidarity that relies on an expanded sense of "us" is potentially an imperialist, misguided, individualist effort that rests on a continued primacy of whiteness (among other things), forcing real differences to become legible as false sameness. It is thus hardly solidarity at all.

AGAINST EMPATHY

If we ought to build solidarity beyond the terms of shared enemies and without expanding a circle of "us-ness," what can we turn to? People across political fields recommend empathy as a way to nurture being good to someone else, in Jordan's terms, and to forge commonality: self-identified Christian conservatives deploy the injunction to "do unto others as you would have them do unto you," and liberals invite us to imagine how we would feel in some particular other person's shoes. These discursive strands at work everywhere from the playground to the church also manifest as theoretical trends in studies of racism, whiteness, and antiracism. One place to see these trends is in the sociological literature on racism and antiracism, which foregrounds both empathetic and cognitivist approaches. On my view, they are dangerous on several counts—in their reliance on empathic models, in their attachment to promulgating change at the propositional level, and in the conception of solidarity-through-sameness I see in Rorty's discussion.

Eduardo Bonilla-Silva's widely influential book *Racism Without Racists* is an important example of one strand of thinking on racism and antiracism. Its primary analytic contribution centers around the idea that people can be, and are, far more racist than they acknowledge—and that the very arguments for so-called color blindness are in fact modes of perpetuating pernicious racialized inequity. I agree with Bonilla-Silva's analysis on this count. For the purposes of this discussion, however, I attend to a theme of his work that is less overtly argued: the roots of antiracist action.

Bonilla-Silva offers one example of an argument that providing people more, or different, information will evoke antiracism, particularly among white people (2003, 184). This call for expanded information is often accompanied by a sense that while having certain information is important or relevant, it is meaningless if it doesn't lead to action. As Bonilla-Silva writes: "Being an antiracist begins with understanding the institutional nature of racial matters and accepting that all actors in a racialized society are affected materially (receive benefits or disadvantages) and ideologically by the racial structure. This stand implies taking responsibility for your unwilling participation in these practices and beginning a new life committed to the goal of achieving real racial equality" (15). Bonilla-Silva here foregrounds two bases for antiracist action: understanding and acceptance. These grounds are, in his account, not personalized—we are to understand and accept the institutional racialization of our society through knowing more about the material and ideological effects of racialization. But Bonilla-Silva thinks that they result in a personal change in activity, in which actors take responsibility and begin a "new life committed to the goal of achieving real racial equality" (16).

Notice the emphasis here on propositional knowledge. There is an assumption that the kind of information provided in Bonilla-Silva's book, and in analogous works, will create the conditions for the relatively radical steps of taking responsibility for how one is situated in the current racist order and beginning life anew—tasks that would in fact require complex changes on the level of implicit understanding. His program of work puts emphasis on: education about racism, particularly its "color-blind" form; overt acknowledgment of the actual racial situation in the United States;[3] research to provide counterexamples and arguments against the various "frames" of

---

3. "Whites' collective denial about the true nature of race relations may help them feel good, but it is also one of the greatest obstacles to doing the right thing. In racial matters as in therapy, the admission of denial is the preamble for the beginning of recovery" (183).

color-blind racism;[4] the documentation of color-blind racism; challenging whiteness "wherever it exists"; and creating a new, militant civil rights movement (183–84). These programmatic steps remain for the most part (with the exception of the recommendation to create a new, militant movement) in the realm of information, claims about the world, and explicit acknowledgement of the manifest racial circumstances of our lives. They are articulate, defensible, and accessible by reason.

Several prominent sociologists working on antiracism argue that the source of antiracist praxis is the experience of white empathy with the plight of those subject to racism. The sociologist Joe Feagin's work is exemplary of this strand of sociology of antiracism. This approach would seem to provide a potentially richer account of the causes and conditions under which people move toward antiracist praxis. Perhaps it gives a bit more traction in explaining the leap that people—especially ordinary people—might make between having information about racialized inequity and taking action for racial justice.

Feagin, Vera, and Batur define antiracism as "an active confrontation of racism by people of varied religious and political ideologies who wish to build a better society. Talking back, being an interruptor of racist commentary, and developing interpersonal empathy are key steps in an antiracist strategy. For whites in particular, empathy is an integral element of antiracist action" (2001, 240). They argue here that the roots of active antiracism are in an empathetic relation with individuals in racialized "out groups." On this account, actions springing from these roots range from "talking back" to other, less personalized strategies, such as agitating for reparations, working toward the more vigorous enforcement of civil rights legislation, and working toward a new constitutional convention in accord with the UN's Universal Declaration of Human Rights. Beyond its importance to these accounts in sociology, notice the weight that affect—in this case empathy—is given here. I want to attend to the prominence empathy is given here, then, because this case is an example of one place implicit understanding is framed as central to political transformation, but also because of the troubling implications of the specific formulation of empathy as a route (or root) for political change.

Feagin argues that empathy is central to antiracist work, involving the "capacity to sense deeply the character of another's torment and to act on that realization" (2000, 254). Feagin extends this notion further, to articulate

---

4. These are abstract liberalism, naturalization, cultural racism, and minimization of racism (28).

what he calls "autopathy"—a step beyond empathy, an understanding and feeling in which a white person has intentionally put her- or himself, if only partially, into the racist world experienced by the oppressed, and thereby not only receives racist hostility from other whites but also personally feels some of the pain that comes from being enmeshed in the racist conditions central to the lives of the oppressed others (255). Feagin actually defines racism as "the destruction of natural human empathy; it means a lack of recognition of the humanity of the racialized other" (254). If racism is a result of an inability to identify across the color line, and empathy a paradigmatic form of such identification, it would indeed make sense to understand antiracism as importantly tied to empathy.

These sorts of accounts of empathy usefully point to the affective and interpersonal entanglements that do seem to arise in the pursuit of solidarity work. There are at least three difficulties, however, associated with foregrounding empathy in this way. First, it is not clear whether it's possible to think about institutional empathy, empathy between groups of people, or between individuals and groups. It seems that the possibility of empathy assumes a relation between one individual and another—a relation in which one person steps into another's place and feels what they feel. This model does not accommodate the kind of antiracism work involved in, for example, church groups offering sanctuary to racialized political refugees whom the U.S. or Canadian state attempts to deport. It does not encompass the work involved in the Black Panther Party providing food to the diverse disabled activists sitting in for twenty-six days in 1977 San Francisco for disability civil rights. It does not speak to what is happening when groups declare themselves in solidarity with individual (current or former) political prisoners like Mumia Abu-Jamal, David Gilbert, Leonard Peltier, Kathy Boudin, Assata Shakur, or Marilyn Buck. While some individuals in these groups might be motivated by hearing stories about particular individuals in groups with whom they stand in solidarity, there is something more encompassing going on than a simple empathetic relation between individuals. That is, while empathy might be an ingredient in these cases, it cannot encompass the breadth or complexity of the affect and politics involved.

Second, the emphasis on empathy assumes a kind of non-entanglement prior to the realization of empathic pain, as though the formation of empathy itself is the source of the entanglement and not simply the marker of an already thorough enmeshment in the processes of racialization. Feagin gives the example of white parents with black children experiencing autopathic pain as a stage of antiracist evolution beyond empathy. In many ways he is not wrong to point to these accounts as important. They provide a kind of limit case in which it's very clear that there are dense networks of racialization, power, and co-constitution in relationships between people. It is important, though, to recognize the ways that we are all already enmeshed in complex networks of racial formation; although particular affective relationships frequently work to bring these networks into view, they were there before the feeling arose. Jane Lazarre's frequently cited memoir *Beyond the Whiteness of Whiteness* explores her coming to consciousness about race in and through her relationships as a white mother with black sons. She writes, "This is the story of a change in a white person's vision through self-discovery to conscience." In characterizing this journey, however, Lazarre says that it has been

> a long journey, and it is still going on, an incremental journey which demands that I think and rethink my experience, moving constantly, often accompanied by a kind of psychic vertigo, from the present moment to the past and back into some further extended enlightenment. I did not begin with crass racial prejudices and move to the realization that "all people are alike," to a state of color blindness that many white people still believe to be the essence of a nonracist perspective. . . . Like any Black person I have ever known, I now perceive both obvious and subtle racism in the immediate world around me every single day. (1996, xx–xxi)

Notice Lazarre's depiction of her journey as complexly mediated across time and as resulting in an attention to the daily nature of racialization. It is not that forming close relationships with her African American husband's family, or having black children, creates an entanglement in racialization that was not there before—though it may well have amplified such an entanglement. That entanglement has, rather, shifted and revealed some of the enmeshments that were already present. That is, the experience of empathy might work against some of the occlusion of racial workings in the world, but is does not, all on its own, create entanglements between white people and racialized others. Those entanglements have been there for hundreds of years.

Third, there is a sense in which the focus on empathy re-centers whiteness and white experience. As Saidiya Hartman argues, when we successfully empathize with another's suffering, it turns out that "empathy is double-edged, for in making the other's suffering one's own, this suffering is occluded by the other's obliteration" (1997, 18–19). Empathy requires us to imagine how we might feel were we in another's place, an imaginative projection rooted in one's own experience. It is a process of making analogies between experiences we've had and ones we haven't, seeing a quality of sameness in them. In principle, this process is unproblematic. When it is applied to experiences of racialized inequity, though, the power of analogy might break down. Because so much of white people's experience appears as a norm to us, the work of making the experiences of racialized others analogous to white experience threatens to recapitulate a dynamic in which whiteness is the norm against which otherness is measured, defined, and understood. That is, on an empathetic account, white people are to come to racial consciousness through projecting analogies between aspects of experiences we've had as white and experiences racialized others have had in relation to racism, white privilege, and the cultural norming/universalizing work of whiteness. But this trajectory ignores the real sense in which white experience—even of some other axis of oppression—is different than the experience of racism (in any of its forms). A fruitful account of how affect is involved in racial re-formation will need to avoid a reduction of real difference into analogous sameness. It will need to de-center white experience, rather than attempting to bring "otherness" into relation with a white norm.

Sandra Lee Bartky offers a valuable feminist theory of sympathy and solidarity, drawing on and offering correctives to Max Scheler's account of the role and use of sympathy and arguing against empathy as a route to political change. Scheler's idea of *Mitgefühl* might, Bartky suggests, give us some traction in thinking about transformative knowing. This term can be translated as "sympathy," or "fellow-feeling," or "feeling-with." Feeling-with might be read to maintain a certain cognitive distance from the other whom we are feeling-with. It is important for Scheler, as Bartky presents him, that feeling-with is not the same as empathy. Empathy, for Scheler, requires us to consider how we would feel were we in the place of the person we're empathizing with. It is, in effect, a way of imagining ourselves in the other's place, and it thus re-centers our own egoistic concerns. Feeling-with, in part through imagination, always implies a kind of distance between people who are attempting to act in solidarity with each other. I take this distance to be particularly important in white people's attempts to feel-with people of color in antiracist praxis. The notion of distance encoded in feeling-with can, on Bartky's view, "act against the temptation on the part of the advantaged one to believe that her oppressor's guilt can be overcome through heroic acts of ego-identification" (2002, 80).

At the same time, the act of imagination draws the felt-with into a closer relation than can mere cognitive understanding. For example, if I think someone has acted in racist, transphobic, or classist ways, and I call on them to change their actions, I am not supposing that all they need is more or different information. Rather, I am calling for a shift in how they move through the world—their inarticulable or unspoken, dynamic, generative framework of understanding. Bartky frames this as a knowing that "transforms the self who knows, a knowing that brings into being new sympathies, new affects as well as new cognitions and new forms of intersubjectivity" (2002, 71–72). The idea here is that building solidarities across lines of politically demarcated difference requires a special framework of understanding—and this is not a solely conceptual or propositional thing. It moves our understanding from a propositional mode of "knowing that" something is happening or has happened to someone to a state that "causes these circumstances to come alive in the theater of my mind" (85). This kind of understanding of another's circumstance—this kind of sympathy—might be the grounds for responsible solidarity.[5] Still affective, but refusing the conflation of self encoded in the notion of empathy, this sort of political feeling-with is central to solidarity. For something to come alive for me is for it to engage me holistically, engaging and transforming my whole corporeal sensorium, my feelings, my prejudices, my ways of being in the world. Where empathy might model a limited engagement of affect in political work, solidarity calls for a more comprehensive shift across all forms of knowing.

5. It is possible that the novelist Russell Banks read Scheler too. His novel *The Darling* is about Liberia, and a woman, Hannah, who is first a member of the Weather Underground, flees to Liberia and eventually starts a chimpanzee sanctuary. Discussing her relationship to her wards (whom she dubs "dreamers"), she describes first thinking them less evolved than humans, then as bearing a close semblance to humans, at which point, she writes, "I came to believe that I could empathize with the dreamers." Later, she comes to "see the built-in limitations of empathy." She muses: "Perhaps because of my relationship with Carol, and the rivalry with Zack, and because I am a woman, I came for the first time to believe that even the best-intentioned man, one who truly does empathize with women, is nonetheless incapable of knowing how the relations between men and women *feel* to a woman. Mainly, he is incapable of knowing how he is perceived by her. And therefore, despite her likeness to him, she remains opaque to him, unknowable." Thinking about her relationship to nonhuman primates in analogy to a sighted person's relationship to a blind person crossing the street, she says: "I'm talking here about the difference between *empathy* and *sympathy*, between feeling *for* the other and feeling *with* the other. The distinction came to matter to me. It still does. When you abandon and betray those with whom you empathize, you're not abandoning or betraying anyone or anything that's as real as yourself. Taken to its extreme, perhaps even pathological, form, empathy is narcissism" (Banks 2004, 325–26).

RACE TREASON

People familiar with the political approach exemplified in the journal *Race Traitor*, or the book of the same name, might hold a "race treason" model up as exemplary of "white" solidarity work through a kind of sympathy. I think this would be a mistake, and explaining why will set the ground for articulating a more compelling solidarity. *Race Traitor* expresses, it is true, an alternative to passive or tongue-tied white guilt, and offers an action-oriented, somewhat optimistic, program. Their motto, "Treason to whiteness is loyalty to humanity," is one way to express their mandate: the "abolition of the white race."[6] *Race Traitor* names "the white race" in order to refute the existence of both "whiteness" and "race," arguing that both are social constructions and calling for the disruption and eventual destruction of the institutions and ways of being that maintain whiteness as a privileged location. It is worth exploring and critiquing this model in some detail because it is a significant player in the field of activist critical work on whiteness, and the site of perhaps the most coherent theoretical elaboration in that field.

Like many aspiring white antiracists in North America, I find much of the race traitor model appealing. It does a better job than many available theories of thinking about how class and race intersect, and it aims at a feminist ethos. It names some important truths about the prevalent racialized order, especially in the United States and Canada. It situates racial formation as contingent and therefore potentially mutable. The race traitor model thereby offers both a deep critique of how race happens and offers one of the only responses to white supremacist systems that is not based on the spectrum of white guilt: through our action, proponents of this model argue, we can repudiate whiteness and the unwanted privileging and oppression that attend it. Finally, the rhetoric of Noel Ignatiev and John Garvey, editors of *Race Traitor*—and, indeed, many of the people in this lineage and associated with this model—is refreshingly outspoken. It projects and instantiates

---

6. Or, as their affiliated society (the New Abolitionist Society) puts it: "The key to solving the social problems of our age is to abolish the white race—in other words, to abolish the privileges of the white skin. Until that task is accomplished, even partial reform will prove elusive, because white influence permeates every issue, domestic and foreign, in U.S. society. The way to abolish the white race is to challenge, disrupt and eventually overturn the institutions and behavior patterns that reproduce the privileges of whiteness, including the schools, job and housing markets, and the criminal justice system. The abolitionists do not limit themselves to socially acceptable means of protest, but reject in advance no means of attaining their goal" (http://racetraitor.org/naindex.html, accessed April 15, 2010).

a frank critique of the current racial order without hedging or apology and in a tone not common in white antiracist writing. Indeed, Ignatiev and Garvey argue that they are calling for stances other than those "normally taken under the banner of 'anti-racism.'" They say, "We mean a challenge to the institutions that reproduce race as a social category—a challenge that disrupts their normal operation" (1996, 3). They might argue that one "normal operation" of a number of antiracist institutions is the perpetuation of the assumption (and corollary rhetoric) that white people cannot, in fact, turn traitor to our whiteness.

The race traitor model has recently been taken up by a collective called "Bring the Ruckus." I take them as a useful current example, weaving older material from *Race Traitor* into this discussion. Bring the Ruckus (BTR) says of themselves:

> We seek to build a revolutionary organization of organizers, committed to an anti-statist, revolutionary feminist, and anti-capitalist vision of a new society. We place a strategic focus on combating racial oppression. We believe that [the] separate deal the white working-class has struck with capital has prevented the full participation of white workers in the struggle for liberation. Only combating racial oppression and attacking institutionalized white privilege and white supremacy can break that separate deal. Only a directly democratic, revolutionary movement led by the working class can truly remake society. (http://www.agitatorindex.org, accessed November 19, 2004)

BTR is a cadre organization aiming its work at revolutionary social change; they set delimited membership terms, requiring a political and financial commitment of their members. The political commitment is to a feminist, class-based, antistatist form of action, taking an opposition to white supremacy as the key leverage point in bringing down other oppressive systems. Like *Race Traitor*, BTR argues that individual white people's actions have the potential to dismantle racist systems, thereby addressing other forms of injustice.

A case in point, and one that has been the site of some controversy: Roy San Filippo, a member of the BTR collective and frequent contributor to the writing posted on their site, wrote an article called "The Color of Authority," in which he presents a common race traitor trope—an individual white person going against systemic racialized expectations of his actions as white. Mitchell Crooks, a white vacationer to Inglewood, California, videotaped the police beating of Donovan Jackson, a young black man, and made the tape public.[7] San Filippo (2003) writes that "Crooks's act was an instance of race treason—when a white person violated an unspoken rule of whiteness by actively opposing the state's attempt to enforce the color line, a transgression of the norms of whiteness that the state took so seriously that Crooks was promptly incarcerated." San Filippo leverages this example to argue that these kinds of actions profoundly destabilize state and disciplinary power structures, which rely on white people's implicit acceptance of massive injustice perpetrated on people of color in the United States and abroad. So, San Filippo argues, Crooks violated the norms of whiteness—thereby opening the possibility for racist structures, instantiated in individuals, to no longer rest quite so surely or stably.

A key claim in much of this model is that when agents of the state become unable to assume compliance to the norms of whiteness from people they identify as white, the structures they enforce won't hold up. This is because of the implied answers to the questions asked in a *Race Traitor* editorial, "Abolish the White Race":

> If enough of those who looked white broke the rules of the club to make the cops doubt their ability to recognize a white person merely by looking at him or her, how would it affect the cops' behavior? And if the police, the courts, and the authorities in general were to start spreading around indiscriminately the treatment they normally reserve for people of color, how would the rest of the so-called whites react? (Ignatiev and Garvey 1996, 13)

So, the argument goes, if a relatively small number of people socially identified as white acted against the interests of whiteness and repudiated the privileges

---

7. There are a number of features of this case that were very salient on its own terrain, and which do not come out in the discussion below. At the time of this case, there was emphasis placed—particularly by Jackson's family and lawyer—on Jackson's developmental disability, which caused him, according to the case, to have delayed reaction time and difficulty responding appropriately to police instructions. His case was picked up by a variety of sources, and used for various ends—from the conventional news media to sectarian socialists to disability news sites to anti-police-brutality work. Of course, San Filippo's (2004) and Ajani and Aguilar's (2004) articles also make use of the case for their own ends. The two officers initially charged with assault in the case had the charges dropped in February 2004 and have brought a suit against their police department on grounds of reverse discrimination. An important aspect of these discussions of the case is how the context of the original, complicated events drops out. For example, I wonder what it would do to San Filippo's analysis to take seriously how disability functioned (actually and discursively) in the case.

that go along with it, it would become impossible to generalize about white people. This might result in a kind of suspension of white privilege, revealing the armatures of political discrimination normally masked by that privilege. And this unmasking would, in a race traitor model, result in a majority of white people ceasing to go along with a system of persistent racialized injustice. This is one reason that recounting the actions of individuals—like Mitchell Crooks—has such rhetorical significance in a race traitor model: such actions read as early tremors in a major collapse of the current racial order.

Despite its appeal, there is a lot that troubles me in the *Race Traitor* model.[8] I have three critiques: I think it assumes too much voluntarism; it remains too individualized, despite assurances to the contrary; and it too quickly collapses the necessary distance of feeling-with (in Bartky's sense) important to responsible solidarity, thereby short-circuiting meaningful intersectional praxis. I think that *Race Traitor* and its allied groups exemplify an attempt to feel-with by being-against-together, in Bartky's terms, or to reduce solidarity to fighting a common enemy, in June Jordan's account.

Voluntarism names the assumption that individuals, or a small group of people, can by act of will change the political circumstances in which they work. Race traitor politics are voluntarist, then, in that they suggest individual white people can bring down white supremacy as a global system of domination simply through their personal actions, thoughts, and interventions. This is problematic not only because it is politically wrongheaded but also because it reinscribes white primacy. That is, because white people can choose when and how to make interventions in situations we identify as racist (and, of course, these identifications are usually quite partial), our participation in race traitor politics is something we can choose. Indeed, it is something that we would have to choose on a case-by-case basis—in order for race traitor politics to "work," white people must be going against others' racialized social readings of us. And this implies that we are, in a deep way, maintaining precisely the white privilege that the model aims to undo. In fact, structurally we must maintain that privilege if we are to effect the kind of destabilizing change that is supposed to result from not acting the way white people are supposed to act. The deep problem, then, is that a race traitor model retains and reifies the whiteness of its actors through a voluntarist

---

8. One difficulty I have in making this critique is that many of the people who criticize the journal are white supremacists and racists of the most overt stripe. Their reading of *Race Traitor*'s mandate is almost enough to make one believe that its very assertion does some of the work Ignatiev and Garvey aim at (see, for example, http://www.whitefuture.com/html/traitor.html, accessed November 23, 2004).

ideal of white antiracist action. This problem is compounded by the sense in which white people can't change (usually) how they are read socially.

The problem of voluntarism is enmeshed with a problem of individualism. The individual actor—Mitchell Crooks, here read as a fictionalized white race traitor—holds paradigmatic status in much race traitor–style politics. Over and over again, it is the story of one person's action against a racist order, often resulting in some cathartic transformation in the self or in the order.[9] This notion of a catharsis implicit in the attempt to act as a race traitor is important, and I explore some of its implications below. There is, in any event, a clear predilection in this cluster of articles toward writing about individual actions and a striking lack of writing about collective or coalitional work for racial justice. Ignatiev and Garvey respond to this critique, saying, "If *Race Traitor* suffers from a shortage of accounts of collective struggles against whiteness, it is because few such struggles are taking place involving so-called whites" (1996, 3). One response to this defense is, of course, that while individualized, voluntarist actions are where we tend to find white people acting against the structures of white supremacy, their singularity doesn't imply that those are the most effective actions; individualist voluntarism might, in fact, be the very thing we want to oppose as white people working for racial justice. It might be precisely what inhibits meaningful solidarity. Further, this mode also ignores the cohesion of most white people's collective investment in white supremacist worlds.

Finally, though, consider a troubling aspect of the race traitor model: the idea that white people can meaningfully cast off white skin privilege, and by extension their whiteness, and stand with people of color in an unmediated solidarity. Joel Olson's "Police-Assisted Homicide" makes half this point. Olson discusses the case of another individual white man, twenty-three-year-old Steven Cole, shot to death by police in South Minneapolis. It is worth quoting Olson at length:

> At least for those brief few moments when he stood against those white cops with big guns, Cole was not playing white. He had quit the "club" of white supremacy, exchanging his membership card for two kitchen knives and a last stand.
>
> To be the shooter, to be the cop, to be the reporter, to be the fancy car with the windows rolled up and the doors locked as you speed by the crowd, THAT is to be white. To be the shot is to

---

9. One question is whether this amounts to a kind of expressive politics.

be not white—at least for that moment—no matter what your skin color. . . . We whites in the crowd were outraged at the police with everyone else, and although we were not Black or Chicano we were, for a moment, not really white, either. Of course, abandoning one's white privilege to join the rest of humanity is usually a fleeting, temporary thing. (1996, 140–41)

One difficulty here is that Olson's depiction makes it look like Cole was making a last stand against white supremacy, while the details of the case don't point toward this conclusion. But the main problem is Olson's assertion that to be positioned as the victim of white supremacist state violence, or to stand in common outrage at such violence, makes a person "not really white." He wavers on some of the implications of this notion—he's not asserting that there was real solidarity among the crowd that happened by the site of Cole's shooting. But he sees the potential for solidarity with "the crowd" in the white people who expressed outrage at the police, and that potential is a result of their capacity to abandon their white privilege.

This example demonstrates the individualism and voluntarism common to many such testimonials. More, though, it demonstrates a wish to collapse white identity into a "not really" whiteness—an identity that floats free of social positioning through the formerly white person's identification with the putative struggles of people of color. Olson here collapses the space that must stand between political groupings in order to produce meaningful solidarity. Intersectional praxis falls out of this equation. The actors involved become the people of color, and the formerly white agents somehow become, well, not exactly people of color themselves—but something that exists only in reference to them. It is as though people of color become a prism in the presence of which white folks can manifest the rainbow of their humanity. In Bartky's terms, Olson's move here erases the kind of true sympathy that would allow for solidarity; the way that he frames the work of standing together erases the actual (and necessary) distance between him and the crowd around him. If this is race treason, it is very partial and very unsatisfying.

SOLIDARITY OUT OF DIFFERENCE

The idea of the race traitor, in the positive way *Race Traitor* and Bring the Ruckus use it, is a category that has analytic meaning for (some) white people: those who identify as aspiring race traitors; perhaps those who identify as aspiring antiracists; those who have acted against white privilege and experienced some repercussions; and, as I note above, some white people who identify as white supremacists and who see *Race Traitor* as a genuine threat to "their race." What resonance is here is not necessarily something to spit on. When white people transgress racialized boundary lines, often we do have a palpable sense of having crossed a line—of acting against a racial order that "expected" us to act in accord with white supremacist logic. Sometimes white people, individually, do cross these lines in ways that retain a consciousness of difference.

I am thinking, for example, of a well-known image from the 1968 Olympics in Mexico City: The medalists from the two-hundred-meter race stand on the Olympic medal platform. The gold medalist, Tommie Smith, and the bronze medalist, John Carlos, hold black-gloved fists high, bringing, as *Z Magazine* writer Dave Zirin (2006) writes, "the Black revolution into that citadel of propriety and hypocrisy: the Olympic games." The silver medalist, Peter Norman, just stands there. When I've talked to friends about this image, usually someone comments on how the white guy in the picture is oblivious to the moment of history he's standing next to: a blank, totally checked out and clueless. Zirin's obituary for Peter Norman notes:

> He is hardly mentioned in official retrospectives, and people assume him to be a Forrest Gump–type figure, just another of those unwitting witnesses to history who always end up in the back of famous frames. Only the perceptive notice that this seemingly anonymous individual is wearing a rather large button emblazoned with the letters O-P-H-R, standing for the Olympic Project for Human Rights. Only those who see the film footage notice that he never throws a furtive glance back at fellow medal winners as they raise their fists. He never registers surprise or alarm. At a moment that epitomized the electric shock of rebellion, his gaze is cool, implacable, his back ramrod straight, a fellow soldier proud to stand with his brothers.

Zirin frames Norman's act, and his life in Australia after he went home, in terms of solidarity work. (Also, more strangely, with a militaristic analogy—solidarity as soldiering.) The articles commemorating Norman's life after his death on October 3, 2006, frequently mention his commitment to racial justice and his explicit desire to stand in solidarity with Smith and

Carlos. A statue at San Jose State University in honor of Smith and Carlos leaves the silver medalist's platform blank, so that others can stand in Norman's place. Zirin quotes Peter Norman's response: "I love that idea. Anybody can get up there and stand up for something they believe in. I guess that just about says it all."

I am not derogating the kind of risk Norman took in standing by Carlos and Smith, and in standing up for his action in Australia in the following years (during which time he was blacklisted in the Australian sports world). I do see this as a kind of solidarity work. It can be courageous to step outside these invisible boundaries, and it will always be uncomfortable to try to change racist practice. But crossing these lines does not necessarily have the same valence for the people of color whom we are ostensibly standing in solidarity with. In Peter Norman's case, Smith and Carlos did count his standing with them as solidarity.[10] But Smith and Carlos were expelled from the Olympic Village and immediately sent back to the United States; Norman was not. Perhaps if more white athletes at the 1968 Games had acted in solidarity with black Americans, he too would have been expelled. Beyond the kind of humble yet real opposition to racism expressed in Norman's reaction to his absence from the San Jose State statue, notice the recognition of difference encoded in his action in 1968. There is something very interesting and very important precisely in Norman's stance, arms by his side. He does not raise a black power fist—he does not attempt to collapse himself into Smith and Carlos's expression of opposition to U.S. structural racism. Instead, he stands by them, conscious of spectacle and history. More important, after this moment—a significant moment, but nonetheless only a moment—he returned home and devoted himself to working against racism in sports for the rest of his life. It would be a mistake to understand Norman as a race traitor in the narrow sense because of the collaborative nature of his actions and because his stance does not attempt to collapse real difference into imagined sameness.

One aspect of the kind of distance I'm arguing for is the fact that different understandings resonate with different social positions. For example, generally when white people think we've really hit on something in doing a racial analysis of the world, and the people of color who interact with that analysis think it's flat wrong, it likely is. At the same time, solidarity across racialized difference has to stand on its own feet—white people need to develop thick analyses and praxes for working against racial injustice. Is there a

10. For example, they flew to Australia to serve as lead pallbearers in his funeral.

way for white people who try to be race traitors to do meaningful solidarity work?[11] This is in part a question of intersectional analysis and of the political practices that arise out of it. Angela Davis (2004) has argued that one of the important legacies of women of color feminisms is a methodology of intersectional analysis: invested thinkers working together toward a common end, without erasing the differences between them. Such analysis has emanated from the collective thinking of people who come out of varied social, ethnic, and racialized positions, often in ways they are complexly invested in.

Beginning political work from the point of view that oppression operates along multiple axes—race wrapping around gender pulling on sexuality textured by (dis)ability, to reprise the activist-scholar Eli Clare—would shift what we do and how we do it. It is old hat by now to argue that we need an intersectional anti-oppression or holistic analysis, one that takes into account the way it is different to be gendered depending on how one is positioned in terms of class and race, and how it is different to be racialized depending on one's sexuality or position in relation to a naturalized gender binary structure. But there is an extended way to understand holistic analysis. This is to pursue a politics within which people can live with our whole selves—as political, social, emotional, physical beings who need to be able to find dignity and delight in many different dimensions of our being. That is, a truly holistic analysis will not only take into account the complexities of multiaxial political formation, it will also take seriously the affective and material contexts in which those politics are lived. One problem is that much analysis of whiteness attempts a divestment—a disinvestment—in our position as white. The corresponding methodology has trouble being intersectional because it's attempting to blow up the road by which it has arrived. The question for me, then, is what methodology we might craft that would take whiteness as its object without moving—as I think some antiracism workshops and the race traitor model do—to formulaic white guilt, imperialist empathy, or the fantasy of being not really white.

Audre Lorde offers a compelling argument for a kind of solidarity built out of difference. She argues that difference can be the root of a powerful and transformational politic. Lorde exemplifies a holistic analysis of dominance grounded in praxis. I take up three facets of her discussion: the idea of interdependence; her analysis of negotiating real difference; and the idea, expressed metaphorically, that no one is free while anyone is in chains.

11. See, for example, Bailey 1998; and Heldke 1998.

First, Lorde takes seriously the idea of mutuality, a way of being in the world that acknowledges difference and relies on systems of support and nurturance—in other words, interdependence. She unpacks this idea primarily in the context of her attempt to think about a multiracial, liberatory, feminist community; she is most interested in dynamics between women who share feminist political ends. Interdependence arises out of mutual, non-dominative difference. Lorde argues that only within "that interdependency of different strengths, acknowledged and equal, can the power to seek new ways to actively 'be' in the world generate, as well as the courage and sustenance to act where there are no charters" (1984, 111). Difference, here, is recognized through seeing different strengths, arising from our being differently positioned. It involves seeing difference without immediately equating difference with inferiority or superiority—which Lorde argues creates guilt rather than solidarity.

Lorde articulates an active approach—willfully seeing difference as a source of creative potential for liberatory change. This is also a case of aiming to understand how difference can be non-dominative. Difference, Lorde argues, must be "seen as a fund of necessary polarities between which our creativity can spark like a dialectic" (111). So, difference becomes a site for mutual support and the often challenging process of transformation through interaction with people who do not share our position. Thus Lorde writes: "As women, we have been taught to either ignore our differences or to view them as causes for separation and suspicion rather than as forces for change. Without community, there is no liberation, only the most vulnerable and temporary armistice between an individual and her oppression. But community must not mean a shedding of our difference, nor the pathetic pretense that they do not exist" (111–12). It will be useful, then, to look at what a non-pathetic acknowledgment of difference might look like, and what sorts of negotiations have to take place in a world where most difference is intertwined with relations of domination.[12]

---

12. Lorde sees global capitalism as importantly related to a rejection (through co-optation, active ignoring, or destruction) of difference. She argues that "institutionalized rejection of difference is an absolute necessity in a profit economy which needs outsiders as surplus people" (115). Capital must manage the instability of individual uniqueness in its production of commodities, workers, and markets. At the same time, there is a movement of creating a surplus workforce, often racialized and outside the norms of already incorporated workers (I think, for example, of undocumented workers in the United States). Further, capital today manages a process of exoticization and exploitation that rests on things being different-but-not-too-different. Lorde's analysis of capitalism's role in the production of difference is under-theorized even by people who write on her work.

Second, addressing the idea of difference, Lorde argues that there are real differences between people, often read as reasons we can't act in solidarity. She sees the refusal to work with these differences as the problem. Solidarity work is impeded by "our refusal to recognize those differences, and to examine the distortions which result from our misnaming them and their effects upon human behavior and expectation" (115). The project is to recognize and explore the difference that is distorted through racism, classism, ageism, and so on—to "recognize, reclaim, and define those differences." One model Lorde sees for this kind of work is the way that feminist women have learned to "deal across" manifest differences between women and men. She sees these differences as ones that are recognized and negotiated, often explicitly, even when this recognition did not shift modes of being dominant or subordinate. We must be able to recognize difference in order to do the political work of addressing inequity.

In the anthology *This Bridge We Call Home*, Indigo Violet echoes some of Lorde's work, arguing that the "work of building solidarity across difference involves facing history and the consequences of our diverse and varied locations in society" (2002, 488). Violet is pointing to the ways that seeing difference is complex, multiply layered, and contingent. Difference is produced significantly through the histories that condition our location; crafting a solidarity that can do justice to the complexity of social relations relies on the recognition of those histories. Arguing for a commitment to alterity and difference, Dawn Rae Davis calls for a feminist ethics that recognizes love as "the impossible experience of knowing across radical difference, and simultaneously, that which requires ethical choice and action even in the face of the impossible" (2002, 146). Taking a recognition of alterity as the basis of solidarity flies in the face of Rorty's call to find sameness; Davis and Lorde offer such a recognition as precisely the root of meaningful knowing and acting across difference.

Finally, Lorde offers an account of freedom as also interdependent. She writes: "I am not free while any woman is unfree, even when her shackles are very different from my own. And I am not free as long as one person of Color remains chained. Nor is any one of you" (1984, 132–33). I read this as an articulation of the kinds of common interests that we might argue white people share with people of color, and as motivation for solidarity work. In some forums, we can argue for the importance of solidarity as something that benefits everyone involved in a struggle. Lorde's conception of interdependent freedom puts it to us that common dignity will only be available to us individually if it is genuinely common to people everywhere. We cannot manifest health if that health depends on systematic degradation and disease. So the self-interest that might provoke white people's solidarity could involve a diffuse, pervasive understanding that we are ourselves diseased by the fact of diffuse, pervasive, palpable inequity and injustice.[13]

WHY FEELING BAD ISN'T A BAD THING

Let me return to the sense in which solidarity is an ideal and an activity that is achieved through struggle rather than something inherently given by any particular social identity. As Rorty and Chanda Talpade Mohanty alike note, solidarity is something that we must work to achieve and expand.[14] This is a useful idea—solidarity as made, not found. I argued in the prior chapter that there is something useable and useful in recognizing that white people attempting antiracist solidarity work sometimes feel shame, and that this kind of negative affect is not automatically something to avoid. In fact, the experience of shame can indicate openings for a transformative recognition of the ways that whiteness functions. As always relational, affect also articulates the potential for a kind of collective (rather than individualist), structurally/socially embedded (rather than voluntarist), holistic, multiaxial praxis. This sort of praxis is the ground for responsible solidarity. I see negative affect as one way to get at a solidarity that acknowledges contingent and historical difference.

Consider this idea from another direction. To the extent that difference is understood in this way—as contingently formed yet real—taking up solidarity work involves active work on the level of implicit understanding. When commonsense presuppositions shift or are revealed to be in conflict with other prejudices, a complex of understanding comes into view. So, two

---

13. I draw inspiration here also from Chandra Talpade Mohanty's words: "I define solidarity in terms of mutuality, accountability, and the recognition of common interests as the basis for relationships among diverse communities. Rather than assuming an enforced commonality of oppression, the practice of solidarity foregrounds communities of people who have chosen to work and fight together. Diversity and difference are central values here—to be acknowledged and respected, not erased in the building of alliances. . . . Solidarity is always an achievement, the result of active struggle to construct the universal on the basis of particulars/differences. It is the praxis-oriented, active political struggle embodied in this notion of solidarity that is important to my thinking" (2003, 7).

14. Rorty frames this mode of solidarity in explicitly utopian futurist terms: such a future would "regard the realization of utopias, and the envisaging of still further utopias, as an endless process—an endless, proliferating realization of Freedom, rather than a convergence toward an already existing Truth" (1989, xvi).

points about solidarity, implicit understanding, and feeling bad. First, solidarity work will always and perhaps even primarily involve implicit understanding in at least a few ways. When people work together, they often develop shared political sensibilities and practices through sharing experiences, feelings, shifting baseline assumptions, and conceptual understandings of the world. The reasons people take up solidarity as a political praxis are never only propositional; they are also passionate, expressing fundamental views about how the world ought to be, and grounded in a particular shared (though perhaps transformed) habitus. I believe that other, less personal forms of political work (lobbying, letter writing) similarly involve implicit understanding—but the import of what goes without saying or cannot be said is particularly salient to the work of solidarity. That is the aspect of solidarity work that might feel good, nourishing, connective, and empowered. Beyond positive affects, though, solidarity "happens" through and with implicit understanding at every level.

But because shaking commonsense apprehensions is disconcerting, and because working in solidarity across difference almost always involves challenge to deep prejudices, doing solidarity work will overwhelmingly involve a whole matrix of negative affect. Feeling bad, particularly for someone coming to (for example) understand herself as the unwitting beneficiary and perpetuator of murderous systems of oppression, can be experienced as a reason to not pursue solidarity work. This may be why the illusory or problematic formations of white solidarity retain some charm—surely it is more comfortable to extend an "us" to the whole world, to feel as others feel through empathetic identification, or to negate whiteness altogether through heroic individual action against systemic oppression. So while negative affect is not necessary to solidarity work, I think it comes up so frequently as to seem almost ubiquitous. Without negating the good feeling of working with others to achieve political change, I thus think we must be able to meet bad feeling as it arises. That is, negative affect might signal success in attempting solidarity rather than its failure—and it is certainly not a reason to abandon the work. In fact, following Bartky, the distance and difference felt through affects like shame, failure, misunderstanding, anger, and so on, paired with political commitments to solidarity work, might defuse the dominative habits expressed through ascribing sameness and empathetic identification.

For white people, this solidarity is grounded on understanding that acting in solidarity is work: continuous, not always a pleasure, sometimes extraordinarily difficult, not about self-gratification, and full of sometimes awkward bridges and seams. The experience of bad feeling marks the kind of distance crucial for sympathy and solidarity; we do not, as white people attempting to generate an antiracist world, easily work against whiteness and for collective dignity. Whiteness, as a social position, involves having a certain kind of dominative power, regardless of whether one desires it. As I discussed regarding *Race Traitor*, one aspect of this privilege is the (voluntarist) possibility of changing how we move through the world. But these possibilities themselves are structured by a system we oppose. Any action we take is deeply fraught. This means that we might never feel good when we attempt to work for radical equality—in fact, if we do feel uncomplicatedly good or righteous, we're probably making a mistake. But there is a sense in which naming and "owning" the kind of negative affect associated with this fundamentally problematic position of the antiracist white person opens the possibility for solidarity across difference and despite feeling bad.

SIX

A KNOWING THAT RESIDED IN MY BONES

"Knowledge for social movements must move us," writes Avery Gordon; it must be "sensual and magical." I find this an evocative and intuitively compelling call to action. What might happen when we understand our conceptual experience of social worlds to interact with and be conditioned by our embodied experience? I extend Gordon's categories to think about sensuousness as material, embodied understanding that structures our experience and capacities for action. The sensuousness I care about here comes out of the aesthetic tradition I consider in chapter 3: a non-reductive bodily experience that is all about sociality.

We can see the significance of sensuous knowledge in the disciplinary formations Foucault unpacks in *Discipline and Punish* (1994), among other works. For example, we might have a sophisticated theoretical understanding of the futility and brutality of the prison-industrial complex, but that understanding acquires a different depth if we are in jail. The strictures governing how we move through space, how we behave socially, how we feel comfortable all manifest on conceptual, affective, and sensuous levels. The importance of our bodily comportment is highlighted perhaps when we step outside "normalcy," and those of us who are negatively racialized, fat, disabled, or gender-ambiguous, for example, step outside those norms without

---

1. "Knowledge" is often understood to name a subject's (*S*'s) true and justified belief that something (*p*) is the case. Thus "*S* knows that *p*" if and only if *S* is justified in her belief that *p*, and *p* is true (perhaps with appropriate responses to Gettier problems). Within those terms "sensuous knowledge" may strike some readers as a misnomer: sensuousness makes no propositional claims about the world. In much of the discussion below I use the term "sensuous understanding" to acknowledge debates around nonrepresentational content in experience, and to assert the epistemic salience of socially situated embodiment. I also use "sensuous knowledge" out of respect for my archive: the writers and activists I engage use the terms "knowing" and "knowledge" in their work in ways that contest a definition of knowledge as limited to an epistemic subject's propositionally mediated relationship to the world.

moving a toe. In other words, the importance of the sensuous dimension is sometimes most visible when it is least liberatory.

In this chapter, however, I attend to the liberatory dimensions of sensuous understanding. I argue for the importance of sensuousness for social movements, focusing on transliberationist and genderqueer movements as both object and theoretical wellspring for this work. Implicitly, I set sensuousness against a liberal model of personhood. Susan Babbitt has argued that the standard liberal, Rawlsian conception of individual rational choice leaves out a kind of nonpropositional knowledge—"knowledge people possess in the form of intuitions, attitudes, ways of behaving, orientation, and so on" (1996, 50). If we were to understand the decision to transition from a liberal standpoint, we would have to radically flatten the ingredients of that transformation—centrally, its implicit, felt aspects. In what follows, I argue that trans flourishing depends on transformations of the world—and, as Babbitt points out, often people have to transform themselves in order to access resources for full human flourishing (46). Sensuous knowledge is precondition, ingredient, and result of a mutual transformation of the self and social worlds. The account I offer of sensuous knowledge is indebted to Babbitt's articulation of relational, multiple, and contingent personhood (1996, 2001).

In chapter 3, I traced a theoretical genealogy that could flesh out Gordon's call for a sensuous knowledge for social movements, aiming to fill in some of the theoretical history she gestures toward. In the other chapters of this book, I have offered a grounding for the category of understanding that goes unspoken, or that is in some way unspeakable. The intuitive appeal of Gordon's claim, in the context of this book, is clear: she draws out some of the political stakes involved in my articulations of commonsense formations, of shame and solidarity, and of the background context for knowing and being in the world. The sense in which such knowing might be sensual and magical, however, is new to this chapter. Gordon's work on sensuous knowledge is connected to the lineage of Marxist aestheticists articulating the importance of sensuous knowledge to forming and re-forming subjects as laborers, as "human," as social. Ultimately, proponents of this approach argue that these processes of sensuous formation are also important to ruptural experiences that might form a ground for heterodox or antiauthoritarian social movements. Recall Bourdieu's interest in the revolutionary possibilities of bodily hexis. In this chapter, then, I extend my inquiry in this strand of Marxist aesthetics to think about how a social, embodied way of being in the world is created and recreated.

In the second section, I draw attention to the fact that people point to how their bodies feel as an indication of political or social movement spaces they want to pursue. Sensuous knowledge shows up as the motor, impetus, or reason for social movement. In the third section, I draw on Eli Clare's important work to evidence the kind of sensuous knowledge I am interested in. I then investigate the trope of being at home in one's body to indicate that sensuous understanding is relational and often political. The desire to feel at home in one's body makes a call back to social movements. In the final section, I examine the importance of sensuous knowledge to our theorization of social movements, arguing for a reciprocal and energizing relation between social movements and sensuous knowledge. The experience of participating in social movements—attending a strike, direct action, or mass demonstration, for example—can evoke an antiauthoritarian understanding of one's situation. Political, relational, and social movement situations can and do open sensuous spaces in people's experience of their lives: politically and relationally situated embodiments that call for or result from social change. Reciprocally, the role of socially situated embodiment in trans social movement shows us that nurturing sensuous understanding as a practice of freedom is crucial to social movements more generally.

SITUATING SENSUOUSNESS

In *Ghostly Matters*, Avery Gordon examines the experience of cultural haunting and the relationship between unacknowledged knowledge and power. She situates sensuous knowledge as "receptive, close, perceptual, embodied, incarnate. It tells and it transports at the same time. Sensuous knowledge is commanding: it can spiral you out of your bounds. . . . Sensuous knowledge always involves knowing and doing" (1997, 205). Gordon's understanding of sensuous knowledge involves pleasures and pains, sensations we can name and ones we have no language for, and ways of being constrained or freed in the world. Sensuousness names a socially situated experience of one's embodiment. It is a "different kind of materialism, neither idealistic nor alienated, but an active practice or passion" (205). Sensuous knowledge opens possibilities for embodied transformation. Gordon explicitly traces her use of the term back to Marx's aesthetics in the lineage I laid out in chapter 3.

I share Gordon's interest in knowledge for social movements: this understanding or way of being has a purpose. It is good for something, which here means that it does some good for someone. It is not, that is, extractable from its context. The knowledge that comes out of socially mediated embodiment is situated, invested, directed toward something; knowledge for social movements is knowledge in favor of social transformation and also knowledge that aims to be useful to social movements. It is knowledge that carries an imperative. It must move us. The knowledge Gordon cares about here is not only invested in some kind of social transformation, it is itself transformative of its knower. To know in this way, or to know these things, is to be moved. The knower may be affected, as in response to a moving story, and so this understanding relates to our affective and emotional relations with the world. Knowledge that moves us is both affective and transformative, complexly emotional and political. This is a kind of knowing that, in Sandra Bartky's words, "transforms the self who knows, a knowing that brings into being new sympathies, new affects as well as new cognitions and new forms of intersubjectivity" (2002, 71–72).

Gordon's notion of sensuous knowledge can be usefully situated in the terrain of feminist activism and texts, queer spaces and people, and trans-liberationist movements. Second-wave feminist theory placed importance on the role and liberation of the body. Queer activists and theorists, especially those working against gender binary social relations, offer complex accounts of heterodox sensuousness. Much transgender and transsexual memoir and theory offers rich analysis and accounts of a liberatory politics co-constituted between a lived bodily experience and a political community. I read this politics in terms of sensuousness. A notion of "the body," of the politics of socially embedded embodiments, and of a bodily way of knowing, have been put forth in these overlapping fields of discourse, practice, and activism. Trans narratives and theories offer a rich and important terrain.

But I have hesitations around precisely these sites. It is too easy to mine trans stories, in particular, to back up academic points; I am leery of participating in the ongoing hip academic concern with trans issues, narratives, and (sometimes) actual people. I am not trans, and I am conscious of some of the dangers associated with writing about trans memoirs in support of an argument about sensuous knowledge. No number of trans friends and lovers can mitigate those dangers. But it is important that how I think about sensuousness, and a reason that it is a compelling analytic category for me, is a result of reading and talking to trans writers and activists. I mean what examples and analysis I offer as a form of respect. This discussion is also completely embedded, as are many trans narratives themselves, in a history of feminist and queer thinking—categories I occupy with less difficulty.

Language is important here, and an additional source of hesitation. Our language indicates political stakes, lived contradictions, and networks of dialogue. In the preceding paragraphs, for example, I quickly slipped from the phrase "transgender and transsexual" to the floating prefix "trans." Terminologies carry histories. In this chapter, I follow the fraught use of "transsexual" to name people who were assigned one gender and sex at birth and have or are transitioning to another through changes in their bodies, social interactions, or appearance. The term "transsexual" is loaded with medical histories that have enabled, constricted, and torqued transsexual gender expression. Marking this, some trans people use the spelling "transexual," refusing these medicalized labeling practices. Read in these histories, transsexual/transexual people have completed gender reassignment surgery—by implication meeting the World Professional Association for Transgender Health's Standards of Care, fulfilling accounts of a psychological gender dysmorphia laid out in the DSM-IV, and having a particular orientation to gendered genitalia.[2] My use of the term, however, includes self-identified transsexuals/transexuals who do not necessarily enact the strict medical sense of the definition.

Since 1996 or so, "transgender" has been framed as an umbrella term encompassing a range of gender crossers—from people who experience discomfort with how people expect them to express their gender, to intersexuals, to cross-dressers, to genderqueers (who explicitly reject a gender binary system), to transsexuals, to other gender-variant people. "Transgender," in this usage, is contested by theorists and activists who argue against a conflation of transgender and transsexual experience. Viviane Namaste, for

2. Formerly the Benjamin Standards, authored by the Harry Benjamin International Gender Dysphoria Association, which is now the World Professional Association for Transgender Health. In 1966 Benjamin authored the first major study of sex reassignment and transsexuality, *The Transsexual Phenomenon*. In 1979 an organization named itself in honor of his work, and produced Standards of Care that regulated both doctors who provide sex-reassignment surgery and "consumers" who want to transition using surgery, among other tools. These standards of care now intersect with the *Diagnostic and Statistical Manual of Mental Disorders* of the American Psychiatric Association, in which Gender Identity Disorder is included. Some people have been able to leverage a GID diagnosis to get their insurance companies to pay for their transitions. Many critiques have been leveled at both the DSM's classification of GID and the Benjamin Standards of Care: the first can be seen as pathologizing what is a nonpsychiatric medical situation (the wish for hormonal or surgical intervention in gender expression), and the latter a rigidly heteronormative gender narrative. There is also substantial critique from many points of view of a perceived reification of genital surgery as the be-all and end-all of trans happiness.

NAVIGATING TRANSFORMATIONS | 130

example, strongly critiques what she sees as a reduction of transsexual embodied experience to transgender-qua-queer, arguing that to read "transgender" together with "queer" renders invisible transsexual people who identify as straight. Further, Namaste—writing in a Québécois context—examines the Anglo-centrism implied in the use of a term virtually unique to English (Namaste 2000, 2005).

The question of language is tied to a deeper question of embodiment and to debates in trans circles on language and labels. For example, trans theory and memoir offer divergent analyses of the narrative of being trapped in the wrong body. Jay Prosser, for example, writes: "My contention is that transsexuals continue to deploy the image of wrong embodiment because being trapped in the wrong body is simply what transsexuality feels like. . . . The image of wrong embodiment describes most effectively the experience of pretransition (dis)embodiment: the feeling of a sexed body dysphoria profoundly and subjectively experienced" (1998, 69). Sandy Stone argues, on the contrary, that we have not "taken the step of problematizing 'wrong body' as an adequate descriptive category. In fact 'wrong body' has come, virtually by default, to define the syndrome. . . . So long as we, whether academics, clinicians, or transsexuals, ontologize both sexuality and transsexuality in this way, we have foreclosed the possibility of analyzing desire and motivational complexity in a manner which adequately describes the multiple contradictions of individual lived experience" (1997, 353).

My account attempts to bridge the competing explanations for the "wrong body" narrative. As Prosser argues, we do ill to dismiss the felt, embodied experience of "wrongness" or "rightness": some bodily experience is always with us, and sensuousness attempts to name this. At the same time, I offer sensuous knowledge as a name for that experience of contingent freedom that comes with a socially situated embodiment, where being in the "right body" has more to do with our social world than with any individuated experience of our bodies. That is, we might feel like we're in the wrong body because there is a problem with our world.

Finally, transliberation as social movement both partakes in a long history and is still very much in process. I am thinking of trans social movement as collective political work to change existing social relations, even when this work shows up on a relatively small scale. Identifying as trans, or being identified as gender-variant, doesn't make a person a social movement of one. Individual actions do, though, contribute to the kind of collective work that makes up social movements. Trans movements in the

United States, even with Namaste's caution against flattening trans people into one huge transgender community, clearly demonstrate some classical social movement markers. There are trans marches, organized direct action, political lobbying, health initiatives, grassroots education, and solidarity organizations. These actions relate to and create the possibilities for new forms of socially situated embodiment, and these social movement activities come out of and craft what Avery Gordon calls sensuous knowledge for social movements.

EMBODIMENT AND SOCIAL MOVEMENTS

To come close to telling a social movement history of the complex sites of trans activism would require a radical intervention into the very sites of social movement studies and theory. For one thing, much of the activity I would situate as political trans work might not be recognizable from a social movement studies point of view. For another, it is not possible to trace a continuous history of trans social movement, even in a particular geopolitical sphere. Indeed, the paucity of research within Anglo North America on trans activism outside North America highlights a myopia in current scholarship structured in collusion with and resistance to how sex and gender "happen" in these sites. There is, then, no singular savvy, anti-imperialist, transnational history of transgender, transsexual, and genderqueer lives and political activism. The history I look toward in thinking about trans social movements takes seriously everyday trans lives and the theoretical work that ordinary trans people produce. It shows continuities while not erasing disjunctures. Though there is no simple account of this developing history, there is a great deal of both historical and current thinking on trans and genderqueer social movement.

An overview of trans social movement histories and narratives traces a story line something like this: Medical advocacy for sex reassignment surgery, along with limited analysis of the social conditions creating gendered inequity, began in Germany in the 1920s with Magnus Hirschfeld's Institute for Sexual Science. Advocacy, of a sort, continued with Harry Benjamin's work in the United States in the wake of Nazi destruction of Hirschfeld's institute and his inauguration of the Benjamin Standards of Care as guidelines for both transitioning patients and the psychiatrists and surgeons helping in their transitions. Legal and political battles for trans rights intersected to some extent with this medical work, as more people accessed medical resources for transition and enacted new forms of public personhood. In the canonical histories there are whispers of people who didn't and don't fit neatly into the framework of access to trans rights. For example, Namaste repeatedly calls for theorists to hold the reality of transsexual sex workers in mind when thinking about surgery, social justice, and gender theory. Queer trans identity equally troubles many of the assumptions about (straight) sexual orientation and gender (normative) identification implicit in the Benjamin Standards.

I read the everyday political work of trans men and women helping one another survive as the root and branch of trans social movement. More than many other movements worth the name, trans people foment social change through complex interactions with microstructures of interpersonal relationships and macrostructures of legal, political, and economic realities. In the United States, the late 1960s saw an upwell of conventionally identifiable trans social movement in concert with what became a gay and lesbian liberation movement. Often this work is historicized in moments like the Stonewall riots, or the formation of the Queer Nation or Transexual Menace organizations. This periodization symbolically begins with Stonewall in 1969, and symbolically (and perhaps actually) ends in 1973 when the firebrand trans activist Sylvia Rivera, credited with throwing the first brick at Stonewall, was forced off the stage at one of the first Pride rallies by opponents of trans inclusion under the "gay and lesbian" banner. Trans social movement "came back" into view in the early 1990s with the advent of riot grrrl music scenes, genderqueer activists, and academic attention to queer theory. Trans people, of course, existed all along, and many of them are still invisible or oppositional to the punk, genderqueer, and queer scenes that may be more visible. The fact that it is difficult to "see" trans social movements aside from these periods may tell us something methodological. Namaste suggests that responsible research methodologies must "recognize that there is not one large 'transgendered community,' but rather several small networks of transsexual and transgendered people, as well as many TS/TG people unaffiliated with other individuals like them" (2000, 266–67). Can we take seriously a nonhomogeneous and sometimes atomized group of transsexual and transgender people and still understand trans political work under the rubric of social movement? I think we must.

Let me give two examples from the archive of trans social movement, in part for their mythmaking properties. First, STAR House. STAR House was a refuge for trans youth in New York, coming out of the Street Trans-vestite Action Revolutionaries. Sylvia Rivera (herself a mythmaking and pe-riodizing figure, as I note above) says, "STAR was born in 1971 right after a sit-in we had at New York University with the Gay Liberation Front [GLF]. We took over Weinstein Hall for three days." This sit-in happened after NYU stopped renting space for queer dances; Rivera explains that STAR House was "born out of the Weinstein Hall demonstration, because there were so many of us living together" (2002, 83). Though STAR House was short-lived, it not only expressed radical social movement activities; it was also engaged in conversation with a revolutionary, radical moment. For ex-ample, the (then) gay movement's goals included wholesale transformation of social conditions in the United States; Rivera and others were deeply in-volved with organizing for gay and lesbian rights at a moment when politi-cal rights for trans people were explicitly on the table. As she notes, STAR came out of a GLF direct action. At the same time, Rivera and others had connections with the Young Lords and the Black Panthers. STAR House manifested the sensibilities of this time in its "liberated" free food, com-munal rent sharing, support for people getting off the street or being safer on the street, and an unapologetic commitment to street queens and pros-titutes. Transy House, a safe house opened in the mid-1990s for transsexual and transgender people in Brooklyn, continues this tradition. STAR House functions colloquially as a kind of utopian reference point for many people who pursue cooperative, queer houses (though they are not, themselves, of-fering free housing to homeless young trans sex workers).

Histories of trans and queer activism in the United States likewise frequently reference STAR House, and not only because of the Rivera con-nection. Though it might not be immediately legible as a social movement activity, this attention to daily needs for housing, food, and community highlights the political valence of formations like STAR House and Transy House. In basic ways, these spaces help create the conditions for a livable life. In more overtly critical ways, they manifest a critique of individuated consumer capital, lack of social services, and the overwhelming social apathy that makes trans lives less secure than non-trans lives. More obviously "social movement–ish" things are also often connected to collective houses (they might provide meeting spaces, places to congregate and make banners, or reference points when actions or campaigns are in full swing), but I would argue that their everyday work is every inch a social movement activity, and one more widespread than will ever be documented.

Second, the 1966 Compton's Cafeteria riots give an example of overtly militant action coming out of and sparking more sustained organizing. This event has been only recently "recovered" as prehistory by the GLBT historical society and by Susan Stryker and Victor Silverman's 2005 film *Screaming Queens*. Three years before the Stonewall rebellion, Compton's Cafeteria was the site of a confrontation between the police and gender-variant customers, drag queens, and "hair fairies"—who in stories about the events are simply called "gays." The proximal reason for the rebellion seems to have been police harassment of several Compton's patrons. But there were more complex conditions producing this conflict and then stabilizing it as symbolically significant. Trans activist organizing had begun to coalesce in the face of intensified police attempts over the previous year to clean up the Tenderloin district of San Francisco, producing a youth organization called Vanguard that had been picketing Compton's for a month before the August conflict. The broader crackdown focused on clubs perceived to be homosexual havens, on street sex workers, and on homeless youth. In the Tenderloin, this focus was squarely on trans and gender-transgressive people. After the Compton's riots, the organizing against gentrification, lack of support for trans people in San Francisco, and the policing of trans communities resulted in several transgender activist organizations with ties to national transliberation agendas.[3] Gay Shame and FIERCE are among the current activist formations rooted in genderqueer sensibilities that often explicitly trace roots to trans social justice organizing. In fact, FIERCE is a New York–based group of youth of color who organized in response to crackdowns on queer use of the same public spaces Sylvia Rivera had lived in years before. While these examples specify the contexts of political organizing to keep gender-variant people safe in ways that extend beyond physical survival, they are homologous with and in direct solidarity with other social justice organizations. In the concluding section of this chapter, I will consider some ways that sensuousness might be useful to thinking about social movements more generally. Such activities come out of and craft what Avery Gordon calls sensuous knowledge for social movements. And crafting sensuous knowledge for trans social movement, to reprise Naomi Scheman (1996), recognizes that transsexual lives are lived, and so must be understood as livable.

3. For one of the most thorough accounts of this history, see "MTF Transgender Activism in the Tenderloin and Beyond" by members of the Gay and Lesbian Historical Society of Northern California (1998).

SENSUOUS KNOWLEDGE AS MOTIVATION
FOR SOCIAL MOVEMENTS

How we live is important, and many trans lives could be more easily livable. The threat of beating or death palpably attends being read as trans or genderqueer, and this shapes the texture and possibilities of everyday life. If you are not clearly read as one of two genders, you can be killed; and in this world, you will inevitably suffer to at least some degree. In other words, even when gender-variant people are not murdered or assaulted, they experience the torquing, friction, discomfort, and disfiguration involved in resisting norms of gender binary straight whiteness, among other things, just by living. Even people who transition and pass seamlessly bear the history of this work. The most obvious, and least speakable, result of trans and queer hating is the production of social worlds in which trans and genderqueer people suffer radically impoverished possibilities for flourishing, a felt sense of group vulnerability, and comparatively desolate conditions for the expression of dignity. This is a sensuous problem: living well involves a socially contingent comfort in one's body. In this context, flourishing without fitting established norms requires a transformation of the world so that living is more possible. The kind of embodiment that this section illustrates through the writings of Eli Clare takes seriously the givenness of the feel of things: sensuousness marks a complex embodiment, related to the social world we inhabit. As I hope to show, it can be a resource for praxis.

In the following passage from *Exile and Pride: Disability, Queerness, and Liberation*, Clare evokes a complex relation between embodiment and the social and interpersonal practices involved in the experience of "knowing gender":

> Our bodies are not merely blank slates upon which the powers-that-be write their lessons. We cannot ignore the body itself: the sensory, mostly non-verbal experience of our hearts and lungs, muscles and tendons, telling us and the world who we are. My childhood sense of being neither girl nor boy arose in part from the external lessons of abuse and neglect, from the confusing messages about masculinity and femininity that I could not comprehend; I would be fool to claim otherwise. But just as certainly, there was a knowing that resided in my bones, in the stretch of my legs and arch of my back, the stones lying against my skin, a knowing that whispered, "not girl, not boy." (1999, 129)

Clare figures a knowing that is both socially crafted and emerging from an experienced body. This knowing whispers ambiguity: a gender that is trans, but not stably "between" or "crossed over"—a verb rather than noun. This knowing comes from a body that contributes to and initiates understanding, that communicates. The "sensory, mostly non-verbal" experience of our embodiment tells us who we are, and, in Clare's account, it tells the world who we are. This telling is thoroughly related to the external lessons and messages from our social worlds about gender. But the impetus for knowing arises from the interrelation between one's body, its communication, and the political arenas it moves through.

In Clare's work, what we might be tempted to read as an essentializing call to the feel of the body is always nuanced and deepened by his intersectional account of what it is to be embodied—in his case, a queer, transgender, disabled, white, mixed-class, childhood sexual abuse survivor, butch embodiment. Moreover, this embodiment incorporates nonbody elements as part of itself. Clare writes: "At 13, my most sustaining relations were not in the human world. I collected stones. . . . Those stones warm in my pockets, I knew them to be the steadiest, only inviolable parts of myself" (124). In the realm of the sensuous, there are always stones, landscapes, radically other-than-ourselves ingredients in the "body." This body is never singular, simple, one-dimensional, or reducible to its materiality, though its bodily being is also not abstract. As Clare writes: "The stolen body, the reclaimed body, the body that knows itself and the world, the stone and the heat which warms it: my body has never been singular. Disability snarls into gender. Class wraps around race. Sexuality strains against abuse. This is how to reach beneath the skin" (137). The sensuous knowledge I see Clare and others articulating is clearly embedded in political realities that make bodies and worlds feel the way they do. It also motivates transformation of those very worlds.

Some of the bodily legacies echoing into the present from the relatively complex accounts of a mind-body/sensate-rational distinction we find in the aesthetic history I explore in chapter 3 remain important here. I say "relatively complex" because I think there is a real way that these accounts evade some of the flat-footed critique we might level at Descartes' mind/body split. Baumgarten, Kant, and Schiller, each in his own way, offer the aesthetic experience as an account of a kind of understanding that bridges, or stitches together, what they see as very different ingredients in experience: the rational and the sensual. They thus give an unprecedented recognition to the place of sensual experience, and this is what I like about their stories. At the same time, their accounts contribute to a hardening of the categories—fixing sensate and rational knowledge on either side of the bridge of aesthetic judgment. Some trans and gender-variant literature offers examples of more complex, and more adequate, ways to think about sensuousness, highlighting the way in which conceptual and physical knowings can never be disentangled. There are, at the same time, troubling homologies between these eighteenth-century accounts and current trans origin stories. The nature/culture split implicit in these sensual/rational classifications is also expressed in accounts arguing for a genomic basis for transgenderism and transsexualism. "The body" is in danger of becoming a reified entity, divorced from the social conditions that make up our experience of embodiment.

Take, for example, Deborah Rudacille's 2005 book *The Riddle of Gender*, a popular-science text framed as a shared exploration into trans identity and history in which the assumed reader is like Rudacille—liberal, non-trans, interested in understanding the transgender movement, and skeptical about the notion of a social construction of gender. While Rudacille says she believes in complex and multifaceted gender expressions, she adamantly argues for an "inborn gender identity" that produces these multivalent gender expressions (xxiii). Rudacille is particularly compelled by arguments that an increase in various estrogen-mimicking environmental toxins, or similar estrogen-mimicking hormone supplements, is responsible for trans gender variation.[4] While most of her conclusions are framed as questions, Rudacille's argument for a link between endocrine-disrupting chemicals or hormones and trans identity is clear. Looking at research on chickens and frogs that show some estrogen "imprintation" on genes, Rudacille notes that "it does lead one to wonder what might [be] the effects on human fetuses whose gene expression may have been chemically altered by exposure to estrogens in the womb and who are then re-exposed again and again to estrogenic chemicals in the environment" (269). Ultimately, she argues: "If the stories contained in this book teach us anything it is that gender variance is neither a fad nor a revolution. It is a biological fact" (276).

Now, without doubt, the stories contained in her book teach us many things—and some of them explicitly and consciously contradict the flat biologism Rudacille trumpets here. But what I mean to draw out here is a

---

4. It is not clear how Rudacille understands these arguments to account for "female" to "male" gender variation, since they essentially argue for estrogen-mimicking chemicals deleterious effects on the forceful push, at the site of in utero sex differentiation, of androgen's man-making powers.

familiar harmony; Rudacille articulates a freedom implied in synchronizing bodily (sensate) imperatives imprinted on us by the hormones we were exposed to in our mother's womb with rationally chosen (reason) cultural expressions. To quote at length from the book's conclusion:

> If gender identity is, as seems increasingly certain, hardwired into the brain at birth, and if the way we choose to express our sense of ourselves as gendered beings is dependent on cultural norms, shouldn't culture follow nature's lead and celebrate variety? Difference can be, as Susan Stryker points out, "a real source of pleasure," if only we can overcome our ancient suspicion of diversity. In an era in which Americans are fighting and dying purportedly to free other people, perhaps we might take this one small step toward freeing ourselves by finally outlawing discrimination based on gender expression. What is freedom, after all, if it is not the freedom to be one's self? (292)

Mobilizing nationalist tropes (admittedly against a particular nationalist moment), Rudacille here articulates a freedom rooted in harmonizing mute biological imperatives toward gender expression with the cultural ingredients available when we exercise our rational capacity to overcome ancient suspicions—the triumph of reason over superstition through harmonizing their imperatives. The "freedom to be one's self" is a freedom to express a gender we are bodily—hormonally, chemically—bound to. I see homologies here to the harmonization and corollary freedom Schiller and Baumgarten saw as the essence of the aesthetic moment. To be clear: I am not objecting to Rudacille's examination of possible biological bases for gender variance. It may well be that there are substantial ways we are "hardwired." And just as the "gay gene" theory is being contingently used to combat homophobia, some are excited at data that show genetic variation in trans people's biology.[5] But to take gene expression to automatically produce gender expression evacuates the specificity and the politics of gender. I object to Rudacille's conflation of gene and gender—even when it might be a politically useable move—for three reasons. First, I worry about the call for "culture to follow nature's lead";

5. I have a friend who is managing a million-dollar ad campaign in Colorado Springs to convince people that being gay is genetic. Colorado Springs is one of the most dangerous places to be queer; perhaps this campaign will help. At the same time, some of the very people this ad campaign is intended to convince use the same data to argue that if being gay is genetic, we ought to find a genetic "cure." See http://borndifferent.org/ and http://narth.com/ (accessed May 8, 2010).

our conceptions of "nature" are deeply intermixed with our cultural categories in mutually informing ways, such that it is not easy to imagine how we could disentangle them enough for one to follow the other. Second, I draw from debates on the "gay gene" the worry that, as in that case, transphobes will call for genetic therapy or abortion for genetically gender nonconforming people. Third, though this is clearly not Rudacille's intention, the "s/he can't help it, it's in hir genes" account ends up making gender-variant people show up as uniquely susceptible to nature's call, uniquely "odd," and in a context that by extension folds more normalized gender expressions back into biological determinist frameworks. Women should act like women, by this account, because we're naturally nurturing, child-rearing, and so forth.

The medicalized discourse that trans folks often have to deploy in order to access gender reassignment surgery echoes much of Rudacille's account of the body. This frame of meaning is significant in part because people are called to frame their memory toward a particular end. To "count" someone as authentically trans, doctors and therapists often require a story of gender dysmorphia beginning in childhood, and continuing in a persistent desire to live as the opposite gender (along with a number of other preconditions, more than adequately explored elsewhere). And while I find, in conversation and in memoir, that these frames are deployed with apparent ease, it is clear that this narrative also misses many people's felt sense of inchoate gender expression.[6] And the ease with which these narratives emerge may mask the work it has taken to construct them as ready to hand in narrating always messy lives. Lived gender is often not so simple, nor so binary, as the current gender model claims.

I am emphasizing this point because the sensuous knowledge I am interested in is not this kind of harmony between two disparate categories of being, a bodily/genetic/sensate body and reason/cognition/chosen expression, one pushing up into the other. Nor am I advocating a speaking body that might craft and clarify our political and personal projects, all on its own. We need an account of the sensuous that understands the import of embodied experience, socially embedded and situated in language even when unspeakable. I follow Teresa de Lauretis in trying to think about experience as "a process by which, for all social beings, subjectivity is constructed. Through that process one places oneself or is placed in social reality, and so

6. Sue Campbell's (1997) important scholarship on the availability of nonnormative feelings for meaningful expressive work illuminates some trajectories along which orthodox narratives become stabilized, naturalized, and personal.

perceives and comprehends as subjective (referring to, even originating in, oneself) those relations—material, economic, and interpersonal—which are in fact social and in a larger perspective, historical" (1984, 159). Experience is the engagement with the frameworks that attend and make salient various facts and events in the world. Marx offers one axis along which we might see experience in this way—a sensuous knowledge arising from close, attentive relations with the objective world.

Many memoirs hold out a far less determined sense of what was "wrong," of what would be "right," or even of what gender one was and what gender one longs to be, than provided by the standard medical model of trans experience. Genderqueer and thirdsex accounts complicate and contradict the telos implied in a nostalgia for a fixed-gender-one-wasn't, opening the possibilities for yet unnamed gender positions. Kate Bornstein articulates a view of gender as a transformative process—gender as transformation—explicitly not thinking in binaries. Thus she talks about the frame of being "trapped in the wrong body": "I understand that many people may explain their pre-operative transgendered lives in this way, but I'll bet that it's more likely an unfortunate metaphor that conveniently conforms to cultural expectations, rather than an honest reflection of our transgendered feelings. As a people, we're short of metaphors, any metaphors, and when we find one that people understand, we stop looking. It's time for transgendered people to look for new metaphors" (Bornstein 1994, 66). Bornstein points to the reality that the metaphors available to us sometimes fail to make available how things feel. Articulating, let alone living, in ways that do not conveniently conform to cultural expectations would require different frames of meaning.

In a chapter called "Stones in My Pockets, Stones in My Heart," Eli Clare unpacks some of the nonbinary, still inchoate, work of gender in this mode:

> I want to enter as a non-girl-not-boy transgendered butch—gendered differently than when I first came out, thinking simply, "This is how I'll be a woman," never imagining there might be a day when the word woman was too small; differently from the tomboy who wanted to be a hermit; but still connected to both. Enter with my pockets and heart half-full of stone. Enter knowing that the muscled grip of desire is a wild, half-grown horse, ready to bolt but too curious to stay away. (1999, 138)

I quote this passage in part for Clare's metaphorical richness. But more, it's important to see how sometimes words are too small, roles too small—entering differently from the tomboy, the hermit, the woman—but also how self-formation can be still intimately connected to frames of meaning that don't accommodate a way of being. Clare searches for ways to write "not about the stones, but the body that warmed them, the heat itself" (124). But writing about the body that warms the stones turns out to be impossible without writing about the stones as well—they become the sign of splitting off from his body in order to live in the face of childhood sexual abuse, in the face of queerphobia and ableist bigotry. At the same time, crucially, the stones also signal a hope for non-reductive, complex embodiment. And so when Clare writes, "the stones rattling in my heart, resting in my pockets, were my one and only true body," I reach to understand the path toward reclaiming an embodiment "full of pride and pleasure" that includes the pleasure of stones warm against skin. This self-formation includes picked-up stones as part of one's being and crafting a heat that can warm them.

Sensuous knowing in Clare's text carries the sense of knowing "what feels right"—complexly and transformatively. It is "knowing that whispered 'not girl, not boy,'" and "wanting to enter . . . gendered differently." Sensuousness is centrally tied to the interaction with others and the world. Another way to talk about sensuousness as a motivation for social change is in terms of the erotic, as Lorde articulates it (discussed in chapter 1). The erotic is "firmly rooted in the power of our unexpressed or unrecognized feeling" (Lorde 1984, 53). It has to do with embodied, heterodox joy, and recognizing our own capacities for joy (57). The erotic names a rejuvenating memory and experience. I argued that an experience of the erotic is first a kind of litmus test for liberatory potential. This is the erotic as "an internal sense of satisfaction to which, once we have experienced it, we know we can aspire. For having experienced the fullness of this depth of feeling and recognizing its power, in honor and self-respect we can require no less of ourselves" (54). Knowing sensuously here carries the sense of knowing "what feels right"—complexly, transformatively—or, in other words, Clare's body that knows itself. Second, the erotic carries a sense of working in concert with others to "pursue genuine change within our world" (59). Sensuousness, as I explored in chapter 3, is centrally tied to both sensus communis and the interaction with others implied in a collective purposiveness, without predetermined or inborn purpose. In the context of transliberationist movements, I see sensuousness as unpacking the practical conditions for creating and transforming our socially situated, embodied experience.

Bodies, understood as politically situated, show up often in writing about political transformation of our way of existence, particularly in queer and trans narratives. And the notion of being at home in one's body, of refusing to "live outside ourselves . . . on external directions only" (58), is important. Many people write about the work of making their bodies homeplaces, though the explanations for how this happens varies from needing to make the outer body match a coherent inner self to needing to find social spaces for ambiguous, queered bodily expression of gender. Throughout, though, I find a sensuous indication of the enmeshment of bodies and politics, well exemplified in the language of the body-as-home.[7] I draw an example, once again, from Clare.

Clare writes about the different "homes" a body can be, articulating the deep enmeshments that produce these homes. Clare looks at a relation between the physical worlds he moves through and the social worlds of a political queer community: "My queer body: I spent my childhood, a tomboy not sure of my girlness, queer without a name for my queerness. I cut firewood on clearcuts, swam in the river, ran the beaches as Battle Rock and Cape Blanco. When I found dykes, fell in love for the first time, came into a political queer community, I felt as if I had found home again" (1999, 10). Clare's body is queered largely through ambivalence—being a tomboy not sure of girlness, queer without a label. His ambivalence is figured through activity: cutting firewood, swimming, running. And somehow, finding a political queer community feels like finding home again. Even when you've never been sure of home, when you find it, it returns as though it were a memory. Clare's queer body arises as such out of the clear-cuts, the rivers, the beaches, and the years of going without a name. It finds a home. But this body is complex—it is a home only in the context of a relationality, a community. It can only be home if we understand that "bodies are never singular, but rather haunted, strengthened, underscored by countless other bodies . . . that place and community and culture burrow deep into our bones . . . that language too lives under the skin" (10–11). This is what it is for a body to be sensuous as the ground for liberation: completely irreducible to any simple or asocial body, but also completely material in its effects and realities. Clare tells stories about bodies in this complex register—the sentence closing his book

7. Jay Prosser examines Leslie Feinberg's *Stone Butch Blues*, illuminating this yearning for "home." He looks at the "emergence of transgender on the fault lines and tensions between transsexual and queer" and argues, "within this project, home may prove a powerful organizing trope"—though not always in the same ways for everyone (Prosser 1998, 177). Lucas Crawford's (2008) work on the location of "home" and gender offers a significant supplement to Prosser's discussion, as does Aren Aizura's (2006) critique of Prosser's views.

calls for more "bold, brash stories about reclaiming our bodies and changing the world" (136). Trans stories offer a lodestone for some ways of being where, in order to reclaim a body, the world has to change—and where in order to change the world one has to complexly incorporate a body. Being-at-home always involves other people and can involve whole networks of sociality.

For example, Gavriel Alejandro Levi Ansara writes: "I tried to be happy as a butch woman, but the woman part just wasn't me. . . . I am transitioning because I feel most comfortable when people refer to me in male terms and because I feel most comfortable and liberated in my body as a man" (2004, 92–93). These accounts articulate the felt body in relation to succeeding or failing to be comfortable, to be at home. Being-at-home is explicitly an achievement, something one can come into; it is also always socially embedded. For Ansara, comfort comes as much from how other people relate to him ("when people refer to me in male terms") as from a particular experience of embodiment ("I feel more comfortable and liberated in my body as a man"). In Clare's sense, he enters as a man, and this constitutes a significant part of his being-at-home.

The feeling of "being at home" marks one way that personal and political experience is inextricably enmeshed. The embodiment that can feel like home doesn't have to be stably gendered, or completely accepted in the social world. Juan-Alejandro Lamas writes about "genderfusion"—a kind of other-genderedness. For Lamas, refusal to settle on being a man or woman did not preclude having top surgery (double mastectomy and chest reconstruction)—"it was seeing myself on the outside how I do on the inside" (2004, 118)—though this surgery was not in the mode of gender reassignment. Still, this reshaping has sensuous effects. According to Lamas:

> Why, if I cut them off, must I choose male? Why must it be gender reassignment? Why must I choose anything? "Top surgery," mastectomy, whatever you want to call it—I cut my breasts off. No therapy, no permission, no regrets, no sadness. Only joy, and a feeling of pure ecstasy, freedom, and connectivity with my body that I had never felt before. Today I love my body and it feels right to me, it feels mine—a really weird thing for a person like me to say, believe me. (120)

This felt body is clearly politically placed for Lamas—it is called to manifest as legible within a gender binary system, with social, medical, and legal frameworks to back it up. So Lamas's feeling of ecstasy, freedom, and body connectivity makes a political call back to those systems, a sensuous experience that requires political change. In this case, the political change necessary would create a space other than the gender options now available (beyond even relatively transgressive options like "gender reassignment"). Lamas's sensuous experience grounds the question "why must I choose anything?" and thus is the impetus and motor for political change. Sometimes the experience of sensuousness arises from the kind of freedom Lamas feels, while sometimes it arises as resistance or rebuttal to felt structures of domination.

Toni Morrison offers the metaphor of home as a space of resistance to racist structures; without reducing gender structures to racial formations, I read her account as important to the conception of home I am forwarding here. In her article "Home," Morrison writes that several questions have troubled her work: "How to be both free and situated; how to convert a racist house into a race-specific yet nonracist home. How to enunciate race while depriving it of its lethal cling? They are questions of concept, of language, of trajectory, of habitation, of occupation" (1997, 5). We can put these questions into conversation with some others: How to "have" gender in ways that acknowledge its socially stabilized nature, destabilize it, and yet be safe enough? How to find comfort within or despite a gender binary system in which one is awkwardly situated? How to find deep physical comfort in transitioning and passing yet still fight gender normativity? Michelle O'Brien writes, for example, about her transition: "I began to realize that if I was going to be a part of a revolution, I'd have to begin by figuring out myself. I'd have to begin with an understanding of this body that exceeds my words, that eludes their categories, that demands a world beyond my imagination" (2002–3, 3). Making the "house" we've been given "home," claiming that it can be home, involves understanding one's present situation clearly, transforming it, and finding the possibility of always contingent joys. As Jay Prosser argues, "Home is, on some level, always a place we make up, [and] belonging is ultimately mythic—for all of us perhaps unreachable without some act of sweet imagination" (1998, 205).

SOCIAL MOVEMENTS AND THE CREATION OF SENSUOUS KNOWING

Social movements are a good place to think about sensuous knowledge in part because they reveal the centrality of this thread in the fabric of our experience. They are sites of sweet imagination, of worlds beyond our imagination, where sensuousness involves thinking hopefully and gestures toward the kinds of freedom dreaming I'm ultimately committed to. A significant aspect of Audre Lorde's argument for the erotic is its commitment to change rooted in joy. But last, and most important, I think the realm of sensuous experience could be fruitfully explored in theorizing social movements. Social movements might create circumstances that transform our sensuous knowledge; they can create new knowledge or give us a way to organize our felt politics differently. Conceptually, it can be satisfying to see that other people hold similar analyses of the situation. Indeed, when political actions and the creation of new ways of being are successful, they articulate and show that a number of people share some intersecting analysis of a problem. These analyses don't have to be coherent: all they have to do is overlap enough that people are moved to come to the action, write a letter, and so on.

This conceptual satisfaction also has an emotional facet—the felt, affective texture of participating in an action of social worlding.[8] It is also sensuous—a complexly embodied, social experience. As much as any theoretical or intellectual work, many oppositional manifestations (demonstrations or direct actions) "happen" in our emotions and our bodies. There is an element of social movement activity that is deeply affective and sensuous. People feel connected, inspired, alienated, angry, loved, loving, confused, righteous, scared, empowered, bored, and much more. And many of these responses are created in the action itself. The episodic experience of a mobilization or march is, in some movements, woven into a fabric with more duration and social interconnectedness than might be visible in a one-time action or speech. In the context of long-term organizing, or when we activists understand ourselves as inheritors of histories of struggle, these kinds of one-time experiences acquire resonance and texture. Accounts of the U.S. queer liberation movements highlight pivotal marches, interactions with police, and direct actions as episodically significant in transforming people's felt sense of their political topographies. Taken together and narrated, these one-time experiences become part of the process of placing oneself as a social being and in relation to history.

Cultivating sensuous knowledge for social movements implies changing our habitus, what feels natural to us, and what places us in a social realm.

8. See Deborah Gould's (2009) important work on the affective component of social movements, focusing particularly on ACT UP.

Such transformations involve an integrated reconstruction of our cognitive, affective, and sensuous knowledges. Eli Clare, answering the question how to write about his body reclaimed, writes:

> In queer community, I found a place to belong and abandoned my desire to be a hermit. Among crips, I learned how to embrace my strong, spastic body. Through feminist work around sexual violence—political activism, theoretical analysis, emotional recovery—I came to terms with the sexual abuse and physical torture done to me. And somewhere along the line, I pulled desire to the surface, gave it room to breathe. Let me write not about the stones, but the heat itself. (1999, 134)

Most tangibly, transformations in sensuous understanding involve a shift in how we identify and follow longings, in Gordon's terms—a cultivation of the subjective factor such that our felt responses line up along new priorities. And lining up along these lines requires, too, new objective conditions— the work of sensuous knowledge is political and motivated. Clare's capacity to write about a reclaimed body, covalent with the capacity to reclaim that body, comes out of queer and disability rights and feminist social movement work. This is, as Gordon notes, a transformation of worldview, of our way of existence.

If sensuous understanding sometimes calls for a political transformation, social movement and political spaces also create or nurture new sensuous knowledges. Narratives of sensuousness moving in this direction are harder to find—we all have a tendency to be able to find and articulate individuated experience. Still, it is clear that the social-sensuous practices we participate in are significant for how we see and feel our own sensuous experience. Eli Clare's feeling of finding home comes significantly out of finding a political queer community—it was not perfect, but it opened a space for feeling differently. Sometimes a single person can open that space: for many people, Christine Jorgensen's 1950 gender reassignment surgery, and the extraordinary media storm that surrounded it, opened a public discourse about transsexuality.[9] This discourse, of course, was for the most part extremely transphobic and implicitly mobilized against transgender yearnings. Still, as Leslie Feinberg writes about Jorgensen: "Just as her dignity and cour

---

9. Joanne Meyerowitz (1998) offers a detailed account of the relation between media attention and a public space for trans imaginings.

age set a proud example for the thousands of transsexual men and women who followed her path, she inspired me—and who knows how many other transgendered children. . . . Christine Jorgensen's struggle beamed a message to me that I wasn't alone" (1996, 7). Feinberg goes on to draw out the importance of spaces like gay bars in the early 1960s to forming oppositional genders and sexualities—even for people who did not identify as genderqueer, gay, or lesbian. Having these collective spaces—discursive and actual—fuels individual and collective political transformation. They become the space into which we can enter as someone we feel at home being, and without which we cannot craft the joy and connectivity Lorde theorizes as the erotic. The work of writing memoirs and histories likewise situates what could otherwise seem like isolated struggle in wider context—and even knowing that others have walked a path makes it feel newly possible and workable to tread there ourselves. This is one sense in which social movement spaces nurture new sensuous understandings.

Desire is important here—an erotics of indeterminacy, intensely curious and embodied. Avery Gordon calls for a felt knowledge of worlds beyond what we now know, while noting that we as yet lack the craft experience to produce this embodied knowledge. The sensuous experience of worlds conducive to freedom and happiness might be more limited than cognitive or affective experience of their potential. Perhaps one result of life under current regressive political conditions is that it is easier to imagine or long for worlds beyond what we know today than it is to sensuously know those worlds; the body experiences the present moment, and this present moment is limited, at least, by the world as it is.

There are, though, felt experiences of embodied freedom; anecdotal reports range from the feeling of bringing one's entire living room set into the street for a Reclaim the Streets party to the goodness of harvesting one's own potatoes. Robin D. G. Kelley, asking how social movements "actually reshape the dreams and desires of the participants," describes attending a conference on the future of socialism during which

> a bunch of us got into a fight with an older generation of white leftists who proposed replacing retrograde "pop" music with the revolutionary "working-class" music of Phil Ochs, Woody Guthrie, preelectric Bob Dylan, and songs from the Spanish Civil War. And there I was, comically screaming at the top of my lungs, "No way! After the revolution, we STILL want Bootsy! That's right, we want Bootsy! We need the funk!" (2002, 10–11)

On the one hand, the fact that we'll still need the funk after the revolution is about recognizing the importance of imagining current pleasure as part of a longed-for future (you can dance to it). On the other, I take Kelley to make the deeper point that in thinking about social justice movements, intellectuals do ill to minimize explorations of freedom and love. According to Kelley: "I have come to realize that once we strip radical social movements down to their bare essence and understand the collective desires of people in motion, freedom and love lay at the very heart of the matter. Indeed, I would go so far as to say that freedom and love constitute the foundation for spirituality, another elusive and intangible force with which few scholars of social movements have come to terms" (12).

If we take seriously the idea that experiences are always embodied, that embodiment is always social, and thus that sensuousness is important to social movements, we might also begin to be able to address a range of ecstatic and socially created collective spaces. I am thinking of how bodily ecstasy in fundamentalist Christian spaces today can calcify a politically retrograde affective state—like Marxism, sensuousness is without guarantees. But since embodiment figures in many politically conservative contexts as a site of restriction, discipline, and individualized liberal selfhood, the kind of socially situated, relationally constituted body and self I see as essential to sensuousness opens space for radical, "progressive" social change. Our bodies can exceed disciplinary strictures of the present, and perhaps this excess expresses an embodied experience of radically transformed futures. The kinds of craft competencies people practice can themselves function as a critique of the notion that we need to pay someone else to do things for us or buy something new because anything broken is irreparable. This craftiness might also turn against what Herbert Marcuse (1978) frames as living as though we were our function—and accepting other people's constraint to their function; to the extent that we proliferate capabilities, we refuse instrumental and mechanistic conceptions of what any given person is good for. Finally, sensuous knowledge as craft attends to the pleasure involved in doing this for nonfunctional reasons. What is the purpose of a truly fine shot of espresso? It is not simply its caffeine: we develop a craft experience of drinking good coffee, which relies on the craft experience of making good espresso. These things refuse a functionalist reduction and affirm an erotics that is also political. When we dwell in sensuous experience, we engage a nonutilitarian pleasure that in its nonutility might itself proliferate dreaming. In other words, when Kelley holds out for Bootsy, he is in part rejecting an instrumental conception of folk music and in part appreciating the funk. Craft competencies can thus be inherently a critique of planned obsolescence and capitalist markets, and at the same time manifest noninstrumental pleasures important to not-yet-fully-manifest words.

SENSUOUSNESS AS CRUCIAL TO
POLITICAL TRANSFORMATION

Within a given present, Gordon argues, there are fugitive longings, or longings that read as extreme. These point to a "subjective factor" in subject formation that opens the possibility for a "willing subject [to] change itself and its way of existence." This is the process "by which an unfree actor is changed in the *here and now* so that she or he vitally needs to be free and acts on this need today—not later, not after the revolution, not when the system says it's OK, not after the time is right" (Gordon 2004, 124). This self-change constitutes the sensuous work of re-narrativizing the world.

Gordon is talking about a cultivated, acquired shift in our first-pass responses to our world. She draws on Marcuse, who names this shift the "cultivation of an instinctual basis for freedom," a phrase that does not evade the worries we might have with the language of human instincts. Marcuse explicitly calls on a kind of biological rebellion against life under domination. The idea is that we can nurture a way of being that identifies longings and turns them into vital needs "we cannot and will no longer live without." As Gordon puts it, "Cultivating an instinctual basis for freedom is about acquiring the sensual knowledge that our survival depends on sacrificing only what is blocking the satisfaction of those vital needs, without which we would otherwise fall apart" (125).

Acquiring sensual knowledge toward freedom might then be rendered as nurturing new first-pass impulses and longings, which Gordon frames as an "instinct for freedom." I would reject the strong ontological claim implied in this notion: to cultivate an instinctual basis for freedom is to express fundamental needs and desires, encoded in the nooks and crannies of our brain, which are shared by all mammals and cause us to freak out when someone puts us in a cage. This is one colloquial conception of the term; "instinct" is freighted with a range of biological deterministic naturalizations that I find troubling and, within the context of thinking sensuousness, also unnecessary. A far more compelling notion is what I term the weak ontological claim for an instinct for freedom: we can cultivate new impulses—things that act like the bad popular biologism's idea of instinct. This cultivation might originate from our conceptual understandings, our emotional frameworks, our bodily experience. We have an immediate impulse toward the fulfillment of our acquired, newly identified vital needs. New needs and wants become "natural" to us. This is a form of redrawing our desires, first-pass responses, and so on, and the possibility of redrawing them demonstrates that they are not at all "natural." Rather, the plasticity of these "instincts" signals that they themselves are already socially formed and situated. I would argue, then, for this more complex understanding of an instinct for freedom—a torquing of Marcuse's work, perhaps. What I take from this notion is the idea that sensuous knowledge is important in reframing our embodied experience of political spaces. To denaturalize our sensuous understanding of alienation, as Marcuse argues the aesthetic form does, is to find ourselves alienated from things that were familiar, drawn to things that would otherwise feel strange.

When people say they are working at "building a new world within the shell of the old," I think they are pointing toward the kind of sensuousness Gordon calls for, a utopia that is precisely not a "no place." Rather, this utopia is a "longing for nonsacrificial freedoms and exuberant unforeseen pleasures," a sensuous excess and evasion of structures of domination. Gordon sees this utopian impulse in the "things we are and do that exceed or are just not expressions of what's dominant and dominating us" (129). This utopia is sensual—a way of living in the here and now—and it is daily and ongoing. And there is both joy and discomfort in such dailiness. I read the domain of joy in sensuousness—not evacuated of politics or fundamentally inexpressible, but rather a reason why it feels good to struggle. As Gina Dent argues, "The experience of joy, of the erotic, is another kind of knowledge, and we must learn to account for its insights because, in theory, it is a domain to which we all have access" (1992, 17). I might push Dent to think about the possibility that the erotic is in practice a domain to which we all have access.

Sensuous knowing offers a way to think about knowledge that moves us, and that calls for movement—knowledge that moves others. The formation we call gender ripples recursively between individuals and their social-political ontologies. Gender has thus been one of my optics in trying to think practically about sensuousness and how it might show up in people's actual lives and struggles. This is because gender is a mode that can also reveal a non-dualistic experience of mind and body, un-fixity, and collective joy—though, of course, it usually, overwhelmingly, fails to fulfill these roles.

Sensuous knowledge marks a site where gender norms and their potential reworkings are stitched together and discomfited. Sensuous knowledge for social movement, then, shows up as one site of creating a livable world—a complex home, without guarantees. It is a resource for change, a site of praxis, an unspeakable but deeply political social and ethical mode of being. Sensuousness, then, is one way to talk about joy as a resource for social change.

I have focused on ideas of what it would be to feel good in one's body and the sense of being-at-home. Attention to sensuousness can indicate sites where social movements still have work to do. This "work" can be what we usually understand as social movement work, addressing injustice in the world. It can also indicate work that needs to happen in the social movement context itself. In trans and genderqueer social movement spaces, race, ethnicity, and class divisions are often marked by their manifestation on a sensuous plane. So, for example, Clare describes such a disjunction in coming to queer community where what he read as class markers were rendered fashion statements: while they were helping a friend move, an urban butch mentioned being happy to be wearing her steel-toe boots. Clare says, "I asked where she worked, assuming she'd have a story about forklifts or hi-los, a warehouse, bailer, mill, factory, or mine." Instead, "Leslie said, 'I just bought them as a fashion statement.' I felt as if I'd been exposed as a hick yet again, caught assuming she was someone I might have grown up with. A fashion statement. What did I have in common with Leslie? I felt the stones in my heart grind deep" (Clare 1999, 135). The presumption that queer identity is urban is woven together with the presumption that it is middle class, and these presuppositions inform the embodied experience of living in these communities. Thus sensuous experiences should be seen as a site for connection or disjunction.

And, as I explored in chapter 2, commonsensical presuppositions arise out of and contribute to the realities of queer and trans lives. Viviane Namaste unpacks rhetorics of nationhood and race in current trans writing and examines how these rhetorics connect to discrepancies in service provision by social service agencies. Namaste examines an analogy frequently drawn between trans experience and African American experience, taking Susan Stryker as a representative example of a more general rhetorical trend. She looks at Stryker's comparison of a trans art movement in San Francisco with the Harlem Renaissance, and then at Stryker's comparison of transsexual narratives of transition with classic slave narratives, which Stryker argues have a tripartite form: "'African freedom,' a transitional period of enslavement, and 'a new kind of freedom after slavery'" (Namaste 2000, 120). As Namaste explains it, Stryker presents a corollary tripartite form: "Transsexual autobiographies, [Stryker] claims, begin with one's life before transition, present the process and effects of transforming one's body, and conclude with 'post-transition life experiences in a new gender'" (120). There are a number of things to trouble us here. First, as Namaste notes, the analogy Stryker draws is based on an observation about form (tripartite) and content (freedom, process, new freedom). But the deeper content, the content that matters, is elided; in an extensive evocation of a "transsexual renaissance" in San Francisco we might expect some significant meditations on how race and racism shaped the Harlem Renaissance. Also, the kinds of "freedom" we see at either wing of the narrative triangle are different in more than kind; following the analogy would require that we take pre-transition lives as "freedom," transition as equivalent to chattel slavery, and post-slavery freedom as equivalent to post-transition freedom. Since these experience are in fact very different, drawing such analogies is politically troubling.

Second, as Namaste argues, "Stryker's argument rests upon the assumption that freedom—for the (white) transsexual as for the African-American—can be found in the urban centers of the U.S., an assumption questionable for African-Americans, transsexuals, and African-American transsexuals" (123). This assumption is classed, as Eli Clare discusses in relation to queer culture, and also bears out Namaste's claim that much current theory erases the experience of transsexuals generally, and poor transsexuals and transsexuals of color in particular. Not only is that freedom not ensured in cities, but imagining the city—whether San Francisco or New York—as a queer and trans haven reinscribes every place that is not the city as unlivable for queers and trans folks. And while the relative safety of these places is debatable, a trans social movement could reasonably be called to work for livable conditions wherever trans people live.

Finally, the persistent comparison between sex and race serves to elide race as an axis of trans and queer experience—trans people are only posited as being like people of color, and almost never understood as people of color. Structurally, the metaphor of transsexuals as a category of people just like a racialized minority perpetuates an erasure of "the actual presence of African-Americans [and other racial and ethnic groups], since race only stands in to represent gender" (125). It matters that the operative narratives some trans people and their allies use to explain and theorize trans experience effect these erasures. Indeed, in this respect trans social movements replicate some of the epistemic and material violences of second-wave U.S. feminist movements.[10] Evan B. Towle and Lynn M. Morgan have explored further implications of the use of racialized Other cultures to offer explanatory resources to (mostly white) Western audiences thinking about nonbinary gender categories. They examine the use of a "third gender" concept, arguing that "unfortunately, the popularization of 'third gender' concepts often contributes to ethnocentric assumptions about other cultures, even when the authors' intentions are liberatory, progressive, and transcendent" (2002, 470).

Wyatt Swindler's reflection on being a black man offers a final caution in thinking about trans and queer sensuous knowledge. He writes:

> I know what is acceptable once I leave the comfort of my gender-queer microcosm where self-identification takes precedence of body parts, voices, and names. I know that there are ways that I can act, ways that I can present myself when I step outside my door so that people will not question who I am. It's hard not to fall into that. It's a battle I face everyday and it's a different battle depending on who, what, when, and where. (Swindler 2004, 67)

Swindler is addressing the complex intersection of self-identification and social sensuous materiality—the sites where body parts, voices, and names matter. He addresses what it means to be offered ways of being a black man that no one will question, while at the same time wanting to challenge a racist understanding of what it is to be a black man. He writes: "At night I was the kind of man I thought I had to be to be accepted. I would set my jaw, walk my brother's standard issue gangsta walk, look straight ahead and through anyone who might have even glanced at me" (68). But when he didn't want to enact this stereotyped black masculinity, whole systems of assumption and presupposition snap into place. And, as he notes, these battles are different depending on socially contingent features. If there are scarce metaphors and thick stories for white trans people with some money or class privilege, there are even fewer models and discursive communities

---

10. And this is ironic, given the intense anti-trans current prevalent in so-called radical feminism, a descendant of the second-wave radical feminism exemplified by virulent transphobes Janice Raymond and Sheila Jeffreys. These theorists' refusal of trans identities functions, I would argue, to stabilize the bounds of gender within radical feminist spaces—to delimit who counts as a "real woman"—in part as a re-entrenchment of gender categories muddied by third-wave feminists' call to theorize intersectional gender formation, with particular attention to race. And so when radical feminists rail against trans identity, they recoup a white-centered feminist identity in part through the erasures trans narratives of racial comparison enact.

for reflecting on how racialized trans people's specific experience is framed or understood and what metaphors are available to them. As I have argued, the crafting of sensuous knowledge is in part a means of crafting collective accounts of forming livable lives. But the sensuously experienced obstacles to being at home in a social world likewise obstruct the transformation of those worlds. This is a reason why Joshua Mira Goldberg's call for understanding trans issues as intrinsically about issues coded along class or race or disability lines is relevant to trans social movements. He writes:

> I think of Jewish liberation as being more than just fighting anti-Semitism—instead I feel it to be intimately connected to land issues, colonialism, and cultural survival in a multiethnic diaspora. . . . On a global level, struggles about gender are more about colonialism, capitalism, and racism than about individual identity. There is a lot of talk about the "interconnectedness of oppressions," but are we carrying that through to how we fight for justice as trans people? (2004, 157)

I think that Goldberg is right to argue for intersectional trans social justice fights, and he's right to argue that gender is about far more than gender. And at the same time, calls like these need a bit more grounding in how and why trans identities are involved in all these other struggles. Paying attention to sensuous knowledge offers a first step in thinking about socially embedded embodiment in all its complexity.

Trans narratives of being-at-home underscore the fact that sensuous joy, or the erotic, is often a socially mediated achievement. The conditions for flourishing are at root a freedom-from—freedom from gender-based harassment, assault, murder. They are also a freedom-to—a relational uptake of transitioning, of genderqueer narratives, of new or other pronouns. Transgender, transsexual, and genderqueer living partakes of relational agency, in which autonomy is contingently crafted through things like being addressed by one's pronoun of choice. Doing justice to dignity and the possibilities for flourishing shows that sensuousness is a concern for social movements generally. Trans social justice movements are a good place to start in thinking about sensuousness and political change because they show the enmeshment of political and embodied experience as a mode of becoming. That is, at the very site often figured as a prototypical liberal individualist project, in which trans people "get" to make the decision to transition all on their own, or in which they're incapable of making such a decision at all, we see that there is no such thing as individualized agency or apolitical embodiment. Trans social movements turn out to be not a social movement focused entirely on the body and one's own comfort in it, but a cluster of movements focused on an interpenetrating dynamic between embodied experience and political social worlds.

Feeling good in one's body and the world is not a voluntarist project. Rather, the transformation of one's implicit understanding expressed in sensuous knowledge is dependent on broader political change, on having access to what hormones and procedures bring one's bodily experience into line with one's projected self, on the basic physical and psychic safety that many people take for granted, and on bigger categories. Sensuousness, stitching together sociality and embodied experience, names one aspect of the complex, agentful living implicit in flourishing. If we are to do justice to this living, we must take into account its affective and embodied aspects and pay attention to implicit understanding as a measure for multifaceted, complex transformation.

REFERENCES

Aal, William. 2001. Moving from guilt to action: Antiracist organizing and the concept of "whiteness" for activism and the academy. In *The making and unmaking of whiteness*, ed. Birgit Brander Rasmussen, 294–310. Durham: Duke University Press.

Adamson, Walter L. 1980. *Hegemony and revolution: A study of Antonio Gramsci's political and cultural theory*. Berkeley and Los Angeles: University of California Press.

Adleman, Jeanne, and Gloria M. Enguidanos, eds. 1995. *Racism in the lives of women: Testimony, theory, and guides to antiracist practices*. New York: Haworth Press.

Adler, Judith. 1976. "Revolutionary" art and the "art" of revolution: Aesthetic work in a millenarian period. *Theory and Society* 3, no. 3: 417–35.

Aizura, Aren Z. 2006. Of borders and homes: The imaginary community of (trans)sexual citizenship. *Inter-Asia Cultural Studies* 7, no. 2: 289–309.

Alcoff, Linda, and Elizabeth Potter, eds. 1993. *Feminist epistemologies*. New York: Routledge.

Allen, Theodore W. 2002. *The origin of racial oppression in Anglo-America*. Vol. 1 of *The invention of the white race*. London: Verso.

Allison, Dorothy. 1988. *Trash*. Ithaca, N.Y.: Firebrand Books.

———. 1994. *Skin: Talking about sex, class, and literature*. Ithaca, N.Y.: Firebrand Books.

———. 1996. *Two or three things I know for sure*. New York: Plume.

Althusser, Louis. 1969. *For Marx*. Trans. Ben Brewster. London: Allen Lane.

———. 1971. *Lenin and philosophy, and other essays*. Trans. Ben Brewster. London: New Left Books.

Anderson, Benedict. 1983. *Imagined communities: Reflections on the origin and spread of nationalism*. London: Verso.

Ansara, Gavriel Alejandro Levi. 2004. Transitioning. In *From the inside out: Radical gender transformation, FTM, and beyond*, ed. Morty Diamond, 91–93. San Francisco: Manic D Press.

Anthias, Floya. 2001. Diasporic hybridity and transcending racisms. In *Rethinking antiracisms: From theory to practice*, ed. Floya Anthias and Cathy Lloyd, 22–43. London: Routledge.

Anthias, Floya, and Cathy Lloyd, eds. 2001. *Rethinking anti-racisms: From theory to practice*. London: Routledge.

Antony, Louise M., and Charlotte Witt, eds. 2001. *A mind of one's own: Feminist essays on reason and objectivity*. 2nd ed. Boulder, Colo.: Westview Press.

Audi, Robert. 1998. *Epistemology: A contemporary introduction to the theory of knowledge*. New York: Routledge.

Babb, Valerie Melissa. 1998. *Whiteness visible: The meaning of whiteness in American literature and culture*. New York: New York University Press.

Babbitt, Susan E. 1996. *Impossible dreams: Rationality, integrity, and moral imagination.* Boulder, Colo.: Westview Press.

———. 2000. *Artless integrity: Moral imagination, agency, and stories.* Lanham, Md.: Rowman and Littlefield.

Babbitt, Susan E., and Sue Campbell, eds. 1999. *Racism and philosophy.* Ithaca: Cornell University Press.

Baier, Annette. 1985. *Postures of the mind: Essays on mind and morals.* Minneapolis: University of Minnesota Press.

Bailey, Alison. 1998. Locating traitorous identities: Toward a view of privilege-cognizant white character. *Hypatia* 13, no. 3: 27–42.

Banham, Gary. 2000. *Kant and the ends of aesthetics.* New York: St. Martin's Press.

Banks, Russell. 2004. *The darling.* New York: HarperCollins.

Bannerji, Himani. 1995. *Thinking through: Essays on feminism, Marxism, and anti-racism.* Toronto: Women's Press.

———. 2000. *The dark side of the nation: Essays on multiculturalism, nationalism, and gender.* Toronto: Canadian Scholars' Press.

Barad, Karen Michelle. 2007. *Meeting the universe halfway: Quantum physics and the entanglement of matter and meaning.* Durham: Duke University Press.

Bartky, Sandra Lee. 1990. *Femininity and domination: Studies in the phenomenology of oppression.* New York: Routledge.

———. 2002. *"Sympathy and solidarity" and other essays.* Lanham, Md.: Rowman and Littlefield.

Batur-VanderLippe, Pinar. 1999. On the necessity of antiracist praxis: An experience in teaching and learning. *Teaching Sociology* 27, no. 3: 274–85.

Baumgarten, Alexander Gottlieb. 1954. *Reflections on poetry.* Trans. K. Aschenbrenner and W. Holther. Berkeley and Los Angeles: University of California Press. (Orig. pub. 1735.)

Bennett, Tony, Graham Martin, Colin Mercer, and Janet Woollacott, eds. 1981. *Culture, ideology, and social process.* London: Open University Press.

Berlant, Lauren. 1997. *The queen of America goes to Washington City.* Durham: Duke University Press.

Bernasconi, Robert. 2001. Who invented the concept of race? Kant's role in the enlightenment construction of race. In *Race*, ed. Bernasconi, 11–36. Malden, Mass.: Blackwell.

Bernasconi, Robert, and Tommy L. Lott, eds. 2000. *The idea of race.* Indianapolis: Hackett.

Blum, Lawrence A. 2002. *I'm not a racist, but . . . : The moral quandary of race.* Ithaca: Cornell University Press.

Bolin, Anne. 1988. *In search of Eve: Transsexual rites of passage.* South Hadley, Mass.: Bergin and Garvey.

Bonilla-Silva, Eduardo. 2001. *White supremacy and racism in the post–civil rights era.* Boulder, Colo.: Lynne Rienner.

———. 2003. *Racism without racists: Color-blind racism and the persistence of racial inequality in the United States.* Lanham, Md.: Rowman and Littlefield.

Bornstein, Kate. 1994. *Gender outlaw: On men, women, and the rest of us.* New York: Routledge.

Botwinick, Aryeh. 1986. *Participation and tacit knowledge in Plato, Machiavelli, and Hobbes.* Lanham, Md.: University Press of America.

Bourdieu, Pierre. 1977. *Outline of a theory of practice.* Trans. Richard Nice. New York: Cambridge University Press.

———. 1984. *Distinction: A social critique of the judgement of taste.* Trans. Richard Nice. Cambridge: Harvard University Press.

———. 1990a. *In other words: Essays towards a reflexive sociology.* Trans. Matthew Adamson Pierre. Cambridge, Mass.: Polity Press.

———. 1990b. *The logic of practice.* Trans. Richard Nice. Stanford: Stanford University Press.

Bouson, J. Brooks. 2000. *Quiet as it's kept: Shame, trauma, and race in the novels of Toni Morrison.* Albany: State University of New York Press.

Boylan, Jennifer Finney. 2003. *She's not there: A life in two genders.* New York: Broadway Books.

Brandom, Robert. 1994. *Making it explicit: Reasoning, representing, and discursive commitment.* Cambridge: Harvard University Press.

———. 2000. *Articulating reasons: An introduction to inferentialism.* Cambridge: Harvard University Press.

Brevard, Aleshia. 2001. *The woman I was not born to be: A transsexual journey.* Philadelphia: Temple University Press.

Brewer, Bill. 1999. *Perception and reason.* New York: Oxford University Press.

Brison, Susan. 2002. *Aftermath: Violence and the remaking of a self.* Princeton: Princeton University Press.

Buck-Morss, Susan. 1995. *The dialectics of seeing: Walter Benjamin and the Arcades Project.* Cambridge: MIT Press.

———. 2000. *Dreamworld and catastrophe: The passing of mass utopia in East and West.* Cambridge: MIT Press.

———. 2003. *Thinking past terror: Islamism and critical theory on the Left.* London: Verso.

Buhle, Paul. 1981. Herbert Marcuse, surrealism, and us. *Socialist Review* 28, no. 1: 141–44.

Bulkin, Elly. 1984. *Yours in struggle: Three feminist perspectives on anti-Semitism and racism.* New York: Long Haul Press.

Butler, Judith. 1989. *Gender trouble: Feminism and the subversion of identity.* New York: Routledge.

———. 1993. *Bodies that matter: On the discursive limits of "sex."* New York: Routledge.

———. 1997. Performative acts and gender construction: An essay in phenomenology and feminist theory. In *Writing on the body: Female embodiment and feminist theory,* ed. Katie Conboy, Nadia Medina, and Sarah Stanbury, 401–17. New York: Columbia University Press.

———. 2004. *Undoing gender.* New York: Routledge.

Caine, Barbara, Elizabeth A. Grosz, and Marie de Lepervanche, eds. 1988. *Crossing boundaries: Feminisms and the critique of knowledges.* Boston: Allen and Unwin.

Califia, Pat. 1997. *Sex changes: The politics of transgenderism.* San Francisco: Cleis Press.

Campbell, Sue. 1997. *Interpreting the personal: Expression and the formation of feelings.* Ithaca: Cornell University Press.

———. 1999. Dominant identities and settled expectations. In *Racism and philosophy,* ed. Susan E. Babbitt and Susan Campbell, 216–34. Ithaca: Cornell University Press.

———. 2003. *Relational remembering: Rethinking the memory wars.* Lanham, Md.: Rowman and Littlefield.

Chanter, Tina. 2006. Abjection and the constitutive nature of difference: Class mourning in *Margaret's Museum* and legitimating myths of innocence in *Casablanca. Hypatia* 21, no. 3: 86–106.

Chiari, Joseph. 1977. *Art and knowledge.* New York: Gordian Press.

Chisholm, Roderick M. 1957. *Perceiving: A philosophical study.* Ithaca: Cornell University Press.

———. 1982. *The foundations of knowing.* Minneapolis: University of Minnesota Press.

———. 1989. *Theory of knowledge.* 3rd ed. Englewood Cliffs, N.J.: Prentice Hall.

Cirese, Alberto Mario. 1982. Gramsci's observations on folklore. In *Approaches to Gramsci,* ed. Anne Showstack Sassoon, 212–15. London: Writers and Readers Publishing Cooperative Society.

Clare, Eli. 1999. *Exile and pride: Disability, queerness, and liberation.* Cambridge, Mass.: South End Press.

———. 2007. Body shame, body pride: Lessons from the disability rights movement. April 2. http://pitbull-poet.livejournal.com/21560.html (accessed June 23, 2007).

Clifford, James. 1988. *The predicament of culture: Twentieth-century ethnography, literature, and art.* Cambridge: Harvard University Press.

Code, Lorraine. 1987. *Epistemic responsibility.* Hanover: University Press of New England.

———. 1991. *What can she know? Feminist theory and the construction of knowledge.* Ithaca: Cornell University Press.

———. 2006. *Ecological thinking: The politics of epistemic location.* Oxford: Oxford University Press.

Collins, Arthur W. 1967. The epistemological status of the concept of perception. *Philosophical Review* 76, no. 4: 436–59.

Crawford, Dan D. 1974. Propositional and nonpropositional perceiving. *Philosophy and Phenomenological Research* 35, no. 2: 201–10.

Crawford, Lucas. 2008. Transgender without organs? Mobilizing a geo-affective theory of gender modification. *Women's Studies Quarterly* 36, nos. 3–4: 127–43.

Crow, Graham. 2002. *Social solidarities: Theories, identities, and social change.* Philadelphia: Open University Press.

Cuomo, Chris J., and Kim Q. Hall, eds. 1999. *Whiteness: Feminist philosophical reflections.* Lanham, Md.: Rowman and Littlefield.

Cvetkovich, Ann. 2003. *An archive of feelings: Trauma, sexuality, and lesbian public cultures.* Durham: Duke University Press.

Dancy, Jonathan, ed. 1988. *Perceptual knowledge.* New York: Oxford University Press.

Davis, Angela Y. 2004. Legacies of women of color feminisms. Paper presented at Center for Cultural Studies Colloquium Series, October 6, Santa Cruz, Calif.

Davis, Dawn Rae. 2002. (Love is) the ability of not knowing: Feminist experience of the impossible in ethical singularity. *Hypatia* 17, no. 2: 145–61.

de Lauretis, Teresa. 1984. *Alice doesn't: Feminism, semiotics, cinema.* Bloomington: Indiana University Press.

de Sousa, Ronald. 1987. *The rationality of emotions.* Cambridge: MIT Press.

Dei, George J. Sefa. 1996. Critical perspectives in anti-racism: An introduction. *Canadian Review of Sociology and Anthropology* 33, no. 3: 247–67.

———. 1999. Knowledge and politics of social change: The implication of anti-racism. *British Journal of Sociology of Education* 20, no. 3: 395–409.

Dent, Gina. 1992. Black pleasure, black joy: An introduction. In *Black popular culture: A project by Michele Wallace,* ed. Dent, 1–20. Seattle: Bay Press.

Doane, Ashley W., and Eduardo Bonilla-Silva, eds. 2003. *White out: The continuing significance of racism.* New York: Routledge.

Dretske, Fred. 1969. *Seeing and knowing.* London: Routledge.

———. 1993. Conscious experience. *Mind* 102, no. 406: 263–83.

———. 2000. *Perception, knowledge, and belief: Selected essays.* Cambridge: Cambridge University Press.

Dreyfus, Hubert L. 1983. *Michel Foucault: Beyond structuralism and hermeneutics.* Chicago: University of Chicago Press.

———. 1985. Holism and hermeneutics. In *Hermeneutics and praxis*, ed. Robert Hollinger, 227–47. Notre Dame: University of Notre Dame Press.

Du Bois, W. E. B. 1940. *Dusk of dawn: An essay toward an autobiography of a race concept.* New York: Harcourt, Brace.

Dufrenne, Mikel. 1987. *In the presence of the sensuous: Essays in aesthetics.* Ed. Mark S. Roberts and Dennis Gallagher. Atlantic Highlands, N.J.: Humanities Press International.

Eagleton, Terry. 1990. *The ideology of the aesthetics.* Cambridge, Mass.: Basil Blackwell.

Eichstedt, Jennifer L. 1998. Problematic white identities and a search for racial justice. *Sociological Forum* 16, no. 3: 445–70.

Elliott, Terri. 1994. Making strange what had appeared familiar. *Monist* 77, no. 4: 424–33.

Engels, Friedrich. 1935. *Ludwig Feuerbach and the outcome of classical German philosophy.* With an appendix of other material of Marx and Engels relating to dialectical materialism. Ed. and trans. C. P. Dutt. New York: International Publishers.

Eze, Emmanuel Chukwudi, ed. 1997. *Race and the enlightenment: A reader.* Cambridge, Mass.: Blackwell.

Feagin, Joe R. 2000. *Racist America: Roots, current realities, and future reparations.* New York: Routledge.

———. 2001. *Liberation sociology.* Boulder, Colo.: Westview Press.

———. 2003. *The many costs of racism.* Lanham, Md.: Rowman and Littlefield.

Feagin, Joe R., and Eileen O'Brien. 2003. *White men on race: Power, privilege, and the shaping of cultural consciousness.* Boston: Beacon Press.

Feagin, Joe R., Hernán Vera, and Pinar Batur. 2001. *White racism: The basics.* 2nd ed. New York: Routledge.

Feinberg, Leslie. 1996. *Transgender warriors: Making history from Joan of Arc to RuPaul.* Boston: Beacon Press.

———. 1998. *Trans liberation: Beyond pink or blue.* Boston: Beacon Press.

Femia, Joseph V. 1981. *Gramsci's political thought: Hegemony, consciousness, and the revolutionary process.* Oxford: Clarendon Press.

Ferguson, Kennan. 1999. *The politics of judgment: Aesthetics, identity, and political theory.* Lanham, Md.: Lexington Books.

Feuerbach, Ludwig. 1972. *The fiery brook: Selected writings of Ludwig Feuerbach.* Garden City, N.Y.: Anchor Books.

Findlay, Barbara. 2006. Acting queerly: Lawyering for trans people. In *Trans/forming feminisms: Trans/feminist voices speak out*, ed. Krista Scott-Dixon, 145–53. Toronto: University of Toronto Press.

Fine, M., L. Weis, C. Powell, and L. M. Wong, eds. 1997. *Off white: Readings on race, power, and society.* New York: Routledge.

Fischer, Norman. 1997. Frankfurt school Marxism and the ethical meaning of art: Herbert Marcuse's *The aesthetic dimension. Communication Theory* 7, no. 4: 362–420.

Foucault, Michel. 1991. Faire vivre et laisser mourir. *Les Temps Modernes* 46, no. 535: 37–61.

———. 1995. *Discipline and punish: The birth of the prison.* New York: Vintage Books.

———. 1997. *Ethics: Subjectivity and truth.* Ed. Paul Rabinow. Trans. Robert Hurley and others. New York: New Press.

Frankenberg, Ruth. 1993. *White women, race matters: The social construction of whiteness.* Minneapolis: University of Minnesota Press.

———. 1996. When we are capable of stopping, we begin to see: Being white, seeing whiteness. In *Names we call home: Autobiography on racial identity,* ed. Becky Thompson and Sangeeta Tyagi, 3–18. New York: Routledge.

———. ed. 1997. *Displacing whiteness: Essays in social and cultural criticism.* Durham: Duke University Press.

Frater, Lara. 2005. *Fat chicks rule! How to survive in a thin-centric world.* Brooklyn: IG Publishing.

Fricker, Miranda. 2007. *Epistemic injustice: Power and the ethics of knowing.* New York: Oxford University Press.

Frye, Marilyn. 1983. *The politics of reality: Essays in feminist theory.* Trumansburg, N.Y.: Crossing Press.

Gabriel, John. 1998. New contours of anti-racist politics. *Patterns of Prejudice* 32, no. 4: 35–44.

Gadamer, Hans Georg. 1977. *Philosophical hermeneutics.* 1st pbk. ed. Berkeley and Los Angeles: University of California Press.

———. 1986. *The relevance of the beautiful, and other essays.* Ed. Robert Bernasconi. Cambridge: Cambridge University Press.

———. 1989. *Truth and method.* 2nd ed. New York: Continuum.

———. 1994. What is truth? In *Hermeneutics and truth,* ed. Bruce R. Wachterhauser, 33–46. Evanston: Northwestern University Press.

———. 1997. *The philosophy of Hans-Georg Gadamer.* Ed. Lewis Edwin Hahn. Chicago: Open Court.

Gallagher, Shaun. 2005. *How the body shapes the mind.* Oxford: Clarendon Press.

Gay and Lesbian Historical Society of Northern California. 1998. MTF transgender activism in the Tenderloin and beyond, 1966–1975. *GLQ* 4, no. 2: 349–72.

Genoni, Mia Renosio. 2002. The persistence defined and denied: Lynette K. Stephenson's *White Girl* series and post-black art. Paper presented at the Color, Hair, and Bone: The Persistence of Race into the 21st Century conference, September 27, 2002, Lewisburg, Pa.

Gilmore, Ruth. 2007. *Golden gulag: Prisons, surplus, crisis, and opposition in globalizing California.* Berkeley and Los Angeles: University of California Press.

Gilroy, Paul. 1991. *"There ain't no black in the Union Jack": The cultural politics of race and nation.* Chicago: University of Chicago Press.

———. 1992. The end of anti-racism. In *"Race," culture, and difference,* ed. J. Donald and Ali Rattansi, 49–61. London: Sage Publications.

———. 1993. *The black Atlantic: Modernity and double consciousness.* Cambridge: Harvard University Press.

———. 2000. *Against race: Imagining political culture beyond the color line.* Cambridge: Belknap Press of Harvard University Press.

Gilroy, Paul, Lawrence Grossberg, and Angela McRobbie, eds. 2000. *Without guarantees: In honour of Stuart Hall.* London: Verso.

Goldberg, David Theo. 1990. *Anatomy of racism.* Minneapolis: University of Minnesota Press.

———. 1993. *Racist culture: Philosophy and the politics of meaning.* Cambridge, Mass.: Blackwell.

Goldberg, Joshua Mira. 2004. Approaching thirty: Some reflections on survival and activism. In *From the inside out: Radical gender transformation, FTM, and beyond,* ed. Marty Diamond, 155–58. San Francisco: Manic D Press.

Gordon, Avery F. 1997. *Ghostly matters: Haunting and the sociological imagination*. Minneapolis: University of Minneapolis Press.

———. 2004. *Keeping good time: Reflections on knowledge, power, and people*. Boulder, Colo.: Paradigm Publishers.

Gould, Deborah. 2009. *Moving politics: Emotion and ACT UP's fight against AIDS*. Chicago: University of Chicago Press.

Gracyk, Theodore A. 1990. Are Kant's "aesthetic judgment" and "judgment of taste" synonymous? *International Philosophical Quarterly* 30, no. 2: 159–72.

Gramsci, Antonio. 1972. *Selections from the prison notebooks of Antonio Gramsci*. Ed. and trans. Quintin Hoare and Geoffrey Nowell-Smith. New York: International Publishers.

———. 1977. *Selections from political writings, 1910–1920*. Ed. Quintin Hoare. Trans. John Matthews. London: Laurence and Wishart.

———. 1985. *Selections from cultural writings*. Ed. David Forgacs and Geoffrey Nowell-Smith. Trans. William Boelhower. London: Lawrence and Wishart.

Green, Jamison. 2004. *Becoming a visible man*. Nashville: Vanderbilt University Press.

Guyer, Paul. 1979. *Kant and the claims of taste*. Cambridge: Harvard University Press.

———. 1993. *Kant and the experience of freedom: Essays on aesthetics and morality*. Cambridge: Cambridge University Press.

Hall, Stuart. 1983. The problem of ideology: Marxism without guarantees. In *Stuart Hall: Critical dialogues in cultural studies*, ed. Kuan-Hsing Chen and David Morley, 25–46. London: Routledge.

———. 1986. Gramsci's relevance for the study of race and ethnicity. In *Stuart Hall: Critical dialogues in cultural studies*, ed. Kuan-Hsing Chen and David Morley, 411–40. London: Routledge.

Haraway, Donna Jeanne. 1991. *Simians, cyborgs, and women: The reinvention of nature*. London: Free Association Books.

———. 1997. *ModestWitness@SecondMillennium.FemaleManMeetsOncoMouse: Feminism and technoscience*. New York: Routledge.

———. 2003. *The companion species manifesto: Dogs, people, and significant otherness*. Chicago: Prickly Paradigm Press.

———. 2008. *When species meet*. Minneapolis: University of Minnesota Press.

Harding, Sandra. 1986. *The science question in feminism*. Ithaca: Cornell University Press.

———. 1991. *Whose science? Whose knowledge? Thinking from women's lives*. Ithaca: Cornell University Press.

Harding, Sandra, and Merrill B. Hintikka, eds. 1983. *Discovering reality: Feminist perspectives on epistemology, metaphysics, methodology, and philosophy of science*. Boston: Kluwer.

Harris, David. 1992. *From class struggle to the politics of pleasure: The effects of Gramscianism on cultural studies*. New York: Routledge.

Hartigan, John, Jr. 2000. Object lessons in whiteness: Anti-racism and the study of white folks. *Identities: Global Studies in Culture and Power* 7, no. 3: 373–406.

Hartman, Saidiya. 1997. *Scenes of subjection: Terror, slavery, and self-making in nineteenth-century America*. New York: Oxford University Press.

Hartsock, Nancy C. M. 1998. *The feminist standpoint revisited, and other essays*. Boulder, Colo.: Westview Press.

Hein, Hilde. 1976. Aesthetic consciousness: The ground of political experience. *Journal of Aesthetics and Art Criticism* 35, no. 2: 143–52.

Heldke, Lisa. 1998. On being a responsible traitor: A primer. In *Daring to be good: Essays in feminist ethico-politics*, ed. Bat-Ami Bar On and Ann Ferguson, 87–99. New York: Routledge.

Heyes, Cressida. 2003. Feminist solidarity after queer theory: The case of transgender. *Signs: Journal of Women in Culture and Society* 28, no. 4: 1093–1120.

Hill, Mike, ed. 1997. *Whiteness: A critical reader*. New York: New York University Press.

Hill, Thomas. 1991. *Autonomy and self-respect*. New York: Cambridge University Press.

Hill Collins, Patricia. 1990. *Black feminist thought: Knowledge, consciousness, and the politics of empowerment*. Boston: Unwin Hyman.

———. 1991. Learning from the outsider within. In *(En)gendering knowledge: Feminists in academe*, ed. Joan E. Hartman and Ellen Messer-Davidow, 40–65. Knoxville: University of Tennessee Press.

Holzman, Clare. 1995. Rethinking the role of guilt and shame in white women's anti-racism work. In *Racism in the lives of women: Testimony, theory, and guides to antiracist practice*, ed. Jeanne Adleman and Gloria M. Enguidanos-Clark, 325–32. New York: Haworth Press.

Hoy, David Couzens. 1978. *The critical circle: Literature, history, and philosophical hermeneutics*. Berkeley and Los Angeles: University of California Press.

Humphreys, Paul, Peter Dlugos, and James H. Fetzer. 1997. Escaping the propositional prison. *Monist* 80, no. 3: 378–81.

Ignatiev, Noel, and John Garvey, eds. 1996. *Race traitor*. New York: Routledge.

James, Joy. 2000. "Discredited knowledge" in the nonfiction of Toni Morrison. In *Women of color and philosophy*, ed. Naomi Zack, 25–43. Malden, Mass.: Blackwell.

Japaridze, Tamar. 2000. *The Kantian subject: Sensus communis, mimesis, work of mourning*. Albany: State University of New York Press.

Jeffreys, Sheila. 2003. *Unpacking queer politics: A lesbian feminist perspective*. Oxford: Blackwell.

———. 2007. FTM transsexualism and grief. http://www.feminist-reprise.org/docs/jeffreysftm.htm (accessed July 15, 2007).

Jensen, Robert. 2005. *The heart of whiteness: Confronting race, racism, and white privilege*. San Francisco: City Lights.

Jha, Stefania Ruzsits. 2002. *Reconsidering Michael Polanyi's philosophy*. Pittsburgh: University of Pittsburgh Press.

Jordan, June. 1985. *On call: Political essays*. London: Pluto Press.

Juang, Richard. 2006. Transgendering the politics of recognition. In *The transgender studies reader*, ed. Susan Stryker and Stephen Whittle, 706–19. New York: Routledge.

Kailin, Julie. 2002. *Antiracist education: From theory to practice*. Lanham, Md.: Rowman and Littlefield.

Kant, Immanuel. 2000. *Critique of the power of judgment*. Ed. Paul Guyer. Trans. Paul Guyer and Eric Matthews. Cambridge: Cambridge University Press. (Orig. pub. 1790.)

Katz, Judith. 2003. *White awareness: Handbook for anti-racism training*. Norman: University of Oklahoma Press.

Keller, Evelyn Fox. 1983. *A feeling for the organism: The life and work of Barbara McClintock*. San Francisco: W. H. Freeman.

Kelley, Robin D. G. 2002. *Freedom dreams: The black radical imagination*. Boston: Beacon Press.

Kivel, Paul. 1995. *Uprooting racism: How white people can work for racial justice*. Philadelphia: New Society Publishers.

Kleist, Edward Eugene. 2000. *Judging appearances: A phenomenological study of the Kantian sensus communis*. Boston: Kluwer.

Kuhn, Thomas. 1962. *The structure of scientific revolutions*. Chicago: University of Chicago Press.

Lamas, Juan-Alejandro. 2004. Genderfusion. In *From the inside out: Radical gender transformation, FTM, and beyond*, ed. Morty Diamond, 113–22. San Francisco: Manic D Press.

Latour, Bruno. 1993. *We have never been modern*. Trans. Catherine Porter. Cambridge: Harvard University Press.

Lazarre, Jane. 1996. *Beyond the whiteness of whiteness: Memoir of a white mother of black sons*. Durham: Duke University Press.

Lewis, Helen. 1971. *Shame and guilt in neurosis*. New York: International Universities Press.

Lewis, Michael. 1992. *Shame: The exposed self*. New York: Free Press.

Lloyd, Cathie. 2001. Anti-racism, social movements, and civil society. In *Rethinking anti-racism: From theory to practice*, ed. Floya Anthias and Cathy Lloyd, 60–77. London: Routledge.

Lorde, Audre. 1983. *Zami: A new spelling of my name*. Trumansburg, N.Y.: Crossing Press.

———. 1984. *Sister outsider: Essays and speeches*. Trumansburg, N.Y.: Crossing Press.

———. 1988. *A burst of light: Essays*. Ithaca, N.Y.: Firebrand Books.

Lubiano, Wahneema. 1992. Black ladies, welfare, and state minstrels: Ideological war by narrative means. In *Race-ing justice, en-gendering power: Essays on Anita Hill, Clarence Thomas, and the construction of social reality*, ed. Toni Morrison, 323–63. New York: Pantheon Books.

———. 1997a. Black nationalism and black common sense: Policing ourselves and others. In *The house that race built: Black Americans, U.S. terrain*, ed. Lubiano, 232–52. New York: Pantheon Books.

———, ed. 1997b. *The house that race built: Black Americans, U.S. terrain*. New York: Pantheon Books.

———. 1998. Talking about the state and imagining alliances. In *Talking visions: Multicultural feminism in transnational age*, ed. Ella Shohat, 441–49. Cambridge: MIT Press.

Lugones, María. 1990. Structure/anti-structure and agency under oppression. *Journal of Philosophy* 87, no. 10: 500–507.

———. 2003. Playfulness, "world"-travelling, and loving perception. In *Pilgrimages/peregrinajes: Theorizing coalition against multiple oppressions*, 77–100. Lanham, Md.: Rowman and Littlefield.

Malpas, Jeff, Ulrich Arnswald, and Jens Kertscher, eds. 2002. *Gadamer's century: Essays in honor of Hans-Georg Gadamer*. Cambridge: MIT Press.

Marable, Manning, ed. 2000. *Dispatches from the ebony tower: Intellectuals confront the African American experience*. New York: Columbia University Press.

Marcuse, Herbert. 1969. *An essay on liberation*. Boston: Beacon Press.

———. 1978. *The aesthetic dimension: Toward a critique of Marxist aesthetics*. Boston: Beacon Press.

Martín-Alcoff, Linda. 1998. What should white people do? *Hypatia* 13, no. 3: 7–26.

Marx, Karl. 1975. Economic and philosophical manuscripts. In *Early writings*. Trans. Gregor Benton, 279–400. London: Penguin Books.

———. 1998. *The German ideology*. With Friedrich Engels. Amherst, N.Y.: Prometheus Books. (Orig. pub. 1932.)

Marx, Karl, and Friedrich Engels. 1973. *Marx and Engels on literature and art: A selection of writings*. Ed. Lee Baxandall and Stefan Morawski. St. Louis: Telos Press.

Massumi, Brian. 2002. *Parables for the virtual: Movement, affect, sensation*. Durham: Duke University Press.

McCloskey, Deirdre N. 1999. *Crossing: A memoir*. Chicago: University of Chicago Press.

McIntosh, Peggy. 1997. White privilege and male privilege: A personal account of coming to see correspondences through work in women's studies. In *Race, class, and gender: An anthology*, ed. Margaret L. Anderson and Patricia Hill Collins, 76–86. Belmont, Calif.: Wadsworth.

McNeill, Laura. 2004. Anti-racist revolutions. http://colours.mahost.org/articles/mcneill .html (accessed December 8, 2004).

McWhorter, Ladelle. 1999. *Bodies and pleasures: Foucault and the politics of sexual normalization*. Bloomington: Indiana University Press.

Merleau-Ponty, Maurice. 1962. *Phenomenology of perception*. Trans. Colin Smith. New York: Routledge.

Meyerowitz, Joanne J. 1998. Sex change and the popular press: Historical notes on transsexuality in the United States, 1930–1955. *GLQ* 4, no. 2: 159–88.

———. 2002. *How sex changed: A history of transsexuality in the United States*. Cambridge: Harvard University Press.

Meyers, Diana Tietjens, ed. 1996. *Feminists rethink the self*. Boulder, Colo.: Westview Press.

Mills, Charles W. 1997. *The racial contract*. Ithaca: Cornell University Press.

———. 1998. *Blackness visible: Essays on philosophy and race*. Ithaca: Cornell University Press.

Mohanty, Chandra Talpade. 2003. *Feminism without borders: Decolonizing theory, practicing solidarity*. Durham: Duke University Press.

Mol, Annemarie. 2002. *The body multiple: Ontology in medical practice*. Durham: Duke University Press.

Moon, Dreama, and Lisa A. Flores. 2000. Anti-racism and the abolition of whiteness: Rhetorical strategies of domination among "race traitors." *Communication Studies* 51, no. 2: 97–115.

Morley, David, and Kuan-Hsing Chen, eds. 1996. *Stuart Hall: Critical dialogues in cultural studies*. New York: Routledge.

Morrison, Toni. 1989. Unspeakable things unspoken: The Afro-American presence in American literature. *Michigan Quarterly Review* 28, no. 1: 1–34.

———. 1992. *Playing in the dark: Whiteness and the literary imagination*. Cambridge: Harvard University Press.

———. 1997. Home. In *The house that race built: Black Americans, U.S. terrain*, ed. Wahneema Lubiano, 3–12. New York: Pantheon Books.

Moten, Fred. 2003. *In the break: The aesthetics of the black radical tradition*. Minneapolis: University of Minnesota Press.

Mulisch, Harry. 1985. *The assault*. Trans. C. N. White. New York: Pantheon Books.

Namaste, Viviane K. 2000. *Invisible lives: The erasure of transsexual and transgendered people*. Chicago: University of Chicago Press.

———. 2005. *Sex change, social change: Reflections on identity, institutions, and imperialism*. Toronto: Women's Press.

Ngai, Sianne. 2007. *Ugly feelings*. Cambridge: Harvard University Press.

Nguyen, Mimi. 2000. She's a mission irresistible. http://www.worsethanqueer.com/slander/ 120600.html (accessed November 27, 2007).

Noë, Alva. 2004. *Action in perception, representation, and mind*. Cambridge: MIT Press.

———. 2009. *Out of our heads: Why you are not your brain, and other lessons from the biology of consciousness*. New York: Farrar, Straus & Giroux.

O'Brien, Eileen. 2000. "Are we supposed to be colorblind or not?" Competing frames used by whites against racism. *Race and Society* 3, no. 1: 41–59.

———. 2001. *Whites confront racism: Antiracists and their paths to action*. Lanham, Md.: Rowman and Littlefield.

O'Brien, Eileen, and Michael P. Armato. 2001. Building connections between antiracism and feminism. In *Feminism and anti-racism: International struggles for justice*, ed. Frances Winddance Twine and Kathleen M. Blee, 277–94. New York: New York University Press.

O'Brien, Michelle. 2002–3. Whose ally? Thinking critically about anti-oppression ally organizing. http://www.deadletters.biz/ally.pdf (accessed October 31 2004).

Olson, Joel. 1996. Police assisted-homicide. In *Race traitor*, ed. Noel Ignatiev and John Garvey, 135–41. New York: Routledge.

———. 2004. *The abolition of white democracy*. Minneapolis: University of Minnesota Press.

Omi, Michael, and Howard Winant. 1994. *Racial formation in the United States: From the 1960s to the 1990s*. New York: Routledge.

Peacocke, Christopher. 1992. A study of concepts. In *Representation and mind*. Cambridge: MIT Press.

Perry, Pamela. 2002. *Shades of white: White kids and racial identities in high school*. Durham: Duke University Press.

Perry, Pamela, and Alexis Shotwell. 2009. Relational understanding and white antiracist praxis. *Sociological Theory* 27, no. 1: 33–50.

Polanyi, Michael. 1959. *The study of man: The Lindsay memorial lectures given at the University College of North Staffordshire, 1958*. Chicago: University of Chicago Press.

———. 1962. *Personal knowledge: Towards a post-critical philosophy*. Chicago: University of Chicago Press.

———. 1967. *The tacit dimension*. Garden City, N.Y.: Anchor Books.

———. 1969. *Knowing and being: Essays by Michael Polanyi*. Ed. Marjorie Grene. Chicago: University of Chicago Press.

Pratt, Minnie Bruce. 1991. *Rebellion: Essays, 1980–1991*. Ithaca, N.Y.: Firebrand Books.

———. 1995. *S/he*. Ithaca, N.Y.: Firebrand Books.

Probyn, Elspeth. 2005. *Blush: Faces of shame*. Minneapolis: University of Minnesota Press.

Prosser, Jay. 1998. *Second skins: The body narratives of transsexuality*. New York: Columbia University Press.

Protevi, John. 2009. *Political affect: Connecting the social and the somatic*. Minneapolis: University of Minnesota Press.

Rawls, John. 1971. *A theory of justice*. Cambridge: Harvard University Press.

Reed, T. V. 1992. *Fifteen jugglers, five believers: Literary politics and the poetics of American social movements*. Berkeley and Los Angeles: University of California Press.

Rich, Adrienne. 1978. *The dream of a common language*. New York: Norton.

Rivera, Sylvia. 2002. Queens in exile, the forgotten ones. In *Genderqueer*, ed. Clare Howell, Joan Nestle, and Riki Wilchins, 67–85. Los Angeles: Alyson Books.

Roediger, David R. 2002a. *Colored white: Transcending the racial past*. Berkeley and Los Angeles: University of California Press.

———. 2002b. *The wages of whiteness: Race and the making of the American working class*. London: Verso.

Rorty, Richard. 1989. *Contingency, irony, and solidarity*. Cambridge: Cambridge University Press.

Rudacille, Deborah. 2005. *The riddle of gender: Science, activism, and transgender rights*. New York: Pantheon Books.

Ryle, Gilbert. 1979. *On thinking*. Totowa, N.J.: Rowman and Littlefield.

———. 1993. *Aspects of mind*. Oxford, UK: Blackwell.

San Filippo, Roy. 2004. The color of authority. Bring the Ruckus. http://www.agitator index.org/articles/authority.htm (accessed November 23 2004).

Sartre, Jean-Paul. 1992. *Being and nothingness: A phenomenological essay on ontology*. Trans. Hazel E. Barnes. New York: Simon & Schuster.

Sassoon, Anne Showstack, ed. 1982. *Approaches to Gramsci*. London: Writers and Readers.

Scheman, Naomi. 1993. *Engenderings: Constructions of knowledge, authority, and privilege*. New York: Routledge.

———. 1996. Queering the center by centering the queer: Reflections on transsexuals and secular Jews. In *Feminists rethink the self*, ed. Diana Tietjens Meyers, 124–62. Boulder, Colo.: Westview Press.

Schiller, Friedrich. 1967. *On the aesthetic education of man, in a series of letters*. Trans. E. M. Wilkinson and L. A. Willoughby. Oxford: Clarendon Press. (Orig. pub. 1794.)

Schmidt, Lawrence Kennedy. 1985. *The epistemology of Hans-Georg Gadamer: An analysis of the legitimization of Vorurteile*. New York: Lang.

———, ed. 2000. *Language and linguisticality in Gadamer's hermeneutics*. Lanham, Md.: Lexington Books.

Scholz, Sally J. 2008. *Political solidarity*. University Park: Pennsylvania State University Press.

Scott, Ellen Kaye. 2001. From race cognizance to racism cognizance. In *Feminism and anti-racism: International struggles for justice*, ed. Francine Winddance Twine and Kathleen M. Blee, 132–53. New York: New York University Press.

Scott, Lady Drusilla. 1985. *Everyman revived: The common sense of Michael Polanyi*. Lewes, UK: Book Guild.

Searle, John R. 1983. *Intentionality: An essay in the philosophy of mind*. Cambridge: Cambridge University Press.

———. 1998. *Mind, language, and society: Philosophy in the real world*. New York: Basic Books.

Sedgwick, Eve Kosofsky. 1990. *Epistemology of the closet*. Berkeley and Los Angeles: University of California Press.

———. 1993. *Tendencies*. Durham: Duke University Press.

———. 2003. *Touching feeling: Affect, pedagogy, performativity*. Durham: Duke University Press.

Sedgwick, Eve Kosofsky, and Adam Frank, eds. 1995. *Shame and its sisters: A Silvan Tomkins reader*. With a biographical sketch by Irving E. Alexander. Durham: Duke University Press.

Segrest, Mab. 1985. *My mama's dead squirrel: Lesbian essays on southern culture*. Ithaca, N.Y.: Firebrand Books.

———. 1994. *Memoir of a race traitor*. Boston: South End Press.

Serano, Julia. 2007. *Whipping girl: A transsexual woman on sexism and the scapegoating of femininity*. Emeryville, Calif.: Seal Press.

Shanker, Wendy. 2004. *Fat girl's guide to life*. New York: Bloomsbury.

Shelby, Tommie. 2005. *We who are dark: The philosophical foundations of black solidarity*. Cambridge: Belknap Press of Harvard University Press.

Shusterman, Richard. 2008. *Body consciousness: A philosophy of mindfulness and somaesthetics*. New York: Cambridge University Press.

Simon, Roger. 1991. *Gramsci's political thought: An introduction*. Rev. ed. London: Lawrence and Wishart.

Smith, Barbara, and Beverly Smith. 1983. Across the kitchen table: A sister-to-sister dialogue. In *This bridge called my back: Writings by radical women of color*, ed. Cherríe Moraga and Gloria Anzaldúa, 113–27. New York: Kitchen Table, Women of Color Press.

Smith, Chip. 2007. *The cost of privilege: Taking on the system of white supremacy and racism*. Fayetteville, N.C.: Camino Press.

Smith, David Lionel. 1997. What is black culture? In *The house that race built: Black Americans, U.S. terrain*, ed. Wahneema Lubiano, 178–94. New York: Pantheon Books.

Smith, Dorothy. 1987. *The everyday world as problematic: A sociology for women*. Toronto: University of Toronto Press.

———. 1990. *The conceptual practices of power: A feminist sociology of knowledge*. Toronto: University of Toronto Press.

Smith, Michael Peter, and Joe R. Feagin, eds. 1995. *The bubbling cauldron: Race, ethnicity, and the urban crisis*. Minneapolis: University of Minnesota Press.

Smith, T. Alexander, and Lenahan O'Connell. 1997. *Black anxiety, white guilt, and the politics of status frustration*. Westport, Conn.: Praeger.

Somerville, Siobhan B. 2000. *Queering the color line: Race and the invention of homosexuality in American culture*. Durham: Duke University Press.

Spade, Dean. 2004. Once more . . . with feeling. In *From the inside out: Radical gender transformation, FTM, and beyond*, ed. Marty Diamond, 94–98. San Francisco: Manic D Press.

Spelman, Elizabeth. 1988. *Inessential woman: Problems of exclusion in feminist thought*. Boston: Beacon Press.

Srivastava, Sarita. 1996. Song and dance? The performance of anti-racist workshops. *Canadian Review of Sociology and Anthropology* 33, no. 3: 291–315.

Stanley, Jason, and Timothy Williamson. 2001. Knowing how. *Journal of Philosophy* 98, no. 8: 411–44.

Starhawk. 2002. *Webs of power: Notes from the global uprising*. Gabriola, B.C.: New Society Publishers.

Stimson, Karen W. n.d. Fat feminist herstory, 1969–1993: A personal memoir. http://www .eskimo.com/~largesse/Archives/herstory.html (accessed April 14, 2010).

Stoller, Paul. 1997. *Sensuous scholarship*. Philadelphia: University of Pennsylvania Press.

Stone, Sandy. 1997. The empire strikes back: A posttranssexual manifesto. In *Writing on the body: Female embodiment and feminist theory*, ed. Katie Conboy, Nadia Medina, and Sarah Stanbury, 337–59. New York: Columbia University Press.

Sudbury, Julia. 1998. En-gendering anti-racism: Towards a politics of social transformation. *Patterns of Prejudice* 32, no. 4: 21–34.

Sullivan, Shannon. 2001. *Living across and through skins: Transactional bodies, pragmatism, and feminism*. Bloomington: Indiana University Press.

———. 2006. *Revealing whiteness: The unconscious habits of racial privilege*. Bloomington: Indiana University Press.

Sullivan, Shannon, and Nancy Tuana. 2007. *Race and epistemologies of ignorance*. Albany: State University of New York Press.

Swindler, Wyatt. 2004. Whose masculinity is it anyway? in *From the inside out: Radical gender transformation, FTM, and beyond*, ed. Marty Diamond, 66–69. San Francisco: Manic D Press.

Tangney, June Price, and Ronda L. Dearing. 2002. *Shame and guilt*. New York: Guilford Press.

Thobani, Sunera. 2007. *Exalted subjects: Studies in the making of race and nation in Canada*. Toronto: University of Toronto Press.

Thompson, Becky. 1996. Time traveling and border crossing: Reflections on white identity. In *Names we call home: Autobiography on racial identity*, ed. Becky Thompson and Sangeeta Tyagi, 93–110. New York: Routledge.

———. 2001. *A promise and a way of life: White antiracist activism*. Minneapolis: University of Minnesota Press.

Thompson, Becky, and Sangeeta Tyagi, eds. 1996. *Names we call home: Autobiography on racial identity*. New York: Routledge.

Thompson, Cooper, Emmett Schaefer, and Harry Brod. 2003. *White men challenging racism: 35 personal stories*. Durham: Duke University Press.

Towle, Evan B. and Lynn M. Morgan. 2002. Romancing the transgender native: Rethinking the use of the "third gender" concept. *GLQ* 8, no. 4: 469–97.

Townley, Cynthia. 2006. Toward a revaluation of ignorance. *Hypatia* 21, no. 3: 37–55.

Tsing, Anna. forthcoming. Unruly edges: Mushrooms as companion species. In *Thinking with Donna Haraway*, ed. Sharon Ghamari-Tabrizi. Cambridge: MIT Press.

Tuana, Nancy, ed. 1989. *Feminism and science: Race, gender, and science*. Bloomington: Indiana University Press.

———, ed. 2001. *Engendering rationalities*. Albany: State University of New York Press.

———. 2004. Coming to understand: Orgasm and the epistemology of ignorance. *Hypatia* 19, no. 1: 194–232.

———. 2006. The speculum of ignorance: The women's health movement and epistemologies of ignorance. *Hypatia* 21, no. 3: 1–19.

Turner, Stephen P. 1994. *The social theory of practices: Tradition, tacit knowledge, and presuppositions*. Chicago: University of Chicago Press.

———. 2002. *Brains/practices/relativism: Social theory after cognitive science*. Chicago: University of Chicago Press.

Twine, France Winddance, and Kathleen M. Blee, eds. 2001. *Feminism and anti-racism: International struggles for justice*. New York: New York University Press.

Vachon, Wolfgang. 2006. Transforming values engendering policy. In *Trans/forming feminisms: Trans/feminist voices speak out*, ed. Krista Scott-Dixon, 227–34. Toronto: University of Toronto Press.

Violet, Indigo. 2002. Linkages: A personal-political journey with feminist-of-color politics. In *This bridge we call home: Radical visions for transformation*, ed. Gloria Anzaldua, and AnaLouise Keating, 486–94. New York: Routledge.

Wann, Marilyn. 1998. *Fat!So? Because you don't have to apologize for your size*. Berkeley, Calif.: Ten Speed Press.

Ware, Von, and Les Back. 2002. *Out of whiteness: Color, politics, and culture*. Chicago: University of Chicago Press.

Weinsheimer, Joel. 1985. *Gadamer's hermeneutics: A reading of truth and method*. New Haven: Yale University Press.

Weiss, Gail. 1999. *Body images: Embodiment as intercorporeality*. New York: Routledge.

Wellman, David T. 1977. *Portraits of white racism*. New York: Cambridge University Press.

Williams, Patricia. 1997. *Seeing a color-blind future: The paradox of race*. New York: Noonday Press.

Wise, Tim J. 2005. *White like me: Reflections on race from a privileged son*. Brooklyn: Soft Skull Press.

Wittgenstein, Ludwig. 1969. *On certainty*. Trans. G. E. M. Anscombe. New York: Harper & Row.

Young, James O. 2001. *Art and knowledge*. London: Routledge.

Zack, Naomi. 1999. White ideas. In *Whiteness: Feminist philosophical reflections*, ed. Chris J. Cuomo and Kim Q. Hall, 77–84. Lanham, Md.: Rowman and Littlefield.

Zirin, Dave. 2006. Brother of the fist: The passing of Peter Norman. ZNet. http://www .zmag.org/content/showarticle.cfm?SectionID=30&ItemID=11192 (accessed October 18, 2006).

Zita, Jacquelyn N. 1998. *Body talk: Philosophical reflections on sex and gender*. New York: Columbia University Press.

INDEX

political transformation (*continued*)
    implicit understanding and, xviii–xx, xxi, 46
    impossible dreams, 5–6, 26, 27, 47
    individualism and, 5–6
    misrecognition and, 15
    poetry and, 24–28
    refusal of shame and, 91–92, 91n8
    sensuous understanding and, 146–47,
        149–51, 154–55
    shame and, 90–92
    women of color feminisms, 119–22
potentially propositional knowledge, xii. *See also*
    commonsense
    hinge propositions, 20–21
    poetry as, 26–27
    prejudice and, xviii, xx, 7, 8, 11n2, 16–21
    presupposition, 7–8, 15, 15n4, 16n5, 18–19, 98
Pratt, Minnie Bruce, 85, 98
praxis
    aesthetics and, 52, 53, 55, 64, 68–69, 151
    anti-racist praxis, 82, 94–95, 106, 109
    collective praxis, 122–24, 122n13
    intersectional praxis, 114, 116, 119–20
    sensuous understanding and, 151
prejudice
    commonsense and, 122, 123
    implicit prejudice, xviii, xx, 7, 8, 11n2, 16–21
    presupposition and, 7–8, 15, 15n4, 16n5,
        18–19, 98
    racial prejudice, 43–44, 45, 82n6, 108
presupposition, 7–8, 15, 15n4, 16n5, 18–19, 98. *See*
    also commonsense
Probyn, Elspeth, 84, 85, 88, 90, 95n13
productive discomfort, xvi, 74, 80, 87, 99, 150
propositional knowledge, ix
    antiracist transformation and, 105–6
    claim-making and, ix, x
    implicit understanding *vs.,* ix–x
    nonpropositional knowledge *vs.,* xi
    propositionality, x
    racial formation and, xix–xx
    true/false evaluation and, x
    use of language and, x
Prosser, Jay, 130, 142n7, 144

race
    implicit understanding and, xvi
    inarticulate aspects of, xxi
    liberatory spaces and, 152
    nonpropositional knowledge and, xvi, xx
    trans formations analogic to, 151–54
Race Traitor (journal), 111–16, 111n6, 117, 118–19,
    124

Racial Contract, the, 36–37
racial formation
    affect and, xii
    color blindness, 30, 105–6, 108
    commonsense and, xviii, 29, 31–32, 35–36, 44
    feelings and, xx
    gender formation and, 32, 37–38, 40–41,
        44–46
    identity formation and, 78–80
    inarticulate aspects of, xxi
    propositional knowledge and, xix–xx
    Racial Contract and, 36–37
    shame and, 78–80, 86–90, 86n7
    transformative understanding and, 73–77
racialization
    color blindness, 30, 105–6, 108
    commonsense and, 31–32, 33, 40–41
    as onotological process, 86n7
    shame and, 88–90
racism, 82n6
    anger as response to, 94n11
    commonsense and, 31–32
    Gilmore on, 73, 90
    guilt and, 82, 84
    somatic/bodily knowledge and, 43–44
Racism Without Racists (Bonilla-Silva), 105
rationality
    impossible dreams, 5–6, 26, 27, 47
    personhood and, 5–6
    rational decision making, 5–6
    whiteness and, 61–63
Rawls, John, 5–6, 126
Raymond, Janice, 153n10
Reflections on Poetry (Baumgarten), 58
Riddle of Gender (Rudacille), 137–39, 137n4
Rivera, Sylvia, 132, 133, 134
Rorty, Richard, 102–4, 121, 122, 122n14
Rudacille, Deborah, 137–39, 137n4

San Filippo, Roy, 112–13, 113n7
Sartre, Jean-Paul, 24, 80n2
Scheler, Max, 109, 110n5
Scheman, Naomi, 134
Schiller, Friedrich
    aesthetic condition, the, 59, 59n5, 60, 136
    Baumgarten and, 58
    freedom and, 60, 69, 138
    play drive, 59–60, 59n6, 65, 69
Schmidt, Lawrence Kennedy, 19n6
Screaming Queens (2005), 134
Searle, John R., 4, 4n1, 6
Sedgwick, Eve Kosofsky, 77–80, 86, 96, 97
Segrest, Mab, 88